The Politics of Union:

Northern Politics during the Civil War

JAMES A. RAWLEY
University of Nebraska

The Dryden Press
901 North Elm Street
Hinsdale, Illinois 60521

To the University of Nebraska

Acknowledgments

Obligations in the writing of this book have accumulated over many years. My intellectual debts to institutions, scholars, and friends are extensive and diverse. The late Allan Nevins kindled my interest in the politics of the Civil War era and continued a helpful interest in my research and writing.

For this contribution to the Berkshire Studies in American History, I have not provided a formal bibliography, but I hope the *Guide to Further Study* at the end of the volume will make some reparation to the scholars upon whom I have leaned heavily. In addition, Professor Allan G. Bogue of the University of Wisconsin not only allowed me to read his unpublished papers but also generously read and criticized a draft of this book. Frank Klement of Marquette University at an early stage of my research let me read his then unpublished life of C. L. Vallandigham. The late John H. Thurber of the University of Nebraska made available his unpublished study of Zachariah Chandler. Professor Gerald S. Henig of California State College at Hayward permitted me to read his manuscript life of Henry Winter Davis. None of these Knights Hospitalers of the Civil War is responsible for any errors of fact or interpretation that may be found in my book.

Two persons are owed special debts. Robert E. Burke, editor of this series, has given me the benefit of his large experience. And my wife, Ann, has unfailingly borne with me in the long process of research and writing.

Libraries which have been especially helpful include: the Columbia University Library, the Alderman Library of the University of Virginia, the Library of Congress, the New York Public Library, and the Nebraska State Historical Society. Particular thanks are due to students, colleagues, and various administrators of the University of Nebraska from whom I have derived continuing aid and encouragement.

James A. Rawley

Lincoln, Nebraska
July 1973

Contents

Introduction

Surprisingly, no one heretofore has written a one-volume general history of Northern politics during the Civil War. To fill that breach in a vast literature on our nation's greatest travail is the primary aim of this work.

Books aplenty exist on the Civil War: the number of volumes on Abraham Lincoln and on military matters seems illimitable; numerous monographs have appeared on political topics such as the Copperheads, constitutional problems, and the election of 1864; every Civil War politician seems to have found at least one biographer; and the monumental histories by James Ford Rhodes and Allan Nevins give much attention to political subjects. This present book is a synthesis of the research of many scholars and of my own investigations.

Excellent works exist on pre-Civil War politics through

the secession crisis and on Reconstruction. Because it attempts to fill a gap, this work, after a short review of pre-Sumter politics, begins in the spring of 1861 and ends with the death of Lincoln. The reader will find occasional brief reference to Confederate politics, but only for the purpose of offering a comparative view.

The politics of Union holds many historiographical dimensions. The Union president has been a study in historians' contradictions: a Tudor monarch, a constitutional dictator, a politician who drew power from skillful dispensing of patronage, an antagonist of radicals in his own party, an antagonist of the war governors—both captor and captive. The evolution of legislation has too often been seen not in its context of the war and its needs but as a "Second American Revolution," "in which the capitalists, laborers, and farmers of the North and West drove from power in the National government the planting aristocracy of the South."

If historians have sometimes interpreted the authors of this legislation as social revolutionaries triumphant over Lincoln, they have in more recent years reinterpreted the radicals' role, emphasizing consensus instead of conflict in the legislative-executive relationship, sectional interests instead of economic in legislative voting, and party above faction in meeting the exigencies of the war.

The Democrats, once considered Copperheads, if not traitors, have been relieved of accusations of disloyalty, and have been identified variously as the loyal opposition, precursors of the Grangers, and Midwestern Negrophobes.

The organism of Union politics in fact included many divisive elements: states rights Democrats, East-West sectionalism, racism, mob violence, dissenters, Republican factionalism, class and urban-rural friction, and a continuing disagreement between Lincoln and Congress over emancipation, confiscation, and the means of reconstructing the Union.

Throughout the war Northern unity stood beleaguered. The central theme of Northern politics was the effort to maintain Northern unity against the forces assailing it. Lincoln tried to keep an eye single to saving the Union, subordinating all other policies to this goal. But saving the Union required Northern unity; and much of the political effort of the Civil War went toward nullifying threats to the unity of the North, not simply toward subduing the South.

Dissent sometimes threatened Northern success. States, through their governors, legislatures, and courts, often were refractory. Border slave states, especially Kentucky and Maryland, were stubborn. Popular resistance to the draft was widespread. Secret organizations were the source of continuing anxiety. Peace advocates were clamorous, in time actually writing the Democratic platform. The Copperhead C. L. Vallandigham was a problem in himself, being a strident critic of the administration. During the cabinet crisis of 1862, Republican senators challenged the authority of the Republican president.

The study of Northern politics is therefore a study of tensions. In the end the North did hold together and the Union was saved. These tensions were not entirely negative in results; dissent sometimes promoted success. Assertion of states rights permitted local pride to contribute to the war and prevented undue centralization of authority. Insistence upon civil liberties checked further excesses against press and person. Advocacy of peace clarified the conviction that the only path to peace lay in military victory. The functioning of the Democratic party served to curb the extremism of one-party government as well as to unite Republicans, thus reducing factionalism. Republican factionalism was often over ways and means to win the war, a healthy competition fostering efficiency.

Diversity of outlook offered energy and vitality to Northern politics. Civil War politics accommodated and even exploited with great success the natural tensions of the hour, invigorating the war effort instead of debilitating it.

It was necessary during the Civil War that the fighting be prosecuted to a victory, that the privilege of the writ of habeas corpus be suspended, that the government be authorized to draft, and that the slaves be freed. As an abstraction it may have been ideal that the North be of one mind on these points; but in fact these and other issues were divisive.

Political institutions allowed groups and individuals to speak, thus stimulating thought and discussion and making it possible to reach generally acceptable decisions. Ends and means had to be debated. No citizen could relax without fear of losing out to another. The outcome was continuing popular participation in a vigorous national endeavor.

With great wisdom the *New York Times* in 1863 observed: "until the constitution of the human mind is changed, it will be impossible for all true Union men to agree in respect to the precise mode in which the war shall be conducted. Men, however devoted to a common cause, always differ about methods and details; and they have a right so to differ, so long as they will keep clear of factious conduct. Fair discussion is always not only admissible, but profitable."

A new federal partnership emerged in state-nation relations. East and West held together. Dissenters, with conspicuous exceptions, were allowed to have their say. The two-party system demonstrated its viability. The Republican party transformed itself into the Union party, welcoming war Democrats; and became a great extraconstitutional bond of Northern unity, connecting state and nation, congress and president, judiciary and administration. Constitutional government not only survived but it grew in strength. And not least, the slaves gained freedom, after full debate and balloting, with the general agreement of the nation in the necessity and justice of emancipation.

CHAPTER ONE

The Rupture
of the Republic

Fallen soldiers of seventeen Northern states lay buried in acre plots assigned to each state in a portion of the great battlefield of Gettysburg which the governor of Pennsylvania had directed be purchased as their final resting place. And the governors of the Northern states had invited the president of Harvard College to be the orator at dedication day—and as an afterthought the president of the United States to be present and to participate.

Rather unexpectedly, President Abraham Lincoln, though occupied in waging a war and anxious about his ailing son Tad, accepted the invitation. On November 19, 1863, on Cemetery Hill, the tall president, dressed in black, read a brief and immortal speech in his characteristic sharp, treble voice. His words reaffirmed the unfaltering purpose for which he fought the Civil War: "Fourscore and seven years ago, our fathers brought forth on this continent a new nation, conceived in liberty and dedicated to the proposition that all men are created equal. Now we are engaged in a great civil war, testing whether that nation —or any nation, so conceived and so dedicated—can long endure."

The American nation was at stake, and bound up in its salvation was the resolve "that the nation shall, under God, have a new birth of freedom, and that government of the people, by the people, for the people, shall not perish from the earth."

To save the nation and the principles it lived by was the president's overriding purpose. Years before he had foretold that a house divided against itself could not stand. When the house had divided and the flag had been fired on, he as president had accepted war rather than let the Union slide.

For a number of years before the election of 1860, the Union had been breaking. Sectional antagonisms over the expansion of Negro slavery had convulsed the country ever since the Kansas-Nebraska Act had reopened the federal territories to slavery. The Kansas controversy preoccupied American politics for nearly five years; and though the immediate question of freedom in Kansas was resolved in 1858, the long-range questions remained unresolved in 1860.

The Kansas troubles gave birth to a Northern, sectional party whose vital center was opposition to the spread of black servitude. Taking the Jeffersonian name Republican, it had announced as its nationalist aim—in the words of its national chairman, Edwin D. Morgan—to determine "not whether the South is to rule or the North . . . but whether the broad national policy our fathers established, cherished and maintained is to be permitted to descend to our sons."

A partisan and sectional Supreme Court had knocked the props from under the Republican platform in 1857 when the majority had ruled in the Dred Scott decision that Congress had no power to prohibit slavery in the territories. In the same year President James Buchanan allowed a proslavery minority in Kansas to write a constitution that would perpetuate slavery. The author of the Kansas-Nebraska Act, Senator Stephen A. Douglas of Illinois, believing his principle of popular sovereignty flouted, broke with Buchanan. The feud between the pro-Southern Democratic president and the leader of the Northern Democrats deepened the divisions in national politics. Douglas and Lincoln, competing in 1858 in the Illinois senatorial race, offered opposing views of national authority over slavery in the territories.

Though congressional compromise provided for a fresh popular vote in the territory, preventing Kansas from entering the Union as a slave state, the aftermath was Democratic disunity and sectional mistrust. Contributing to anxieties over slavery's meaning to the future of the Union was the resistance of some Northern states to the national fugitive slave law and the proposal of some Southern extremists to reopen the foreign slave trade. To the perplexity of some observers, states rights Northerners were tearing the national fabric, while overheated Southerners were wrapping it about slavery.

At the approach of the pivotal presidential election of 1860, the arrant antislavery zealot John Brown, already responsible for the assassination of five men in Kansas, invaded the slave state of Virginia with a group of followers in a misguided plan to free slaves. Though put to death eleven months before the actual balloting, he became a martyr to some antislavery men and a menacing symbol, in the event of a Northern antislavery government, to many proslavery men.

The chilling drama of "Bleeding Kansas" and the sharp impact of Old Brown produced a crisis of fear in many Southerners. Fear of Northern-enforced emancipation, of slave insurrection, and of the Negro freedman produced paranoia. A Republican victory in 1860 would do more than cost the slave-holding South control of the national government. It menaced, some believed, the foundations of Southern life—a system of labor and race relations based on Negro slavery.

When the disordered Democrats convened in Charleston in April 1860 to select a presidential candidate, Southern extremists demanded a platform guaranteeing national protection of slavery in the territories. Douglas forces insisted on reaffirming the 1856 platform assuring popular sovereignty to territorial inhabitants. Efforts to hold together the national party failed and the Democrats divided into two sectional factions. Northern Democrats nominated Douglas, and Southern seceders nominated John Breckinridge of Kentucky, incumbent vice-president of the United States, each candidate upholding rival positions about national power over slavery in the territories.

When the Republicans—in better array—convened in Chicago in May, moderates composed differences within the party. The "available" man,

Lincoln, won nomination over the leading Republican, William H. Seward of New York, now penalized for twenty years of prominence in controversy. The platform reaffirmed the power and duty of Congress to prohibit slavery in the national territories, and it reprimanded the Democrats for their handling of the Kansas question. It condemned efforts to reopen the African slave trade, while recognizing the rights of states to maintain slavery. It called for national aid to internal improvements and especially to a railroad to the Pacific. Identified in the minds of many immigrants as nativist, the party declared in favor of protecting the rights of naturalized citizens. Widening its appeals to interest groups, it favored a protective tariff and a homestead law. After voting not to repeat its 1856 endorsement of the Declaration of Independence, the convention reversed itself without, however, directly applying the principles of liberty and equality to Blacks. (The Black abolitionist, Robert Purvis of Philadelphia, denounced the Republican party as "the white man's party.")

Considering the generations—old tensions between central and state governments in the Federal Union, it was notable that nearly every paragraph contained the word "nation" or "national," and the platform attributed the nation's success to "the Union of the States." It was also notable that this rhetorical emphasis upon nationalism was offset by an insistence on the maintenance inviolate of the rights of the states, especially over domestic institutions (slavery), as essential to the balance of power on which the perfection of the national political fabric depended.

A fourth party, avowing that platforms had the effect of misleading and deceiving the people, succinctly upheld the principles of the Union, the Constitution, and the laws. When this Constitutional Union party met in Baltimore, it nominated John Bell of Tennessee for president and Edward Everett of Massachusetts for vice-president and sought to rise above geographical and sectional issues.

No party stood for disunion. No party stood for emancipation. No party could have won the election on either principle. The actual canvass produced more heat than light, the two Democratic factions squabbling with one another and Lincoln keeping quiet while ardent "Wide Awakes" demonstrated in his favor and suspicious Southerners feared the "Black Republican."

In November Lincoln won a clear majority in the electoral college. But the true dimensions of the canvass are best seen not in the size of either the electoral or popular vote but in the division of voters into two nations.

Lincoln was not on the ticket in ten slave states, and he carried only two slave state counties—both in Missouri. Breckinridge carried only one county in the free states east of the Rockies, and won all but two of the states that would form the Confederacy.

Portentous for Northern politics during the Civil War were four results. First and foremost, of course, was the victory of the Republican candidate. Second was the small Northern Breckenridge vote, representing the extreme Southern position. Next, the heavy Douglas vote, concentrated in the North, offered an opposition party challenge to the Republicans. And finally, the overwhelming preference of the loyal slave states for Bell and Breckenridge posed problems of peculiar delicacy to Lincoln and the Union Congress.

Beyond all this lay perplexing questions. Would the recent adherence of the Old Northwest to the Northeast withstand the stress of civil war? Would the agricultural interests in the Republican party clash with the emerging industrial interests? Would the coalition of ex-Whigs, ex-Democrats, Free-Soilers, Liberty party men, and Know-Nothings become brittle once victory had been forged and the heat of the campaign had cooled? Would Northern Democrats sympathize with the Confederate resistance to Republican hegemony? Would ethnic tensions, arising particularly among Roman Catholics who had voted almost overwhelmingly Democratic, roil the waters of wartime politics? Would the economic strain between the rich and the poor, aggravated by war profiteering and policies of taxation and military service, be intensified to the point of class strife? Would the large cities, where great numbers of immigrants lived and where the anti-Lincoln vote had been strong, erupt in violence under the stress of war?

"A geographical line has been drawn across the Union, and all the States north of that line have united in the election of a man to the high office of President of the United States whose opinions and purposes are hostile to Slavery," so accused the South Carolina secession convention. Claiming that the national compact had been repeatedly broken by Northern state violations of the fugitive slave clause of the Constitution, complaining of the activities of antislavery societies, and contemplating a war to extinction against slavery, South Carolina—stormy petrel of the South—seceded on December 20, 1860.

This risky dissolution of the Union by a single state found sympathetic response throughout the Lower South. Within six weeks six more slave states, each acting individually under the constitutional theory that the nation was merely a compact of sovereign states, seceded. They quickly recognized, however, the need for unity; and February 4, 1861—one month before Lincoln was inaugurated—they met in Montgomery to frame a constitution and form a new union.

The Confederate constitution was more like than unlike its Federal model. It differed markedly in recognizing the "sovereign and independent character of each state" and the right of property in slaves, in tightening the fugitive slave clause, and in extending national authority over slavery in all territories belonging to the Confederacy. The convention elected as provisional president Jefferson Davis, a distinguished Mississippi Democrat, and as vice-president Alexander H. Stephens, an eminent Georgia Whig.

Davis invoked the American revolutionary tradition to justify secession and confederation undertaken to protect slavery interests of "overwhelming magnitude." Stephens in a notorious vindication of the new government declared: "its cornerstone rests upon the great truth that the negro is not equal to the white man." Economic and racial aspects of African servitude were joined in the Lost Cause.

Was it to be peace or war? The poet Whittier asked

> They break the links of Union; shall we light
> The flames of hell to weld anew the chain
> On that red anvil where each blow is pain?

Statesmen attempted compromise. Three times before, between 1819 and 1850, the Union had been threatened, and compromise had prevailed. Now the hour was late, and the shape of Southern secession and Northern unity had altered. The leading bid for compromise came from Kentucky Senator John J. Crittenden, heir to the Clay tradition of pacification, who proposed a tardy return to the Compromise of 1820, recognizing slavery south of longitude 36°30'. Crittenden's compromise stood at variance with Republican pledges to prohibit slavery in all the territories. President-elect Lincoln advised rejection, believing that compromise would be followed by Southern efforts to extend slavery and add new slave states. A poorly attended peace convention, called by Virginia, failed to find acceptable grounds for national reconciliation. Echoing the Crittenden plan, the convention's work won negligible support in Congress. When Lincoln took office on March 4, hope of compromise had dimmed.

Four urgent tasks awaited the new chief magistrate. Primary was the need to regain the allegiance of the seven seceded states. Only slightly less critical was the need to retain the allegiance of the eight unseceded slave states. Imperative in case of hostilities was maintaining a solid North. And last of all, he must unify the Republican party as the instrument to execute his policy.

His First Inaugural Address delineated Lincoln's policy toward slavery, the Confederacy, and a developing crisis over the Federal forts claimed by the Confederacy, and defined main elements of his political philosophy. As to slavery, he had no intention to interfere with it in the states; and he did not object to a proposed constitutional amendment guaranteeing slavery in the states forever from Federal interference. The fugitive slave law, which he thought ought to be revised to protect free Blacks, would be enforced. Though the Constitution did not say whether Congress may prohibit slavery in the territories, he appealed to the minority South to acquiesce in the majority verdict at the polls.

With respect to the Confederacy, he rejected the political theory on which it rested, branding secession as anarchy. Majority rule, allowing change through constitutional amendment, was the true principle. The Union was perpetual, was older than the Constitution; formed in 1774 by the Articles of Association, it remained unbroken. His course of action, he said, would be to hold the forts and other government property, collect taxes, and deliver the mails unless repelled.

"There will be no invasion," he promised, at the same time appealing to Southern Unionism and faith in the ultimate justice of the American people—the "ultimate tribunal." "In *your* hands, my dissatisfied fellow-countrymen, and not in *mine*, is the momentous issue of civil war," he gave as his last assurance of his pacific purpose.

An unhappy tangle of events, with some discredit on both sides, led to hostilities at Fort Sumter, South Carolina. The resulting four years of civil war tested American political institutions—a written constitution, the president and commander-in-chief, Congress, the military establishment, money, banking, taxing, the judiciary, and the party system.

The sixteenth president of the United States, now entering the fifty-second year of his life, offered unimpressive credentials for his high office and immense responsibilities. Congress was filled with men boasting more glittering political attainments. Besides deficiencies in his formal schooling and a provincial background, he had had little experience in national office and none in an executive capacity. He knew little about the conduct of war. He had served a single term in the House of Representatives, had failed of election to the Senate; and he was in his habits, his secretary said, "extremely unmethodical." His small public reputation in early 1861 had been formed by his debates with the more famous Douglas, his disconcerting "house divided" speech, and his conservative Cooper Union address. In this address he had repudiated Northern extremism, and urged conciliation of the Southern people: "let us determine . . . what will satisfy them."

What no one could foretell at this time was the ardor of his nationalism —the polar star by which he steered the ship of state; the depth of his self-education; the political finesse with which he would keep the Northern political system in equilibrium and motion; and his capacity for growth. The Union above all was his motto. To save the Union he opposed compromise in 1860-61 (all the while perhaps oversanguinely hoping for a peaceable solution to secession), accepted war, opposed abolition, later embraced emancipation, advocated colonization of Negroes, violated the Constitution, amended the Constitution to abolish slavery, and urged passage of a spate of legislation.

His passion for the Union sprang from his belief that it offered the best opportunity for the ideas of the Declaration of Independence to flourish. It lifted the weights of the European past from men's shoulders and held out a vast promise for the future of all mankind. A free society and a free economy were integral to his conception of the Union.

His extraordinary personal appearance put off some persons and appealed to others. Walt Whitman caught a "capital view" of the president-elect as he passed through New York City: "his unusual and uncouth height, his dress of complete black, stovepipe hat push'd back on the head, dark-brown complexion, seam'd and wrinkled yet canny-looking face, black, busy head of hair, disproportionately long neck, and his hands held behind as he stood observing the people."

Lincoln's political sagacity showed in the formation of his cabinet. It was a marble cake, blended of geographical and factional ingredients. He chose three members from the West, two from Border slave states, and three from the East. Most of them had been rivals for the presidential nomination; two of them had been paid off for supporting Lincoln's nomination. In previous party affiliation they represented a fair balance between Whigs and Democrats with a bow in the direction of Free-Soilers. In antislavery conviction they ranged from Border State conservative to ultra-

Republicanism. Unlike President Davis who was concerned about having every state represented, President Lincoln was concerned about having party faction—in thought, region, and past affiliation—represented.

The composition of the cabinet was an important step in unifying the Republican party by identifying some of the strongest politicians in the party with the administration. At the same time, the cabinet had weaknesses and precipitated crises during the next four years. The first secretary of war was incompetent to his great challenge; his successor was almost as cantankerous as he was competent; the secretary of state twice became the center of major crises in presidential leadership; the secretary of the treasury never let up striving to preside over the cabinet; and the postmaster general became a sacrificial lamb to party unity. Only two of the original appointees were left by 1865. On balance, however, the presence of most of these men in the cabinet appears to have brought the government greater strength than it would have had without them.

Secretary of State William H. Seward had been the titular leader of the Republican party before he lost the presidential nomination to Lincoln. A veteran politician, he had won notoriety as a senator with his references to a "higher law" than the Constitution and an "irrepressible conflict" between slavery and freedom. Righteousness and canniness fused in Seward. A patriot and expansionist, he believed in an energetic national government and foresaw a large role for the United States in world affairs. Breezy in manner, occasionally irresponsible, he kindled distrust as well as admiration. He grew in moderation through this period and greatly contributed to the North's political achievement.

At the start of his tenure, Seward made a famous and gigantic miscalculation: of the profundity of Unionism in the slave-holding South, of the measure of the untried president's self-reliance, and of the means to preserve the nation. In a plan to avert civil war, dated April 1, 1861, he privately advised Lincoln to abandon Fort Sumter and delegate presidential authority to some cabinet member, arguing that a dual policy of conciliation toward the South and bellicosity toward foreign nations would change the question before the public from slavery to union. We now know that Seward intended not to keep his plan private but to launch a press campaign, after having secured Lincoln's endorsement, that would be a first step toward pacific reunion as well as evidence of Seward's statesmanship.

Lincoln in reply quietly pointed out that he had his own policy, he did not see how Seward's suggestions would change the question from slavery to union, and as to devolving presidential powers upon a cabinet member (Seward), he bluntly answered, "If this must be done, *I* must do it." From that moment it was plain who was the head of the government. By June, Seward was exclaiming, "The President is the best of us all."

Salmon P. Chase, secretary of the treasury, had little qualification for his post but much qualification for an important appointment. Of all the cabinet he had been slavery's strongest foe, shifting parties with the anti-slavery winds, from Whig to Liberty to Free Soil to Republican. Brought up by his uncle, an Episcopal bishop, he meditated much upon piety as well as upon the presidency. In him religion and political aspiration jostled with one another. As a lawyer defending fugitive slaves, he was called "the attorney-general for runaway Negroes"; and as an author of the "Appeal of the Independent Democrats," he had stoutly opposed Douglas' Kansas-Nebraska bill and had contributed to the making of the Republican party. Governor of his native Ohio in the late 1850s, he had been chosen United States senator in 1860. To his keen disappointment he had won only 49 votes out of 465 on the first ballot at the Chicago convention (Seward had led with 173½). When offered the portfolio by Lincoln, he resigned his senate seat to manage the nation's finances and sit in high council. Until the party came round to abolition in 1864 and until his ambition became overt, Chase was virtually indispensable to the cabinet coalition.

Lincoln had reluctantly lived up to the bargain made by his convention managers with Simon Cameron, the Pennsylvania machine politician, who in exchange for a promise of a cabinet post had supported Lincoln's nomination. As secretary of war during an unexampled emergency, he proved unable to revitalize that fossilized department. Reports of corruption in the letting of lucrative war contracts merely underscored his unfitness for office and contributed to his departure and censure by the House of Representatives.

The organizer of victory in the War Department was his successor, Edwin M. Stanton. Another Pennsylvanian, a Democrat who had been attorney general under Buchanan, he had, apart from his abrasiveness, superior intelligence and prodigious energy. He brought a crabbed genius to his job, and not without occasional error (as in halting recruiting in the spring of 1862), he made the department move. Aggressive and fierily efficient, he stood long hours at his high desk in the War Department, urging on the North's legions. Stanton ended the large-scale corruption, raised a huge army, furloughed soldiers to vote, stood for vigorous prosecution of the war, and served as an important link between the president and a vocal wing of the party which called for strong measures.

Attorney general for the Union was Edward Bates, a conservative ex-Whig from the slave state of Missouri. Cautious in his outlook on slavery and the Negro, he stoutly upheld Lincoln's role as commander in chief, including suspension of the writ of habeas corpus, while taking a chary view of martial rule, treason and confiscation laws, and the partitioning of a state.

The other slave state representative was Montgomery Blair of Maryland. Member of a politically prominent family, he was a son of an adviser to Andrew Jackson and brother to a Missouri leader, Francis P. Blair, Jr., who served during the war as general and congressman. The elder Blair had been a founder of the Republican party and remained a force in politics throughout the war. Early in the Sumter crisis, Montgomery Blair alone in the cabinet unequivocally advised Lincoln to provision the beleaguered garrison. Ardent in his Unionism, he was at the same time the most pronounced in anti-Negro sentiments.

Gideon Welles ("Father Gideon"), the bewhiskered secretary of the navy, came from Connecticut. The sole member from New England, he represented not the abolitionist impulse associated with that region but calm opposition to the extension of slavery. A former Democrat and editor, he had once headed a bureau in the Navy Department. Moderate in his views on constitutional construction and use of governmental power, he was innovative in his supervision of the wartime navy. Methodical in mind, impelled by a keen sense of duty, canny in his judgments of men, with which he filled his salty diary, he won Lincoln's accolade, "Your department has been conducted with admirable success."

Caleb Smith, head of the Interior Department, had gained his office as the price of supporting Lincoln's nomination. A hack who at a fateful moment controlled the Indiana delegation, he proved the least effectual of Lincoln's advisers. Late in 1862 Lincoln appointed him to a federal judgeship and replaced him with a more worthy Indianian—John P. Usher.

An inharmonious ministry of talents, these men were held together by a mutual hostility to the expansion of slavery and a mutual love for the Union. None favored the immediate abolition of slavery. None championed extension of full citizenship to free Negroes. On many questions they differed with one another. But appointment of these diverse men to administer the government achieved a party balance. It also, as one after another learned, created a cabinet that was Lincoln's, controlled by him for his great purpose of saving the nation in his fashion.

The making of his cabinet was the most conspicuous act of parceling out the loaves and fishes of patronage. Lincoln's was the first Republican administration; and office-hungry partisans in the weeks after the inauguration thronged the executive mansion. Preoccupied with the Sumter crisis, the president was appalled that, as he said, while the national house was on fire at one end, he had to be letting out rooms at the other. Vexed when he found that office-seekers left him no time to take a drink of water, he fixed visiting hours, at first from ten o'clock until three and later from ten until one.

The United States did not have a systematic civil service to reduce the clamor for office and smooth the transition from one administration to another. Neither was the Republican party a cohesive organization. In spite of the fact that he had polled but forty percent of the popular vote, Lincoln used the civil patronage not as an instrument of national but of party unity. When war came, he changed his policy with respect to military appointments, realizing he could not even start to suppress a rebellion without assistance from outside the party. In pursuit of his national policy, he appointed a number of political generals, many of whom were Democrats. Ironically, one of these, George B. McClellan, became his Democratic rival for the presidency in 1864.

Northern institutions in 1861 were ill adapted to wage war. Deep-rooted convictions and bitter history had combined to weaken the spring of government. Antigovernmentalism, expressed in a written constitution that rigidly limited the central government, in traditions of states rights, individualism, and laissez-faire, augured badly for a dynamic war state.

The nation's sword had grown rusty and its purse empty. Taxation in recent years had not met expenses. Andrew Jackson's legacy to the nation included a Whig distrust of a strong executive, a decentralized banking system, hostility to paper money, a low tariff, suspicion of federal support of internal improvements, and a spoils system.

Sectional tensions over Negro slavery for a quarter of a century had further debilitated the national government. Not since Jackson, with the exception of the dark horse Polk, had there been a strong president. Not since Jackson had there been a two-term president. Political parties had splintered under the blows of expanding slavery. Third parties had been formed: Liberty in 1840, Free-Soil in 1848, Anti-Nebraska in 1854. Major parties had been reshaped with the defections of Democrats from 1854 to 1860 and the disastrous disruption of the party in 1860, and with the emergence of the Republican party during the controversy over Kansas. The party system of 1861—a divided Democracy and a sectional Republican coalition—was the product of the strife-torn fifties.

Congress had borne up well under sectional stress throughout the 1840s. For a dozen years before 1861, however, it had increasingly wrangled over slavery questions. Three times the House had hung inoperative while factions unable to muster majorities had quarreled over naming the speaker and organizing the chamber. Fisticuffs and duels between members and the sensational caning of Senator Charles Sumner had marked the decade. Legislation concerning homesteads, a transcontinental railroad, and a protective tariff had failed to overcome constitutional and sectional obstacles. Based upon state representation, the Senate was dominated by the South. Befriended by pro-Southern presidents in the fifties, the South was able to frustrate many Northern aspirations. Washington in 1861 had a distinctly Southern flavor.

The Supreme Court for many years had looked southward. The South had more than its share of federal judges, both on the high bench and in the inferior federal courts. Since the days of John Marshall's nationalizing decisions, the high court had moved, not so much as is sometimes said in the direction of states rights, as in the direction of divided government. The principle of federalism—allocating power between central and state government—characterized the thinking of Chief Justice Roger B. Taney. He based his notorious ruling in the case of Dred Scott not on the Calhoun theory of state sovereignty but squarely upon the Fifth Amendment, astonishingly construed to prohibit Congress from depriving owners of slave property without due process of law.

For years many Northerners had deferred to the South in order to maintain national unity. Deference had been the policy of Pierce and Buchanan. Now in April 1861 a separate Southern confederacy had been formed, sundering the nation. An untried president and a new sectional party occupied a divided, warring house. In the early morning light of April 12, the Confederates opened fire upon Fort Sumter and the Civil War began.

CHAPTER TWO

The Appeal to Arms

"To maintain the honor, the integrity and the existence of our National Union," Lincoln by proclamation called up 75,000 militia in mid-April. The militiamen, he said, were intended to suppress illegal combinations in the seven seceded states and to enforce the laws.

"The response of the country was most gratifying," he later rejoiced, "surpassing in unanimity and spirit the most sanguine expectation." Indeed, the free states (a more accurate term than Lincoln's "the country") were a unit for war. Although Northerners had cast one million three hundred thousand votes for Douglas and had given Breckinridge about one-third his total; although many of the great cities had voted against Lincoln; and although the desire to conciliate the slaveholding South had been widespread, the free North almost to a man approved the proclamation and its doctrine of military coercion.

The national quarrel had now broken into open hostility. It required Northern people to ask why they fought. It forced the Border slave states to take sides. It strained the Constitution, drafted without expectation of civil war. It tested not only the manpower and material resources of North and South, but also the political institutions of the antagonists.

What was the North fighting for in 1861? Unlike the Confederacy, it did not have to defend its homes, its property in slaves, a social system that lawfully segregated a large Negro population and successfully prevented slave insurrection. Abolition was not a Northern war aim. Some Northerners, hating war, the South, and slavery, had favored separation in the interest of peace and moral purity.

The firing on the old flag opened the wellsprings of patriotism. Suddenly Northerners seemed to realize that their way of life was bound up in the Union. The nation was a living thing, holding the proud past of the experiment in popular government, the security of the present, and the promise of the future. The welfare of every household, the aspiration of every man was to be found in the organic life of the American democracy.

It was not an abolitionists' war to free the Negro slave, nor a politicians' to perpetuate the Republican party, nor a businessmen's to secure Northern profits. None of these reasons alone will suffice. The fight to preserve the Union had a mystic element as well. "The dream of humanity, the vaunted Union we thought so strong, so impregnable—lo! it seems already smashed like a china plate," mourned Walt Whitman. "The Negro was not the chief thing: the chief thing was to stick together," he said.

Poets and pacifists now cheered the colors. In 1846 James Russell Lowell had been among a minority to oppose the Mexican War. A critic of war as well as slavery, he then had written: "Ez fer war, I call it murder." Now in 1861 he quieted his fears of war's consequences and, siding with the majority, dolefully acknowledged:

> Peace, too, brings tears; and mid the battle-din,
> The wiser ear some text of God divines,
> For the sheathed blade may rust with darker sin.

The American Peace Society surrendered to the war spirit, virtually expiring in 1861. The influential pacifist religious weekly, *The Independent*, praised war as a vital defense of the Constitution, a restorer of national life, and divine retribution for the sin of slavery. William Lloyd

Garrison, the nation's foremost abolitionist, who had preached disunion and peace, now cried, "There is not a drop of blood in my veins, both as an Abolitionist and a peace man, that does not flow with the Northern tide of sentiment."

"No union with Slaveholders!" had been the motto of Garrison and his intransigent colleague Wendell Phillips. "Sacrifice anything to keep the slaveholding States in the Union? God forbid!" Phillips had declared before Sumter. Now in a dramatic reversal he declaimed to an audience of four thousand in Boston Music Hall, "I rejoice . . . that now for the first time in my anti-slavery life, I speak under the stars and stripes, and welcome the tread of Massachusetts men marshalled for war." Abolitionists, who had advocated nonviolence in antebellum years, in this crisis of conscience endorsed war.

Democrats with few exceptions planted themselves by the side of the Lincoln administration. The word *Copperhead* was yet unknown. On the day that the garrison at Fort Sumter, colors flying and drums sounding, surrendered, Stephen A. Douglas sought an interview with his old rival. No other person was in the room of the Executive Mansion where for two hours the North's two chief political leaders conferred. The next morning the Associated Press wires hummed the news that Douglas "was prepared to sustain the President in the exercise of all his constitutional functions to preserve the Union. . . ." He began a series of speeches denouncing disunion. To a cheering crowd in Chicago, where he had once been shouted down, he rapped out, "There can be no neutrals in this war; *only patriots and traitors.*"

Ex-President James Buchanan, Lincoln's Democratic predecessor, declared the administration "ought to be sustained at all hazards." Edward Everett, who had run for vice-president on the Constitutional Union ticket, blamed not Lincoln but the South for inaugurating "the unprovoked and unrighteous war." The Democrat who had been head of the nation when the Kansas-Nebraska Act had been passed, Franklin Pierce, gave lukewarm support to the war, though privately he opposed and characteristically blamed the abolitionists for bringing it on. John Cochrane, New York Democrat, who during the secession crisis had opposed coercion, wanted to "crush the rebellion."

New York City was uniquely important as the mercantile and financial heart of the country. Her ties to the South in trade and credit were strong. "Will she sacrifice her commerce, her wealth, her population, her character, in order to strengthen the arm of her oppressors?" demanded the Richmond *Examiner*. A large portion of the nation's foreign commerce, paying a large portion of the nation's expenses through tariff receipts, flowed through the finest harbors on the Atlantic seaboard. The Brooklyn Navy yard and several forts lay within reach. Great numbers of Irish Roman Catholics, fearful of Republican nativism and antagonistic toward Negroes, lived on Manhattan Island.

In 1860 New Yorkers had voted against Lincoln by a plurality of 29,000. Two months later the Democratic mayor, Fernando Wood, recommended to the city council that New York secede and become a free city. On the day Lincoln called out the militia, the Democratic New York *Herald* urged "the people of this metropolis . . . to make a solemn and imposing effort in behalf of peace." The following day, however, the *Herald* said the time had passed for peace meetings. "War will make the Northern people a unit." In a meeting of national moment held at Union Square, an estimated quarter of a million people heard loyalist speeches from many factions and faiths. Roman Catholic Archbishop Hughes, ill at home, sent a letter endorsing the purpose of the meeting. Mayor Wood enthusiastically put himself and the city on the side of Union: "I am with you in this contest. We know no party now."

The New York gathering, one of many Union meetings throughout the North, gave birth to a Union Defence Committee, one of many voluntary agencies that reinforced political institutions during the war. Created to raise money, provide supplies, and equip regiments, in the early months of the war this non-partisan group helped to enlist the city's resources. The identification of the New York Democracy with the war seemed complete when the party's national chairman, the wealthy New Yorker August Belmont, denounced "the treasonable schemes of the slavery oligarchy."

The free states readied men for dispatch to Washington. Massachusetts, with the best prepared militia in the North, hurried off her Sixth Regiment. The New York legislature authorized enlistment of 30,000 men for two years—two-fifths of the total number requested by Lincoln. Pennsylvania promptly ordered five companies of militia to the nation's capital; carrying only thirty-four muskets and no ammunition, they were little more than a promise of the Keystone State's future aid.

Impelled by a host of motives, young men rushed to the colors. Excitement of the moment, the notion that war is a picnic, need for money, hatred of traitors, idealism—all motivated long lines of men at recruiting offices. An Iowan said he intended to "fight for my country so long as I can shoulder my musket" in order to secure "free Speach [*sic*] , free press and free Governments in general."

If the response of the free states was overwhelmingly on the side of the Union, the situation in the eight slave states that had not joined the Confederacy was another matter. Here the call for troops was widely looked on as coercion of sovereign states; and one by one four additional slave states adhered to the Southern cause. Virginia, whose statesmen had contributed so much to the making of the nation, was the first to go. The Old Dominion's secession convention, which earlier had voted down separation, now passed an ordinance of secession by a vote of 88-55, charging the Federal government had perverted its powers to the injury of Virginia and to the oppression of the Southern states. Virginia's secession cost the Union a pre-eminent commander, R. E. Lee. Offered command of the field forces of the Union, he put his state before his nation—in a dramatic testimony of political principles—and resigned. "Save in defense of my native State," he said, "I never desire again to draw my sword."

The secession of Arkansas, Tennessee, and North Carolina followed quickly, the four new Confederate states adding nearly four million persons to the Confederacy. Though Lincoln had managed to retain the loyalty of the free states, he had been unable to retain the allegiance of the Upper South.

The question remained, however, of the adherence to one side or the other of four slave states: Missouri, Kentucky, Delaware, and Maryland—as well as "western Virginia." Federal forces invaded this portion of the Old Dominion, winning a series of small battles, while an irregular convention in Wheeling, representing some of the western counties, formed a "restored government" of Virginia. Federal troops in Missouri restrained secessionist spirits, but so clumsily as to foster guerilla warfare and require continuing military support of the loyal state government.

Kentucky was for some time in doubt. Tied to the slave-holding South by kinship and commerce, it had given its native son Lincoln only 1364 votes as against 119,000 for Bell and Breckinridge. More than one-fifth of her population was slave. The great rivers that formed her northern and western boundaries flowed southward. Her governor defied Lincoln's call to arms with a ringing: "Kentucky will furnish no troops for the wicked purpose of subduing her Sister Southern States." Her legislators, assuming the pose of a sovereign power in international relations, announced Kentucky would be a neutral. Abandonment of neutrality in favor of the Union, patiently awaited by Lincoln, came only when Confederate troops invaded the state in September.

Tiny Delaware, with no militia and a minuscule number of slaves, was "tied hand and foot" to the North, her distinguished senator, James A. Bayard, observed. Though many citizens sympathized with the Confederacy, opposed coercion, and tenaciously upheld slavery, the governor directed that a regiment of volunteers be mustered into the service of the United States.

The greatest immediate peril in the Border slave states threatened in Maryland. The North's access to the nation's capital lay through the Old Line State. If she should secede, Washington would become an island amid hostile slaveholding states and probably be made capital of the Confederacy. Baltimore, forty miles from Washington, was the third city of the nation. It held half the state population, carried on an extensive business with the South, ranked as the country's fourth port in value of commerce, commanded three railroads, and stood third in manufacturing among slaveholding states.

Only thirty-seven Baltimoreans had voted for Lincoln; and city officials were largely secessionist. Great numbers of foreign-born—Germans and Irish—dwelt in the city. Similarly, the legislators, among whom the Southern slaveholding counties were overrepresented, leaned strongly toward secession, Governor Thomas Hicks, elected in 1857 on the Know-Nothing ticket, was loyal but lacking in spine. Strategic, economic, and political reasons joined to make the allegiance of Maryland urgent.

On April 19, the anniversary of Lexington and Concord, the Sixth Massachusetts, while marching through Baltimore, was attacked by a feverish mob. Four soldiers were killed and perhaps ten civilians. Notorious for urban violence, especially in the Know-Nothing era, when it won the nickname "Mobtown," Baltimore now fell into the hands of Southern sympathizers and Secessionists. A monster rally of anti-Unionists in Monument Square heard the timid governor say (though accounts vary), "I will suffer my right arm to be torn from my body before I will raise it to strike a sister State."

For twenty-four hours or more, secessionists held the city and seemed to control the state. Never was the danger of secession so great. The urge to join the Confederacy was strong. A Baltimore native, who was teaching in New Orleans, on hearing of the riot, composed these lines that became a favorite marching song of the Confederacy:

> Come! for thy shield is bright and strong,
> Maryland!
> Come! for thy dalliance does thee wrong,
> Maryland!
> Come to thine own heroic throng,
> Stalking with Liberty along,
> And chaunt thy dauntless slogan song,
> Maryland! My Maryland!

The state military helped to bring the Baltimore riot under control, but the political situation in the state deteriorated and the danger to Washington deepened. Fearful of the effect of having more Union troops pass through Baltimore, state authorities cut railroad bridges connecting Baltimore and Washington with the North. Lincoln acquiesced to a request not to order further troops through the turbulent city; and arrangements were made to convoy troops to Washington by water.

Disaster had attended disaster. Virginia had seceded on the 17th, the Federal arsenal at Harper's Ferry had been burned on the 18th, Baltimore had broken into murderous violence on the 19th, bridges linking Washington with the North had been burned later at midnight, the Union navy yard at Gosport, Virginia, had been abandoned and destroyed together with its ships on the 20th. The capital stood in peril unmatched since the British captured it in 1814.

In this crisis Lincoln stretched his constitutional powers. On the night of April 21, he issued a series of orders. Among them was an executive appropriation of $2 million to be placed in the hands of three eminent private citizens of New York, to be used at their discretion for the public defense. Before the orders could go out, the telegraph operator at Baltimore reported that secessionists had seized his office. The loyalty of government clerks loomed in question. The next day, Monday, April 22, hundreds of government employees resigned. Governor Hicks foolishly suggested that Great Britain be asked to mediate between North and South, and he called a special session of his legislature, which heretofore he had resisted doing. A special election was required to fill the Baltimore seats then vacant.

Lincoln despaired. On the 23rd, gazing out his office window, looking for the ships bearing troops from New York and other Northern states, he anguished, "Why don't they come! Why don't they come!" Later he sank into irony, "I begin to believe that there is no North." The special election in Maryland the next day offered only a "States Rights" ticket; and with less than one-third of the 1860 voters participating, the slate was chosen.

After six anxious days of isolation, Washington—its windows, balconies, and housetops crammed with cheering citizens—welcomed the New York Seventh Regiment, brought by water to Annapolis and carried to the capital over a hastily repaired railroad.

Danger abated in Washington, but in Maryland secessionist militia were drilling. On the eve of the pro-Southern legislature's meeting, Lincoln stretched the Constitution to the breaking point. Without authorization from Congress, which was not in session, though after taking advice from Attorney General Bates, he authorized, "in the extremist necessity, the suspension of the writ of habeas corpus."

John Merryman of Baltimore County, accused of holding a commission in a rebel company which had destroyed railroad bridges, was taken from his bed by military authorities and incarcerated in a Federal fort. He immediately petitioned the United States circuit court for a writ of habeas corpus—namely, that the authorities be ordered to bring him into court and show why he was being detained. The circuit judge was also chief justice of the United States, eighty-four-year-old Roger B. Taney, a native of Baltimore, a Democrat, and author of the Dred Scott decision that had helped bring on the war.

The Federal general twice defied Taney, who issued the writ. After citing the general for contempt, Taney proceeded to read the president of the United States a lesson in constitutional law. Lincoln's suspension of the writ was unconstitutional, he ruled. Citing court precedent and the fact that the habeas corpus clause is in Article One of the Constitution, which treats legislative powers, the ancient jurist declared only Congress may suspend the writ.

The president is authorized, he continued, to execute the laws, not to make them, and to assist the court in enforcing them, and not to resist it. But in this case, with presidential sanction, the military had gone beyond mere suspension. It had thrust aside the judicial authorities and substituted a military government for civil authority. Lincoln's violation of the Constitution was grave, the issue heavy with meaning which Taney strove to make plain: if the military may usurp power at its discretion, "the people of the United States are no longer living under a government of laws, but every citizen holds life, liberty, and property at the will and pleasure of the army officer in whose military district he may happen to be found."

Lincoln for the moment ignored Taney's condemnation, waiting until he could justify his action to Congress. Maryland still was unquiet. Her legislators, having heard Governor Hicks counsel neutrality, had passed a fourfold resolution imploring the president to "cease this unholy war, at least until Congress assembled"; consenting to the recognition of the Confederacy; protesting the military occupation of the state; and, finally, stating that a secession convention at this time was inexpedient.

Notwithstanding Maryland's failure to secede, the state remained under military surveillance. One of Lincoln's political generals, swashbuckling Benjamin Butler, a Massachusetts changeling who had voted fifty times in the Charleston nominating convention to make Jefferson Davis the Democratic candidate for president, now an ardent warrior against Davis, occupied Baltimore without authorization. He was replaced; but Federal troops stayed in the city. Soon the chief of police was arrested, and the Federal government through the provost marshall took charge of the municipal police.

Baltimore had subsided and Maryland had kept loyal, but at heavy, if perhaps unavoidable, cost to constitutional government. Through the perilous night the flag was still there, but the bright stars and broad stripes continued to stream over Maryland and the loyal slave states only with the military standing by. Arbitrary executive acts, abridgments of personal liberties, suppression of newspapers, military interference with elections would mark the Lincoln administration and feed Democratic opposition. Not until 1863 would Congress authorize suspension of the writ of habeas corpus; not until 1865 would it prohibit military interference in elections; and not until 1866 would the Supreme Court reject martial law where the civil courts were open.

On the day the Confederacy fired on Fort Sumter, President Jefferson Davis summoned his Congress to meet in special session at the end of the month. At this session the Confederate Congress girded for war, providing for its army, navy, finance, and a permanent capital. Davis was empowered to accept volunteers without limit to serve for the duration of the fighting, and to issue letters of marque and reprisal in the absence of a navy. A $50 million loan was ordered, but taxation shunned. The Confederacy prepared for a long war with a short purse. Payment of debts owed to individuals in the free states was forbidden. The newly seceded states were welcomed; and Richmond was designated the new capital.

While these events were taking place, President Lincoln was imposing further strains upon the Constitution. By proclamation he ordered the blockade of the Confederate coast. A "blockade is an act of war, which a nation cannot commit against itself," as the attorney general later wrote in his diary. The president had, in effect, declared war, in spite of the Constitution's stipulation that Congress shall have power to declare war. He would perhaps have been better advised merely to have declared the ports closed, making violators punishable as smugglers under domestic law. "But the attempt to break a blockade works a forfeiture of ship and cargo— must be adjudged under the law of nations, and constantly imperils our relations with neutrals," Bates said in sober afterthought.

Early in May, Lincoln, governing by proclamation, increased the size of the regular army and navy. Again he had trespassed upon the constitutional powers of Congress, to raise and support armies and to provide and maintain a navy. By this bold stroke, which he admitted overreached his authority, he hoped to prepare for a long war, diverting the excessive offers of three-months' volunteers to enlistments for three years. He would have to answer to Congress, jealous of its prerogatives, for all his irregular and extralegal acts.

Often thought of as an exponent of freedom and popular government, Abraham Lincoln since April 15 had played the role of dictator—a Tudor monarch, one historian called him—running the country without Congress, waging an undeclared war, appropriating money, raising an army and navy, suspending the writ of habeas corpus. A German diplomat resident in Washington at this time observed, "One of the interesting features of the present state of things is the illimited power exercised by the government. Mr. Lincoln is, in that respect, the equal, if not the superior, of Louis Napoleon. The difference consists only in the fact that the President rests his authority on the unanimous consent of the people of the loyal States, the emperor his on the army."

As North and South confronted one another in the spring of 1861, the superiority of the North seemed glaring. Twenty-two million people faced nine million, a preponderance of more than two to one. Of the South's numbers more than a third were Negro slaves and ineligible for combat. Of the North's teeming population, fewer than 780,000 were Negroes, free and slave (the latter in the four Border States), all of whom were ineligible for combat service at the outset of hostilities. In white males of military age, the North outnumbered the South more than three to one.

In material resources the North overwhelmed the South. It claimed, according to the census of 1860, 111,000 manufacturing establishments, employing 1,300,000 workers as against 18,000 manufacturing establishments with 111,000 workers in the South. The first of modern wars, the Civil War required iron as well as blood. In 1860 the United States, in the infancy of its great industrial revolution, had 286 iron furnaces, of which more than two-fifths were located in Pennsylvania. The Keystone State led in the production of bar, sheet, and railroad iron. Of the 470 locomotives built in the United States in 1860, all but nineteen—made in Virginia—were built in the North. The value of firearms manufactured in 1860 came to $2,342,700, of which the South's share was only $73,000.

The Civil War, the last of the romantic wars, still required draft animals. The North's supremacy in numbers of horses was partially offset by Southern supremacy in asses and mules. Railroad mileage was divided about seven to three to the North's advantage; but this was partially offset by a war fought within interior lines and by a navigable river system.

If we turn from manpower and material comparisons to political, the North again held the advantage. The constitutions of the two governments were, as we have seen, strikingly similar. The South was to suffer perhaps not so much in the constitutional affirmation of states rights as in the inveterate tendency of her people to insist upon localism and individualism. States rights and personal freedom were strenuously clung to by Southerners despite the centripetal imperatives of war. One historian has judged that the Confederacy died of states rights, while another has judged she perished of an excess of democracy. Resistance to conscription, executive power, and taxation—all weakened the Confederate war effort. Enforcement of national authority proved difficult; and it is probably a meaningful clue to its spirit of anticentralism that the Confederacy never created a Supreme Court.

The place of political parties in the two governments differed. In the first place, the election of 1860 gave a major party control of the Union presidency through a popular vote. Abraham Lincoln was leader of his party as well as president, whereas Jefferson Davis was a president without a party. Originally designated by the Confederate Congress, Davis early in the war was elected to a long six-year term in balloting that allowed voters no alternative. The Confederacy tried to establish a government without political parties, based upon the cooperation of sovereign states and an inchoate Southern nationalism.

The Confederacy in failing to have a two-party system failed thereby to unify a political program, to fix responsibility, to discipline politicians, and to provide a safety valve for criticism by a loyal opposition. Factions without party organization and responsibility developed in the Confederacy. The Davis government was an uneasy marriage, troubled by frequent changes in the cabinet, a lack of focus in congress, and the downright hostility of Vice-President Stephens (who dogmatically advocated state sovereignty) as well as of a number of states rights governors. Davis regarded the patronage as a nuisance rather than the nursemaid of household strength and never developed a civil service commensurate with the needs of a government at war.

The North, on the other hand, was in effect governed by the Republican party, which to be sure made obeisance to War Democrats. The party controlled the presidency, the Congress, and, from the midpoint of the war, the Supreme Court. Lincoln skillfully dispensed the patronage, allowing Democrats to enjoy some of it, but keeping control for administration ends. The Republicans did not hesitate to maintain elections in wartime, thus defining public issues and gaining public support. The presidential election of 1864 was a referendum on administration policies which strengthened the Lincoln government and added impetus to the defeat of the Confederacy and passage of the Thirteenth Amendment.

Though the Republican party suffered from a setback in the election of 1862 and from factionalism on certain issues, it was the central political agency for the actual exercise of power. It enacted, with help as well as hindrance from the Democrats, a legislative program of a high order of statesmanship. It served to bridge the separation of powers in the national government; and it also served to bridge the division of powers between national and state government. It was in these ways integral to the functioning of the Federal Union.

For their part, the Democrats, though temporarily disabled in 1860-61, would reintegrate themselves and demonstrate the durability of a two-party system for the remainder of the war. The point is often lost sight of that throughout the war the North enjoyed the advantages of party government.

CHAPTER THREE

"A Giant Committee of Ways and Means"

The first testing of Northern political institutions was made by the short, extraordinary congressional session of 1861. In it the Republican party had to organize the Congress and to assume the posture of responsibility. The Democrats defined their role as the opposition—loyal to, obstructive to, or united with the dominant party—thereby losing their separate identity. The new Congress had to face the legislative demands of an ongoing war; to consider the unauthorized legislative acts performed by the executive; and to formulate its understanding of the war purpose. The events of the session as well as the voting in state elections in the fall of 1861 offer us an opportunity to observe how well all this worked out and what were the early tendencies of wartime politics.

In his call for troops, Lincoln had also convened Congress into special session for July 4. The legislators were, he said, to "determine such measures as, in their wisdom, the public safety and interest may seem to demand." The long interval of eighty days between the call and the convening allowed the executive to deal with the emergency without the complications of a legislature in session; and it also allowed two crucial Border States time to hold special elections for this unanticipated session.

Maryland met its first electoral test of Unionism in its election on June 13. Though Federal troops made their presence felt, they did not interfere in the election. The day passed without trouble; and all but one of the six newly chosen representatives were regarded as friends of the Union. The future radical congressman Henry Winter Davis lost to Henry May of Baltimore, who refused to take an unconditional Union oath. The future Democratic senator Reverdy Johnson, head of the Maryland bar, who had rejected Taney's reasoning in the Merryman case, at this time denounced secessionism and proclaimed his Unionism. Union candidate votes exceeded the opposition's nearly two to one.

Of greater moment was the canvass in "neutral" Kentucky, where ten representatives were to be named. Here in his native state, Lincoln had refrained from introducing military force, rightly fearing that Federal troops would drive Kentuckians into the embrace of the Confederacy. The venerable political leader John J. Crittenden, who had striven for compromise in Congress, on the eve of the election upheld neutrality and rejected disunionism. Joseph Holt, late a member of the Buchanan cabinet and soon to be appointed Judge Advocate General, denounced neutrality and disunion. On June 20, with less than half as many persons voting as in the presidential election, Kentucky showed her Union sympathies. The Southern Rights party carried only one of the ten districts, polling a little over forty percent of the aggregate vote. Henry Burnett from the western part of the state was the only avowed secessionist elected. Later expelled from the U.S. Congress, he became a senator in the Confederate Congress. The Border State elections had gone well for the Union; and Lincoln's policy of watchful waiting in Kentucky had been vindicated.

Greatness was thrust upon the Thirty-seventh Congress. It met in three sessions, once in the short special session convened by Lincoln, and twice in the regular sessions starting in December prescribed by the Constitution. Made up of men of marked ability, challenged by the crisis of the Union, and uninhibited by Southern lawmakers, it provided the sinews of war, restructured the nation's economic institutions, and changed the face of race relations, simultaneously striving to save the Union and to shape its future.

When Congressmen gathered in their chambers at noon on Independence Day, the most conspicuous sight was the vacant chairs. Assigned to legislators who had seceded, they were visible evidence that only secession had given control of the two chambers to the Republican party. Secession had transformed the Republicans into the majority, with margins of thirteen in the Senate and thirty-two in the House. The Senate was composed of 31 Republicans, 10 Democrats, and 8 Unionists; the House of 105 Republicans, 43 Democrats, and 30 Unionists. Secession contracted the size of Congress by about one-third and of party structure from four to three groups: Republican, Democrat, and Unionist.

In the new Capitol, whose unfinished dome suggested the incomplete state of the Union, the House of Representatives met to name a Speaker. This officer, more than a figurehead presiding over debates, was a man of power, apportioning legislative authority by naming committees, controlling the floor, appointing conference committees, and serving as a link to the executive.

Galusha Grow of Pennsylvania was speedily chosen. A member of the House since 1850, a former Democrat who had helped found the Republican party, advocate of homestead legislation, he was at thirty-seven the youngest Speaker since Henry Clay. Wise and careful in discharge of his duties, he enjoyed Lincoln's confidence as well as his colleagues'. When the Thirty-seventh Congress adjourned nearly two years later, it voted the traditional thanks to the Speaker unanimously—for which there had been only one precedent in the history of the House. An imposing six feet two inches tall, he was strong in physique; with steely eyes and a record of pugnacity, he personified decisiveness and strength.

On the floor of the House, the natural leader was Thaddeus Stevens, also of Pennsylvania. Club-footed, sharp-tongued, a solitude-loving bachelor, he seemed almost a misanthrope except for his love for the Union and his warm espousal of the antislavery cause. At sixty-nine he was a veteran in politics, formidable in appearance, with his huge frame, strong, dark features, and ready scowl. Unswervingly he demanded vigorous prosecution of the war. Crisp rather than eloquent in his speechmaking, he impelled the House to act by his knowledge, sarcastic wit, courage, and parliamentary skill. He had nominated Grow for Speaker and in turn became chairman of the House's most powerful committee—Ways and Means. His committee handled taxes, loans and currency, and appropriations, and in the course of the war added Pacific railroads to its authority. In the last weeks of the war, when the multiform burden had grown great, the House transferred jurisdiction over appropriations, banking and currency, and Pacific railroads to three new committees.

As chairman of Ways and Means, Stevens had to be consulted by all other chairmen whose work required money. He had the privilege of the floor whenever he wanted it. Yet it is possible to exaggerate both his influence and his radicalism during the war. As we shall see, he was more than once frustrated and more than once moderate. His controversial reputation as dictator of the House, scourge of the South, and friend of the Negro better conforms to Reconstruction years than to the Civil War period. He was nevertheless the leader of his party in the House.

The Senate was presided over by Vice-President Hannibal Hamlin of Maine, who had deserted the Democratic party during the Kansas crisis of 1856. Portly in person, lacking in authority, he could look out toward the floor upon the only senator from a seceded state—Andrew Johnson of Tennessee, his successor as vice-president. Shrunken in size to fewer than fifty members, the Senate had lost its experienced committee chairmen: Jefferson Davis, former head of Military Affairs, and now president of the Confederacy; Stephen Mallory, former head of Naval Affairs, and now Confederate secretary of the navy; R. M. T. Hunter, former head of Finance, and soon to be Confederate secretary of state; and James M. Mason, former head of Foreign Relations, and soon to be Confederate minister to the United Kingdom.

At the start of the session, Senate Republicans acknowledged no one as party leader, the position once held by Seward. At the moment the most important committee was Military Affairs, now headed by Henry Wilson of Massachusetts. A cobbler in his youth, self-educated, he had come into the Senate in 1855, delivering his first speech in favor of the abolition of slavery wherever the Federal government had the authority to do so, for example, the District of Columbia and the territories, and of the repeal of the fugitive slave law. Now forty-nine years old, strong and clear in voice, he was earnest in creating a great military establishment and in attaining the aims of his first Senate speech. The quality of his leadership and the quantity of military and pro-Negro laws he sponsored brought their reward with the vice-presidency under Grant.

Sharing high responsibility for direction of Senate measures was William Pitt Fessenden of Maine, chairman of the Finance Committee. Like Wilson and other party leaders, he had gone to Washington during the Lincoln "dictatorship" to consult members of the administration. Experienced in state and national lawmaking, he had served on the Senate Finance Committee since 1857. The illegitimate son of an abolitionist father, precocious as a child, profane in speech (Bowdoin College had withheld his diploma for a full year because of his swearing and other offenses), he had gone over to antislavery slowly. More moderate than Wilson in his views about emancipation, Negro rights, and the powers of the national government, he bore a tremendous burden throughout the war. Together with Stevens in the House, he managed the legislation to finance the war. His committee looked after both revenue and appropriation bills. In spite of ill health, he worked awesome hours to prepare measures in advance of submitting them to the Senate. In spite of the colossal cost of the war and the extensive self-seeking political projects of his colleagues, he strove to hold the ground for economy and businesslike methods. Within a short time he had established his mastery of the Senate in matters concerning his committee. Senator Grimes of Iowa said to his fellows in 1861, "My experience has taught me that it is utterly futile to war against the chairman of the committee on finance. His eloquence, will, and persistency are such that it is useless for me to press an amendment against his wishes. I therefore withdraw the proposed amendment, hoping to receive his support some other time." Sword and purse—essentials of power in a war state—were in capable hands in the two houses of Congress.

On the Democratic side of Congress, a power vacuum existed. Split and defeated in 1860, severed by secession in 1861, discredited by Sumter in April, the Democrats were left leaderless in June by the death of Stephen A. Douglas. As Douglas lay dying, the editor of the New York *Tribune*, Horace Greeley, wrote, "The loss . . . at this crisis must be regarded as a national calamity." Northern Democrats lost their most statesmanlike figure, Lincoln a healthy critic, and the two-party system a spokesman of loyal opposition. The titular leader of senate Democrats now became John C. Breckinridge, the Southern rights champion, who within a few months would be wearing a Confederate uniform. Throughout the Thirty-seventh Congress, no one could be found to organize and institutionalize the senate Democrats, divided into ideological and geographical blocs.

In the House, Democratic disunity was apparent. Democrats shared the opposition with the Unionists (mostly Border State men). John J. Crittenden, the Kentucky Unionist, was the most conspicuous figure, and Speaker Grow gave him the chairmanship on foreign affairs. Ohio offered a large share of vigorous Democrats: the witty S. S. ("Sunset") Cox, George Pendleton (future author of the civil service act), and Clement L. Vallandigham (fated to become the most noted "Copperhead"—a term of reproach suggesting disloyalty if not treason). From New York City came Benjamin Wood, brother of the mayor and editor of the New York *Daily News*, which the postmaster general in August excluded from the mails as dangerous to loyalty. From Albany came Erastus Corning, the wealthy businessman with a predilection for public affairs. Characterized by colorful personalities, the House Democrats remained loosely organized, their influence springing from men more than party.

On the day after they assembled, the two chambers heard the message of the president. A notable state paper, it treated a number of matters— reviewing the secession crisis, explaining and justifying what the president had done since Sumter, recommending measures to be enacted, elucidating Lincoln's conception of the Union and of the issues presented by the war, and finally giving a statement of future policy.

Before he became president, he pointed out, an "illegal organization, in the character of Confederate States," had sprung into being, placing upon him the duty of preventing the destruction of the Union. He had chosen peaceful means, but the attack on Fort Sumter forced the issue, "immediate dissolution, or blood." He was left, he said, no choice but to call out the war power of the government. The alternative was to surrender the existence of the government.

Turning to the sensitive issues of executive action after Sumter, he asserted that his call for 75,000 militia and his proclamation closing Southern ports were "strictly legal." He justified his call for three years' volunteers and for large additions to the army and navy, "whether strictly legal or not," on the grounds of popular demand and public necessity. Coolly he remarked the executive branch had done nothing "beyond the constitutional competency of Congress."

His suspension of the privilege of the writ of habeas corpus, he recognized, had been questioned; and it had been suggested that he had violated the laws. In answer he said nearly one-third of the states were resisting the whole body of laws. "Are all the laws but one to go unexecuted, and the government itself go to pieces lest that one be violated?" he demanded. Beyond all this, he did not believe he had violated any law; the Constitution, despite Taney's reading of it, was silent as to which branch may suspend. He himself could not believe that the framers intended rebellion should be allowed to run its course until Congress could assemble. The attorney general, he announced, would provide an opinion; and Congress could judge whether legislation was needed.

Military and financial legislation was required, he went on, to make "this contest a short and decisive one." He asked Congress to authorize 400,000 men and $400 million, staggering figures which he measured against the manpower potential, the national wealth, the need "to preserve our liberties," and the apparent willingness of the people to save their government.

Secession, considered a constitutional right in the Confederate states, he scored as "an ingenious sophism." Concerning states rights he flatly declared, "The states have their status in the Union, and they have no other legal status."

The war, he said in a global perspective, was not a war between the states. "This is essentially a people's contest . . . a struggle for maintaining in the world that form and substance of government whose leading object is to elevate the condition of men. . . . The plain people [understand] that the destroying of the government which was made by Washington means no good to them."

For the future he did not anticipate that the Constitution would be different after the war from his present conception of it. And finally, in an often overlooked but early hint of his reconstruction policy, he would be guided by the Constitution and the laws in his course after the rebellion.

Lincoln had presented Congress with a fait accompli—an ongoing war, a series of acts which could not easily be repudiated, and a plausible legislative program. The executive had laid a heavy hand on the first Civil War congress. The brief, twenty-nine-day session became, in the words of a member, "a giant committee of ways and means." There was no disposition on the part of Republicans to enact the 1860 platform, to fasten (as some historians have said) an industrial economy on the future, or to feud (as some historians have said) with the president.

The House, which held the pursestrings, swiftly approved a resolution introduced by a conservative Indiana Democrat to restrict the session to war measures. Raising an army was the most pressing matter. In a series of measures, Congress (1) provided for paying the militia and volunteers already called into service and authorized the closing of the ports where obstruction of collection of · revenue existed, without mentioning the blockade; (2) authorized 500,000 volunteers, exceeding the executive request; (3) authorized increase of the regular army by eleven regiments, again exceeding executive request; (4) adopted various proposals to reorganize the army; and (5) strengthened the navy.

This prompt creation of a military machine was the work of the president, who had shown the way, the secretaries of war and navy, who had made recommendations, Henry Wilson, who had steered measures through the Senate, and Frank Blair, who, as chairman of the House Military Affairs Committee, steered the measures through the lower chamber. President and Congress had cooperated to draw the Union's sword.

These military steps of the first session of the Civil War Congress point to certain aspects of military policy. Congress, as a Republican senator remarked, had begun to appreciate the magnitude of the task. The size of the new army shattered tradition; but otherwise the lawmakers seemed tradition bound. The Jeffersonian outlook, stressing distrust of a professional army and a reliance upon states rights, had prevailed. Lincoln's request for 24,000 men to be added to the regular army (as distinguished from state militia and volunteers in the temporary national forces) encountered strong objection. The House Military Affairs Committee thought volunteers could win the war and the question of strengthening the regulars could be postponed until the end of the war. Wilson favored disbanding the regulars and distributing them among the volunteers. The outcome was to attach a proviso to approval of Lincoln's request that with the end of the war the regulars would be cut back to 25,000.

The principle of states rights was upheld by retention of the framework of the militia system. The national government would call for troops and fix state quotas; the state governors would raise the men, appoint the officers except generals, organize the regiments, and exercise control until they were turned over to Federal authority at the point of rendezvous. There were merits at the start of the war in tapping state initiative to produce a national army; but as the war continued, Congress learned lessons of future value about raising a United States army.

Wartime finance in this session affords some instruction in legislative politics. Two measures were enacted. The first was a bill authorizing a loan of $250 million and giving the secretary of the treasury broad discretion about the means of borrowing. Stevens was in command, urging Congress "to give everything the government asks." He moved for a suspension of the rules, then allowed only one hour for debate, and rammed the measure through the House with only five dissenting votes. In the Senate Fessenden indefatigably took the floor to avert delay and amendment and had it passed July 15.

Borrowing money for a future generation to pay (the loan was irredeemable for twenty years) was a popular path toward financing the war and raised little objection. Paying for the war by taxation was another matter, raising objection that crossed party lines. Three modes of taxation were proposed: a direct tax, an income tax, and an increase in the tariff. Lashed on by Stevens, the House approved a bill, 77-60, for direct and income taxes; the large numbers of nays included Republican stalwarts from the West. The Senate added amendments; and there was resort to the important device, a committee of conference. The House now approved the joint committee's recommendations (with 39 nays, of whom all but two were Democrats and Unionists), and the Senate concurred (with 8 nays, all Democrats and all but two from the border slave states).

The financial measures again demonstrated that Congress, gauged against past parsimony in military matters, saw the magnitude of its task by authorizing huge loans and imposing a variety of taxes. The lawmakers, who were both innovators and mossbacks, had for the first time levied a tax upon incomes, small to be sure, but looking in the direction of equalizing taxation, and offering precedent for the future. They had imposed a direct tax, twice tried without much success in previous wars. They had responded with alacrity to the bidding of the president, the secretary of the treasury, and the party leaders. They had shown no bias in favor of protectionism, inasmuch as the tariff duties fell upon noncompetitive items, like tea and coffee, not produced in the United States.

In the middle of the session, the first major engagement of the war—Bull Run—fell like a thunderclap on Congress. Deliberated by the administration, the battle had in large part been determined upon for political reasons—the need to do something decisive and thereby sustain Northern morale. This baptism of fire, which occurred on Sunday, July 21, not far from Washington, came as a shock to Congress. Some members had gaily gone to watch the contest, as if to attend a picnic, and returned from the military reversal somber but resolute. The influential representative

Justin S. Morrill wrote to his wife: "the loss of prestige is not to be computed. We must have more men . . . it will cost much, but we must not flinch a hair's breadth." And he added ominously, "But while it has not been contemplated and is not now, if it becomes necessary, I know that slavery will be handled roughly."

Men, money, morale, and possibly measures against slavery—this was Morrill's forecast of Congress' concerns. Bull Run sounded a note of urgency; it warned of a long war and moved the Republican majority slightly to the left. The comprehensive tax and military program had mainly been broadened by Bull Run. After the battle Congress turned to laws to punish rebels, confiscate their property, threaten slavery, and exact the loyalty of Federal employees. Throughout the North a second wave of patriotism arose.

Whitman wrote:

Beat! beat! drums—blow! bugles! blow!
Make no parley—stop for no expostulation,
Mind not the timid—mind not the weeper or prayer

So strong you thump O terrible drums—so loud you bugles blow.

On the day after Bull Run, the House adopted a pending resolution on the aims of the war. Proposed by the conciliatory Crittenden, the resolution renounced any purpose of oppression, subjugation, or interference with slavery in the states. The war was being waged "to defend and maintain the supremacy of the Constitution and to preserve the Union. . . ." When these objects had been accomplished, "the war ought to cease." Only two members of the House, Stevens keeping silent, voted against this self-denying ordinance: and only five members of the Senate cast nay votes a few days later. Crittenden's resolution was the first congressional commitment on Reconstruction.

On the other hand, the stiffening in the spirit of the laws is perhaps best seen in the confiscation act. The Confederacy had pointed the way to economic warfare by a law confiscating debts due Northerners. The Union law, first of two passed during the war, took as its target only property put to hostile use. The day after Bull Run, Lyman Trumbull of Illinois remarked, "I take it that Negroes who are used to destroy the Union . . . ought not to be restored" to their masters. Asserting Negro slaves had been used by the rebels at Bull Run, he offered an amendment to free slaves employed in resisting the laws of the United States.

Adopted with only dissenters in the Senate, Trumbull's amendment provoked a storm of objection in the House. Remember the Crittenden resolution, the House was admonished. With one-third of the House not voting, the confiscation act passed, 61-48, a sharp division of sentiment. With two exceptions all the ayes were Republicans; seven Republicans cast nays. Nine administration men disappeared from the House just before the vote was taken.

Discord over Lincoln's exercise of personal rule before the Congress had convened was so great that the lawmakers did not act on it until the very end of the session. Even Republicans were strongly disinclined to sanction his increase of the regular military establishment; and a bipartisan majority was hypersensitive to his suspension of the writ of habeas corpus. Breckinridge thought the president ought to be rebuked. John Sherman of Ohio said the Constitution gave these powers to Congress alone.

To press the matter of validating the president's acts might endanger the great military and financial bills that were pending. Enactment of them would tend to sustain the unauthorized acts. But Congress dragged its feet on a joint resolution to sustain him. On the last day of the session, Wilson resorted to the subterfuge of adding an amendment legalizing the president's orders respecting the army and navy to a popular bill to raise army pay and provide relief benefits to volunteers. Sugar-coated, this pill went down, some half dozen senators and nineteen representatives protesting.

Habeas corpus was another matter, though. A Senate bill to regulate the use of martial law provoked antagonism from extreme Republicans and conservative Democrats. James A. Pearce railed against Lincoln's despotism in his home state, troubled Maryland. Day after day the issue was postponed, until the session ended without approval. If Congress was unwilling to concede to the president authority to encroach upon its constitutional prerogative as well as upon the personal liberty of citizens, it did pass a law to punish conspirators against the government and, inaugurating what has been called "the era of the oath," required Federal employees to affirm not only their future loyalty to the Constitution and the government but also their fidelity to the Union irrespective of state claims of sovereignty.

The special session, in summary, had done its work quickly and well. Its central concern had been to provide for the vindication of the national authority. It had more than met the administration's requests for men and money. Postponing discharge of platform pledges, largely suppressing differences, Congress dealt realistically with an unexampled emergency. The Republican machine ran smoothly, operated by able men using expert techniques of law enactment.

Democrats and Unionists had cooperated with Republicans, notably in the bills to raise a quarter of a billion dollars and half a million men. Still there were bad omens for the future of congressional politics. Vallandigham, crying "I am for peace," made an absurd proposal to send peace commissioners South with the Union armies, tried to censure Lincoln, and voted against both finance bills. A list of obstructionists would include Vallandigham, Benjamin Wood, many of the Border State men, and practically the entire Kentucky delegation. The chronic resistance of Kentuckians to wartime legislation is a marked feature of congressional voting.

Among Republicans a tendency toward extremism could be discerned in the passage of the confiscation law and in jealousy of congressional authority. Party strength was also laid under stress by sectional loyalty. In debate over the direct tax to be assessed upon real estate, Western Republicans tilted with Easterners. The tariff, too, fostered sectionalism, as the Columbus, Ohio *Crisis* exaggeratedly complained: "The West has been sold to Eastern manufacturers by the politicians. . . ." If the war should long continue, these fissures might deepen, complicating the cooperation needed for prosecuting the war.

In the state elections conducted in the fall of 1861, efforts were made to unite the parties. The exigencies of war and the signs of harmony after Sumter, Bull Run, and in the special session of Congress gave credence to the movement. Surely, Northerners, devoted to the Union and vigorous waging of the war, could join together in maintaining American nationality. A united political front, it was said, was as important as a united military front.

This attempt to adjourn politics in 1861 met but partial success. The cry for merger clearly came from the dominant Republicans. "No More Party" seemed to mean "No More Democratic Party," complained the Cincinnati *Enquirer*. It was in fact foolish to expect party organizations to abandon their identities. Self-preservation and the need for a loyal opposition argued against it. When the Republican chieftain of New York State, Thurlow Weed, reminded the Democrats of Andrew Jackson's toast,

"Union, now and forever," and invited them to agree on a single state ticket, the Democratic chieftain, Dean Richmond, declined and, in effect, reminded the Republicans that the old Democratic president had coupled Liberty and Union.

It would indeed have been a heroic achievement for the new Republican party to have united the Democratic organization with it. The latter was very old, tracing its ancestry almost to the birth of the republic and boasting as its past leaders Jefferson and Jackson. It was strong in certain states, including Connecticut, New York, New Jersey, Pennsylvania, Indiana, and Illinois, as well as in many cities.

The Democrats, moreover, prided themselves on a creed that was congenial to vast numbers of voters; a creed of individualism, states rights, and laissez-faire. In addition to these political, constitutional, and economic appeals were religious and ethnic loyalties. Catholics, whether Irish or German, Old School Presbyterians, and many Episcopalians—liturgicals in religion—opposed evangelical and nativist elements in the Republican party with their zeal for prohibition, Sunday observance, and antiforeigner laws, as well as antislavery notions.

Moreover, real wartime issues separated many Democrats from Republicans. Staunch Democrats held out the hope for a negotiated peace, suspected Republicans of abolitionism, and denounced the administration for abridging civil liberties. In New York the regular Democrats did, however, respond to Weed's invitation; and the outcome was a Union ticket headed by a former Breckinridge Democrat.

In Ohio, party differences were sufficiently patched over for a Union convention to nominate a former Democrat for governor. The Democratic party wing led by Vallandigham and others put forward an able candidate. The Union party, charged a Democratic newspaper, "is only a mask to cover the deformities of Abolition."

The outcome was Union party victory in New York and Ohio. Voters in the municipal election in New York defeated Fernando Wood and placed the wealthy fur merchant George Opdyke, earlier entrusted with Federal funds by Lincoln, in the mayor's chair. The North's largest state and largest city were in friendly hands. In crucial Maryland, where, on orders from the secretary of war, troops had arrested a number of secessionist members of the legislature, voters elected a Union party governor and legislature. "Our domestic traitors are prostrate," rejoiced Winter Davis. Meanwhile, in Kentucky, the legislature, outraged by Confederate invasion, terminated neutrality; requested the state's Senators, Breckinridge and Lazarus Powell, to resign their seats; and in an emphatic resolution declared that Kentucky will cling to the Union "with unfaltering devotion."

The two-party system kept alive in the autumn of 1861. The brief truce of parties was over. Strong criticism of the Lincoln administration and the Republican party came from the lips and pens of Democrats. But the party of the "outs" enjoyed little success at the polls; nor could the Confederacy find much cheer in the results.

The problems that Lincoln faced in unifying the nation had become immediately apparent. The need to meet the war in the shape it presented itself required him to act before Congress met, and his actions created resentment. Congress went along with his constitutional requests for military and economic legislation, but only grudgingly it accepted his acts which infringed on congressional powers. It refused to condone suspension of habeas corpus, and even in the emergency session, it began to stake out an independent and more forceful position, as seen in passing the confiscation law and in going beyond some of Lincoln's requests.

In addition to the continuing competition between legislative and executive branches, that emergency session also revealed the continuation of East-West sectionalism. At the same time, politics as usual went on in the fall of 1861; but the very opposition of Democrats, as in Congress, helped unify the Republicans, who now were taking the name Union party to help unite the North behind the war effort. Republican conflict with Democrats and Lincoln's competition with Congress, then, from the very beginning pushed the North toward a more effective prosecution of the war than Lincoln might have achieved if unopposed.

At the same time many Northerners shared the belief that the war must be fought to a finish, that the finish would be a victory for the *United* States, and that the Union had a divine purpose. Patriotism, optimism, millenialism were fused together four days after the election by Julia Ward Howe, wife of a reformer and physician, who now wrote "The Battle Hymn of the Republic."

> Mine eyes have seen the glory of the coming of the Lord:
> He is trampling out the vintage where the grapes of wrath
>   are stored;
> He hath loosed the fateful lightning of His terrible swift sword:
>   His truth is marching on.

CHAPTER FOUR

Congress Wages War

Congress reassembled in December 1861, somber in mood and resolute in bearing. The war was in its eighth month and was not going well. The reversal at Bull Run had been followed by a reversal at Ball's Bluff, not far up the Potomac River from the capital, where Senator Edward Baker of Oregon, eloquent enemy of secession, had lost his life. Military mismanagement, critics charged; and there was much grumbling about the generals and the War Department.

A new, young, inspiriting general, George B. McClellan, who had seemed to give the Union a brilliant victory in northwestern Virginia, had been called to Washington after Bull Run. With the retirement of Winfield Scott, McClellan, a thirty-four-year-old moderate Democrat, had been appointed general-in-chief. Now head of an army in excess of half a million, he had put his men to digging trenches and drilling, without giving a sign he would fight the enemy. Readers of the issue of *Harper's Weekly* that came out just before Congress convened found the apt poem, "All Quiet Along the Potomac To-Night," which during the winter was used to taunt the cautious general. In addition to all this, rumors circulated that Cameron in the War Department was handing out preferential appointments and corrupt contracts.

Conviction was hardening that slavery was the root of the war. In late August, John C. Frémont, the first Republican presidential nominee, now commanding in guerilla-ridden Missouri, proclaimed rebels' property in the state confiscated and their slaves freed. Lincoln regarded Frémont's action illegal and impolitic, unauthorized by the confiscation law, and menacing to the loyalty of the Border slave states, particularly Kentucky. Finding Frémont unwilling to retract, Lincoln ordered the clause revoked.

Frémont won wide popularity among moderate Republicans as well as antislavery men; and the incident, as Lincoln's secretaries observed, "to a certain extent raised him to the position of a new party leader." Thus, as early as 1861, events were bringing forward as Lincoln's rivals for the presidency in 1864 both McClellan and Frémont. When, for various reasons, Lincoln later reassigned Frémont and replaced him with Henry Halleck, a Democrat, giving the opposition party command of the two great armies in the East and the West, extremist Republicans were troubled both by the president's slavery and military policies.

As Congress opened, all this stood as background to a stiffening of policy, to starting a controversy over McClellan, to considering emancipation as a war measure, and to vitalizing and purifying the War Department. These circumstances dashed cold water on the *National Intelligencer's* pious hope for harmony and for the restriction of legislation to "the vindication of the Constitution and the restoration of the Union." At the same time, the long, regular session offered opportunity to take a more deliberate look at the financial and military needs of a lengthening war and to enact the party platform.

On the first day of the session, December 2, members of the two houses introduced a series of resolutions attesting to a hostility to slavery, a willingness to resort to strong courses to prosecute the war, and an insistence upon the exercise of its constitutional authority. A blunt question to Secretary Cameron, asking, "Who is responsible for the disastrous movement of our troops at Ball's Bluff?" won unanimity. Lyman Trumbull of Illinois gave notice he intended to introduce a new confiscation bill, freeing rebels' slaves. Stevens introduced a resolution requesting the president to declare free all slaves who should leave their masters or who should aid in quelling the rebellion. There could be no permanent peace and union so long as slavery existed, he said. And a blustering resolution of thanks to a Union naval officer who arbitrarily had removed two Confederate diplomats from a neutral vessel on the high seas was heedlessly adopted by the House. The vessel, the *Trent*, flew the British flag; and the resolution as well as the removal gave insult to the mistress of the seas.

On the next day Congress heard Lincoln's first Annual Message—that constitutionally prescribed state paper which in the twentieth century became known as the "state of the union" message. In actuality it was not so much a state paper as a political document. He began with foreign affairs, without, however, mentioning the crisis occasioned by removal of the enemy's diplomats from the *Trent*. Acknowledging "profound solicitude" about the possibility of foreign intervention on behalf of the Confederacy, he made what he called "a sound argument" that foreign nations could acquire cotton from America more readily by helping to crush the rebellion than by aiding it. Putting the matter more broadly, he appealed to European interest in international trade and tranquility, asking foreign nations to see that "one strong nation promises more durable peace, and a more extensive, valuable, and reliable commerce, than can the same nation broken into hostile fragments."

Of greatest import for domestic politics were disparate passages that recognized the widening spectrum of sentiment over slavery and emancipation among both radicals and conservatives. To the first, he suggested congressional recognition of the Black republics of Haiti and Liberia, spoke of the administration's success in executing laws against the African slave trade, and showed openness of mind about an additional confiscation law. He recommended that Congress encourage states to free their slaves through financial inducements and encourage colonization of free Blacks. The "whole proposition"—liberation under the confiscation law and possible state enactments, combined with colonization—was absolutely necessary, he pleaded, to the perpetuation of the government.

Appealing indirectly to radical Republicans for support of his mild plan of emancipation, he said he had been "anxious and careful" not to let the war "degenerate into a violent and remorseless revolutionary struggle." He had kept as the war's primary aim the integrity of the Union—reminding Congress of the Crittenden resolution—and soothingly said he had left all questions not of vital military importance to "the more deliberate action of the Legislature."

To Northern conservatives, especially white laborers, he made an adroit appeal. The insurrection, he said, "is largely, if not exclusively, a war upon the first principle of popular government." Evidence for this was in the abridgment of the existing rights of suffrage and the denial to the people of all right to participate in the selection of public officers except legislators. The status of labor, in particular, was threatened by the Confederate system, which placed capital above labor. "Labor," he asserted in a ringing sentence, "is prior to, and independent of, capital." Recognition of this fact in the North, under popular government, provided "the just and generous and prosperous system, which opens the way to all, gives hope to all, and consequent energy and progress, and improvement of condition to all." Let laborers, "beware of surrendering a political power which they already possess, and which, if surrendered, will surely be used to close the door of advancement" on them. Americans owed their opportunity, their national growth, their prosperity to popular government.

Lincoln's remarks about labor have sometimes been taken to bear a quasi-Marxist meaning, to be an endorsement of the rights of labor, or to illustrate the "myth" of the self-made man; but it is here suggested, he was in fact speaking in a contemporary context. Popular government, with universal suffrage, was at stake. A Confederate victory, with slavery, would be a sign of "returning despotism." "The struggle *of* to-day is not altogether *for* to-day—it is for a vast future also."

Lincoln the president, then, was urging the radicals to support his "proposition" for emancipation as a means to keep the integrity of the Union; and he was urging laborers to support the war as a means to keep popular government with its securities for free labor and opportunity.

Lincoln's moderation did not meet the new temper of Congress. When it was proposed to reaffirm the principles of the Crittenden resolution, Stevens swiftly moved to table the proposal. In July only two members of the House had voted against the resolution; now fifty-three members who had voted for it voted to table. By a vote of 71 to 65, Border men voting solidly against tabling except Blair, the House refused to reaffirm.

In the short session there had been a series of peace resolutions. In this long session there was but one, and it was never called up for a vote. Zealous Republicans set about expelling disloyal members from Congress. The Senate promptly expelled Breckinridge, who had joined the Confederate Army, both members from Missouri, and one from Indiana; these four expulsions further weakened the Democrats. An attempt to turn out Kentucky's other senator, abetted by Breckinridge's successor, failed. The House, which had in the special session ejected one Missouri member, now eliminated a second and expelled the sole secessionist Kentucky representative.

Congress' insistence that it shared the war power with the president found embodiment in the creation of a joint committee on the conduct of the war. This famous committee originated, taking the long view, in the constitutional war powers of Congress. In the more immediate background lay a series of impulses: military reverses, War Department ineptitude, appointment of Democrats (particularly McClellan) to command, and an abiding civilian distrust of a professional army in the republic. Energetic to the point of being overzealous, exercising powers to the point of irregularity, the committee continued in existence throughout the war.

It is misleading to describe the joint committee as the radical Republican vanguard of industrial capitalism, a handicap to Lincoln, an instrument to torture unsatisfactory generals, and a dangerous precedent for congressional interference with the executive. It is to be noted, on the contrary, that the committee was usually exercising lawful authority, has been absolved of the charge it employed Star Chamber methods, was often used by Lincoln for his own purposes, as a mere committee had no powers to act, and, finally, was possessed of its share of patriotism and concern for racial justice.

The fact is a broad divergence of opinion existed among radicals, among Republicans, and among members of Congress in general. And it is equally true that Lincoln not only never lost control of executive powers, but also after formation of the committee continued to exercise wide discretion. He permanently enlarged the presidency.

Conservative, moderate, and radical—each outlook was represented among Republicans. Though firm lines among these elements may not be drawn, it can be said disagreements took place with respect to policies on the status of the Negro (including emancipation, military service, colonization, and civil rights), confiscation, and reconstruction. Few party members fitted into a neat pattern. It is impossible to portray monolithic factions of radicals or conservatives. Yet as specific questions arose on the policies, groupings appeared and, though often shifting, make it convenient to distinguish a range of Republican views by use of the terms *radical, moderate,* and *conservative.* But above all, Republicans voted as Republicans.

On the other side of the House, the Democrats in this session failed to find unity under varied attempts by such diverse leaders as Crittenden and Vallandigham. The Democrats, too, had factions. The Border States formed a fairly distinct voting bloc on slavery and confiscation issues, Kentucky continuing to be the most obdurate delegation in Congress.

Congress almost immediately upon convening faced a financial crisis which strained party loyalties and made plain that businessmen and bankers were not a monolithic community for whom the Republican party was a front.

Secretary of the Treasury Chase reported that expenses were fast outrunning receipts. He had badly underestimated expenditures in his July report; and now he recommended a modest increase in taxes, a substantial increase in loans, and above all creation of a national bank currency issued by national banks, backed by government bonds. Chase's timidity about taxation coincided with a general concern about an expensive war with Britain over the *Trent.* Deepening apprehension among bankers and capitalists was the effect of Chase's insistence that the treasury notes he was issuing be paid in specie. Congress the preceding summer had freed him from this requirement, making it possible to use the modern system of bank checks and clearing houses. Instead he had accepted only coin as payment to the government, thereby draining gold from the banks. At the end of December, the banks suspended specie payment. The North, so superior in financial capacity to the South, seemed virtually prostrate.

In assessing blame for the crisis, one must recall the traditional American hostility to taxation, reaching back to the origins of the Revolution; the sorry state of public finance in 1861 with an annual deficit; a national debt on July 1 of $90 million; and an annual revenue of but $42 million. Moreover, the economy forming the tax base was mainly agricultural, and expenditures were normally so light they could be met out of revenues from customs and sale of public lands, with the happy effect that Federal taxes were practically unknown to the average citizen. The American aversion to taxes was even more acute in the Confederacy, which raised less than one percent of its war needs by taxation, never made its notes legal tender, and suffered ruinous inflation. The Union, on the other hand, raised twenty-one percent of its needs by taxation. Federal wartime expenditures amounted to $3.3 billion. Loans accounted for the greater part, and paper money which originated in this crisis accounted for only about one-seventh of the total. Future generations were to resort to taxation more readily: thirty percent of World War I and forty-two percent of World War II were financed by taxes.

Secretary Chase of course bears a portion of the blame for this financial crisis, together with his generation and Congress. Inexperienced in finance and banking, a hard-money Democrat by conviction, he held, it has been said, ideas that would have been "practicable during the Wars of the Roses." At the same time he was urging Congress to adopt a new banking system, and he had the capacity of adapting to circumstances. He was at first opposed to issuing paper money in the emergency, swung to a reluctant support, and finally, after crying in anguish, "The Treasury is nearly empty," urged the House to act "today."

How was money immediately to be raised? To enact a tax bill and then to collect the taxes would take time. Early in January the chairman of the Ways and Means subcommittee to frame a national currency bill stated the extremity: "We must have at least $100,000,000 during the next three months, or the government must stop payment." Ideally, a comprehensive fiscal program to finance the war should be enacted, embracing broad taxation, with national banks authorized to issue currency, loans, and legal tender to meet the emergency. But the government was on the verge of bankruptcy, and plans went forward to enact an independent measure, departing from the historic gold standard, authorizing $150 million in notes that would be proclaimed lawful money.

Bankers divided over the merits of printing-press money. A distinguished delegation favored a policy of heavy taxation, interest-bearing notes, and bonds to be sold at market value. Injured by the gold stringency, they could pay off depositors as well as noteholders in greenbacks. Other bankers acknowledged the exigency, considering legal tender to be a necessity, while still others vacillated in their opinions. The argument of necessity counted strongly in Congress in opposing gold orthodoxy, counterschemes, and questions of constitutionality. The subcommittee chairman, E. G. Spaulding, himself a banker, in opening debate in the House pleaded "necessity," and John Sherman, the Ohio financial expert, in making a major speech in the Senate for legal tender, said it was "indispensably necessary."

Republicans also divided over the merits of printing-press money. Party leaders Morrill, architect of party tariffs, Roscoe Conkling, critic of the War Department, and Owen Lovejoy, abolitionist from Illinois, sided with Democrats in opposing the legal tender clause. A crucial House vote on the clause passed, 95-55, with 23 Republicans and 7 Unionists voting with 25 Democrats. Strongly exhorted by Stevens, the House passed the bill and sent it to the Senate.

There Fessenden, chairman of the Finance Committee, disliked the legal tender clause, telling his colleagues it was of doubtful constitutionality, "it is bad faith," and it "must inflict a stain upon the national honor." The Senate's most eminent Republican conservative, Jacob Collamer of Vermont, at sixty-nine the oldest and often considered wisest member, forcefully argued the measure impaired contracts. The Founders had not intended to make paper legal tender; and he offered an amendment to strike out the offending clause.

Analysis of the Senate vote on Collamer's amendment exposes party and sectional divisions. Though the amendment was lost, 17-22, 9 Republicans voted against it, while 4 Democrats or Unionists voted with the Republicans. Senators from New England split almost evenly, those from the Middle States largely opposed, from the Middle West unanimously opposed, and from the Border slave states largely opposed. Failing to defeat legal tender, 5 Republicans switched to support the bill itself, which passed, 30-7. Revised before the two chambers finally agreed on its terms, the Legal Tender Act required importers to pay in coin and the government to pay interest on bonds in coin. Thus the measure fell short of abandoning the gold standard, invited a scramble for gold among importers, and discriminated in favor of bondholders.

But the financial pinch had been eased. Relief was nearly wholesale. Lincoln later told Congress there had been "no other way," urging nonetheless a return to specie at the earliest chance. Congress in July added another $150 million, and in March 1863, a third and last issue of the same amount, making in all $450 million. Abhorrence of the greenbacks waned with each enactment; and by 1863 a more thoroughgoing fiscal program was in view. The struggle over fiat money was handed on to the postwar generation.

Amid the improvisation of legal tender, Congress, looking to a more sound and deliberate fiscal policy, resolved that "a tax shall be imposed which shall, with the tariff on imports, secure an annual revenue of not less than one hundred and fifty million dollars." The Ways and Means

Committee in consequence introduced a tax bill as extraordinary in its provisions as in its acceptability to Congress and the public.

The tax principles which the committee hoped to fulfill, Stevens said, were equalization of the tax burden and realization of the largest sums from luxury articles and "the large profits of wealthy men." The bill was prodigious, running when completed to thirty printed pages and levying, it was said, a tax on everything. Military pressures from the sea and field reduced opposition, with memories of the ironclad warship scare in early March and of bloody Shiloh the day before the House voted. Only fifteen representatives, all but one Democrats, said nay to the mammoth internal revenue bill. In the Senate Fessenden pushed it through with but one nay vote, Powell of Kentucky.

Lincoln on July 1 signed into law "one of the most searching, thorough, comprehensive systems of taxation ever devised by any Government." Rising above party and personality, businessmen, with small exception, had urged it. It nationalized taxation in the North, bringing the tax collector to nearly every household; and it inaugurated new departures in American taxation. Not only was there a heavy duty on liquor and tobacco, but the once detested stamp duty was revived. It raised taxes on incomes, offering more in the social principle of progressive taxation than in the production of revenue. Raised again in 1864, the income tax from 1863 to 1865 yielded only $55 million. The principle of withholding was adopted from Great Britain and applied to Federal employees—military and civil. Social principle also appeared in the first actual precedent for an inheritance tax, which, though raised again in 1864, netted little money. The law suspended the direct tax until 1864, when it was abolished. Of future significance, too, was establishment of the Internal Revenue Bureau. Just as the bill had its nationalizing effects, it had its bureaucratic ones. Realistic and progressive, the new law helped to strengthen the credit of the beleagured Treasury and to redeem Congress from charges of short-sightedness. Passed with minimal disagreement, it had far-reaching consequences. And having been accepted, it formed a base for internal taxation that was built upon during the war. By 1864-65 the internal tax system was producing $209 million per annum—five times the total receipts of 1860.

In his report to Congress, Chase had recommended higher import duties on tea, coffee, and sugar. Within two weeks after the report, Morrill brought in a bill providing these duties; and he informed the House his

Ways and Means Committee later would report a bill covering other articles. In the December crisis this stopgap was passed promptly by both chambers.

It was six months before a comprehensive tariff bill came before the House. When it was taken up in late June, Congress was just completing its work on the internal revenue bill. The two were linked together by Stevens, who told the House his committee primarily intended to raise duties on imports "equal to the tax which had been put on the domestic articles. It was done by way of compensation to domestic manufacturers against foreign importers."

In many cases, however, the finished tariff was protective of American manufacturers. Duties were raised to an average of 37 percent, and the free list was reduced by nearly one-half. Sectional, partisan, and class complaints were heard, but opposition was successfully muffled. The comprehensive tariff bill of 1862 was passed without a roll call, and Lincoln made it a law on July 14. Long a divisive issue, a protective tariff like this one probably could not have been passed but for the exigency of civil war. Like the Internal Revenue Act, this law served as a base for further increase in the stormy year 1864.

Should we carry on a war by subscription, and politely?" asked Emerson. "They will conquer who take up the bayonet, or leave their other business and apply themselves to the business of war."

Taxes in heroic proportion had been imposed by the weight of military misfortune. The Union had won only limited victories. In the West, Federal forces under General U. S. Grant had pushed south through Kentucky and Tennessee into northern Mississippi where, after being struck by the Confederates at Shiloh (April 6-7), they had been too exhausted to continue. Eastern Kentucky remained vulnerable and central and eastern Tennessee continued in enemy hands. Amphibious operations brought the Union mastery of a portion of the North Carolina coast and valuable New Orleans.

The true target for the Union forces—the Confederate Army—stood intact, and much of it was in Virginia. Popular interest concentrated on this theater. The quiet on the Potomac following McClellan's assumption of command had stirred public anxiety. McClellan kept drilling and preparing for an assault upon Richmond while a good portion of the Northern public clamored for action. Northerners were dividing into McClellan and anti-McClellan factions. Late in January, Lincoln, yielding to the general impatience, issued War Order No. 1, fixing Washington's birthday for launching a general Union offensive. McClellan ignored this and later orders from the commander in chief. At length he advanced upon Richmond, not by the frontal movement which Lincoln preferred, but by the Peninsula, leaving the Union capital exposed. The misunderstanding and discord between Lincoln and McClellan deepened as the Peninsula campaign unfolded. Among Republican congressmen mistrust of McClellan was widespread. Fessenden growled that the general was "either totally unfit for his position or worse. . . ."

Nor was there trust between McClellan and Edwin Stanton, the secretary of war, who in mid-January had replaced Cameron. A steam engine of a man, Stanton had brought great force and value to the department. Methodical, tireless, and decisive, he was at the same time impatient, intolerant, and abrupt. Though leaning in the radical direction, he cooperated with Lincoln and shared his concern over whether McClellan could be counted on to fight to victory. In early April, just before McClellan had begun the siege of Yorktown, he had committed a major blunder by closing recruiting offices throughout the North.

On the Peninsula the cautious McClellan, ever overestimating the enemy's strength and underestimating his own, kept calling for more men; crept forward slowly; maneuvered brilliantly; and carried on a recriminatory correspondence with Lincoln and Stanton.

On June 1 General R. E. Lee took command of the Army of Northern Virginia, and before the month was out, he had hurled a bloody offensive against the invading Army of the Potomac. The Seven Days' Battle began June 26, and at 12:20 a.m. on the 28th, McClellan sent the following telegram to Stanton: "I have not a man in reserve, and shall be glad to cover my retreat and save the material and personnel of the army. . . . If I save this army now, I tell you plainly that I owe no thanks to you or to any other persons in Washington. You have done your best to sacrifice this army."

The manpower crisis would not brook delay, but Lincoln feared that a public appeal from him for a huge force would cause "a general panic." He therefore resorted to the subterfuge, executed by the canny Seward, of having the Northern governors petition the president to call for troops. Following through on this plot, Lincoln on July 2 called for 300,000 volunteers for three years.

At the war's start it had been easy to secure volunteers for what was expected to be a short, glorious rout of the rebels. In Ohio after Lincoln's April 15, 1861 call for 75,000 militia so many men had rushed forward that Ohio alone could have met the national quota. First quotas were oversubscribed; and as Lincoln told Congress on July 4, "One of the greatest perplexities of the government is to avoid receiving troops faster than it can provide for them."

The face of war had changed since spring 1861. One after another, loyal governors told Stanton recruiting was difficult. Men did not want to sign up for three years; long service deterred them. One of the war's most stirring songs now sounded: "We are coming, Father Abraham, three hundred thousand more," but in reality men hung back.

On July 8, when the day's senate session was well under way, Henry Wilson took the floor. "I ask the unanimous consent of the Senate to introduce a bill . . . so that we can call it up in the morning." Next day he explained the measure. "This bill contemplates drafting from the body of the militia of the country a force sufficient to support the country. It contemplates calling out the militia in case we fail to obtain the number of men required by the present system of volunteering. . . . It simply provides that the President, if he calls the militia, shall not be limited to the time specified in existing laws. . . ."

The completed Militia Act of 1862 revised the law of 1795. By its terms it authorized the president to call out the militia for nine months (instead of three) and to apportion quotas to the states; it defined the militia as all men from eighteen to forty-five, described a system of exemptions, and authorized bounties for military service. An important clause empowered the president, if state machinery proved defective, to make all necessary rules and regulations. A controversial section, which we shall examine in another context, for the first time authorized Negro soldiers and promised them freedom.

Except for the hot contest on this last matter, the bill moved easily through Congress. Within a week after introduction, the Senate approved the final bill, 28-9, all but one of the nay votes coming from the slave states. The House, after a futile effort by Democrats to table the bill, passed it without a division.

The law, in perspective, maintained states rights, relying on the militia system and the governors, and did not explicitly authorize a draft. It has been criticized by latter-day advocates of military preparedness and of a national conscript army. Yet, remembering the strength of the traditions of states rights and individualism, and taking into account the strenuous resistance to conscription by Northerners for the following year or more, it is doubtful whether Congress at this time could have gone beyond the Militia Act. It was in actuality a step toward a national, conscript army with its coercive clause authorizing the president to make all necessary rules and regulations. More military setbacks, more months of war were to form the background for resort to unpopular conscription.

Congress at this time enacted a far-reaching program for the navy. Looking to modernization and reform and responding to recommendations from Secretary Welles, Congress, in addition to providing for large-scale expansion, authorized a board to study ironclads and subsequently appropriated funds to build them; passed a bill to reorganize the Navy Department that long remained the basis of navy organization; abolished the liquor ration; and created the rank of rear admiral, thus giving the navy a grade equal to the then highest in the army—that of major general.

This liberal legislation was owing in part to the political skill of Secretary Welles and Senator Grimes of the Senate Navy Committee, to military exigency, and to the significant achievements of the navy in waging war on the water. Though Welles did not escape criticism by Congress, he did escape censure, unlike Cameron. His sharpest critic was the Senate Navy Committee's chairman, John P. Hale, who misspent his time attacking the secretary. Hale's duties devolved upon the constructive Grimes, who after Hale was found to be guilty of impropriety and was eventually deposed, assumed the chairmanship.

The navy itself, faced with the task of blockading 3500 miles of coastline and confronted with the challenge of a Confederate ironclad, had begun to seal the Southern ports and had withstood the defiance of the *Merrimac*. Beyond all this, it had set up bases on the South Atlantic coast, cooperated on the rivers with the army, and made possible Federal occupation of New Orleans. Bold David Farragut, hero of this exploit, was made the first rear admiral in United States history.

A mighty military establishment was in the making. The persistency of fighting had impelled Congress to tax and arm citizens beyond the dreams and fears of the Founding Fathers. In this long second session of the Thirty-seventh Congress, there were to be further proofs of zeal to wage the war for the Union, and at the same time the Congress was intent on peaceful development of the Union's landed heritage. What was still to come in this session formed, Charles Sumner said, "enough for an epoch."

CHAPTER FIVE

Liberty and Land

Wars, especially internal wars, always impose great strains upon personal liberty. National security considerations during the Civil War competed with constitutional guarantees of freedom of speech and press. Legislators were in disagreement on the problem of liberty in wartime. Simultaneously occupying their attention was the problem of disposing of the public land with the attendant long-range implications of individual opportunity and a free economy. Political tensions between lawmakers and president, moderate and radical Republicans, as well as Democrats and Republicans, and Eastern and Western members formed a central theme as the second session of the Thirty-seventh Congress wrestled with these issues.

The wartime urgency which caused Congress to make paper money lawful, to impose burdensome taxes, and to sharpen sword and trident, led it to sanction executive censorship of the press. The Constitution's pledge of freedom of the press conflicted with the need for military secrecy. Compounding the problem was the avidity of journalists to report military news on the one hand and the hesitancy of the government to control the press on the other hand. There was no seditious libel law on the statute books, and the nation's unhappy experience with the Sedition Act of 1798 discouraged passage of a new law during the Civil War.

An uncensored press helped the enemy. General Lee studiously read Northern newspapers for the valuable military information he found in them. Beyond this, pro-Southern, if not positively "disloyal," newspapers presented serious problems in areas where secession seemed possible by publishing false information and giving aid and comfort to the enemy. At first tolerant of sheets of questionable loyalty, Northerners after Bull Run frequently took mob action against editors and newspaper offices, destroying type and presses and making bonfires of furniture and paper.

The administration in 1861 had imposed censorship on dispatches from the capital and had sought without success a gentleman's agreement with the press. Legislative authority for War Department censorship of all telegraph lines in the United States was given by a law enacted January 31, 1862. Introduced and defended by Wade in the Senate and rushed through the House by Blair, it empowered the president to take possession of all the telegraph lines in the United States whenever in his judgment public safety might require it. Within a month the War Department took possession of all telegraphic communication for military operations. Though the press promptly complained and the House Judiciary Committee reported telegraphic censorship had gone too far, censorship throughout the war was sparing and ineffective. A Treason Act passed in July was not used against editors.

Apart from the War Department's supervision of the telegraph, military authorities on occasion suppressed newspapers whose loyalty was suspected. The most celebrated examples, however, entailed only brief interruptions—that of the Chicago *Times* for a single issue and that of the New York *World* for three days.

Administration censorship was also imposed by the postmaster general, who ordered certain "treasonable publications" excluded from the mails. The House Judiciary Committee, recognizing that Blair had acted without congressional authority, sustained him, holding that the government "has the most ample power of self-preservation." The committee did not pursue its investigation; and Attorney General Bates subsequently upheld the government's right to exclude from the mails "printed matter the design and tendency of which are to promote insurrection."

The Union press, in actuality, throughout the peculiarly charged atmosphere of a brothers' war, remained surprisingly uncontrolled. Freedom of the press and freedom of opinion, while not unabridged, were not repressed. Lively debate on public issues characterized—and contributed to— the North's conduct of the war. Congress, for its part, though still jealous of its prerogative over the writ of habeas corpus, had in this instance abdicated in favor of the executive.

The same law which permitted censorship of telegraph lines also authorized the president to take possession of the railroads. This double-barreled law pointed to the importance of the telegraph and the railroad in a modern war. The bill had been prepared by Stanton, who, on the eve of an anticipated general offensive, had implored Wade for "immediate action." What Stanton wanted was not, as in the first World War, a means to unify the national network in the interest of efficiency, but a club to hold over the heads of recalcitrant railroad managers. His bill provided for court martial of anyone interfering with its execution.

Wade in debate correctly forecast that most railroads would cooperate, that the power to seize would be invoked only when "absolutely necessary." The threat, he said, "is more radical and sweeping in its terms than it ever will be in its operation." Provision for compensation of seized railroads seemed to placate friends of property rights. Objections that civilians should not be tried by court martial and that authority to take over railroads should be restricted to insurrectionary districts were answered by Wade with a sweeping claim that Congress had "a right to say precisely upon what principles that war shall be conducted from the beginning to the end."

The law passed quickly and by sizable margins, but with seven Republican senators voting no. Though Wade had asserted that the war power resided in Congress rather than in the executive, not all his colleagues shared his opinion. Whatever the source of power, Congress had extended to the executive broad discretion, as in the case of the telegraph, to take possession of private property when he thought public safety demanded.

In practice the government exercised very little supervision over railroads during the war, though Lincoln took formal possession of all railroads in May.

If Congress was willing to concede to Lincoln full discretion to take possession of the telegraph and railroad facilities of the nation, it was not prepared to yield its authority over suspension of the writ of habeas corpus. Arbitrary arrests ordered by the State Department rose in number and notoriety in the last months of 1861 and early 1862. One of Seward's saucy remarks ran that whenever he wanted to arrest anyone, he had but to touch a bell on his desk.

Persons suspected of disloyalty were arrested by the military, incarcerated in Federal forts, and held indefinitely without trial. Lincoln, concerned about preservation of the nation, justified the abridgments of civil rights by arguing that a limb must often be sacrificed to save a life, but a life must never be given to save a limb. Marylanders and Kentuckians, in particular, were seized and detained. The famous cases of John Merryman of Maryland, Charles S. Morehead, aged ex-governor of Kentucky, Charles J. Faulkner of Virginia, former congressman and minister to France, and General Charles P. Stone, commander at Ball's Bluff, won wide criticism.

The administration in actuality was in a dilemma. It feared not to act lest disloyalty overwhelm the government. Having arrested suspects, it feared to prosecute, for a conviction might create a martyr and an acquittal an embarrassment. Meanwhile the administration was the target of sharp attack. Congress also was in a dilemma. It could not readily ignore the president's suspension of the writ of habeas corpus because of the public's concern. But at the same time it could not bring itself to the point of passing a habeas corpus act, resolving the constitutional issue of the president's right to suspend, as well as providing a judicial process for arrested persons.

Lyman Trumbull, chairman of the Senate Judiciary Committee, in mid-December introduced a resolution directing the secretary of state to inform the Senate under what law the arrests had been made and persons imprisoned. "What are we coming to," he asked, "if arrests may be made at the whim or the caprice of a cabinet minister?" After a lively debate the Senate refused a direct vote upon the resolution and, over Trumbull's protest, referred it to his committee, where it languished. Later in the session the House approved an ambiguous habeas corpus bill, which, despite Trumbull's labors, the Senate declined to act upon. The second session of the Thirty-seventh Congress, like the first, failed to agree upon a habeas corpus law. The vexed issue was carried over to the congressional elections of 1862 and to the third session of Congress.

Branded by critics as a Caesar and an oriental despot, Lincoln was constrained to act. In mid-February he ordered the release with amnesty of all political prisoners, on parole, except spies and other dangerous persons. He lodged future authority to make "extraordinary arrests" in the War Department. To execute this order a two-man commission was named, which swiftly set about separating spies and secret agents from political prisoners. The number of fresh arrests shrank and public tension eased, until, as we shall see, draft resistance arose. When the persistent military arrests in Kentucky prompted the Senate in mid-May to request the president to furnish information on them, Lincoln coolly replied that giving such information was incompatible with the public interest. The president, thus, felt free to pursue his policy of military arrests, disregarding the court as in the Merryman case, and denying the request of Congress as in this Kentucky instance. It is worth noting that, though unauthorized by Congress, he was also unchecked by Congress.

All the same, Congress struck at disloyalty in another manner. Federal employees by the law of 1861 were already required to affirm their future loyalty to the Union. In June, Congress took up the problem of excluding rebels from Federal juries. "Will traitors execute the law of treason against traitors?" demanded the sponsor of a bill to require of Federal jurors an oath of both past and future loyalty. Passed with little objection, this bond was followed by yet another, imposing the celebrated "ironclad oath." In final form it subjected every Federal office-holder, except the president and vice-president, to the test of swearing past and future loyalty. Approved by a partisan vote, it became the device through which for the next thirty years rebels could be excluded from Federal office.

The mightiest blow aimed at disloyalty was a multiple weapon to punish treason, confiscate rebel property, and free slaves owned by rebels. We have earlier adverted to the treason provision and we shall later treat the slave provisions. This weapon, the Second Confiscation Act, was not finally approved until the last day of the session. Controversial and divisive, it presented the greatest threat of the session to unity within the

Republican party and to harmony between the Congress and the executive.

The confiscation bill would expand the dimensions of the struggle. It contemplated economic warfare, waged not by the army against soldiers in the field, but by Congress against property owned by persons in rebellion. This legislative assault upon property rights, including slaves, roused strenuous opposition. Collamer, the venerable Vermont conservative, pointed out that the bill, as reported by Trumbull from the Judiciary Committee, violated the Constitution, failed to provide judicial process, and gave the lie to Republican pledges not to free the slaves.

Republicans divided into radical and conservative, the first wishing a more stringent measure and the second a more tempered one. A series of party caucuses failed to find grounds for agreement. At last the impasse was broken by the obscure but powerful New Hampshire senator, Daniel Clark, who arranged for a select committee on confiscation. The Clark committee improved the bill by requiring judicial proceedings before confiscation and by authorizing the president to grant pardon and amnesty to persons who had engaged in rebellion. Differences between Senate and House were smoothed over by a joint committee of conference. The completed measure abated the old mandatory death penalty for treason and allowed punishment by heavy fine and imprisonment. It separated from treason the crime of engaging in or aiding rebellion against the United States and provided penalties of fine and imprisonment. It freed the slaves of all persons convicted of treason or support for the rebellion. The House then approved by the substantial margin of 82 to 42, with only five Republicans (four of these were from Border States) in opposition. The Senate approved, 28 to 13, with only four Republicans (two from Border States) saying nay.

At this stage a new threat to the unity of the party in power loomed. It was understood that the president might veto the bill. Relations between Lincoln and some Republicans had been strained during debate on the bill by a dispute over whether executive or legislature possessed the "war power." Sumner had said, "It is true the President is Commander-in-Chief; but it is for the Congress to make all laws necessary and proper for carrying into execution his powers . . . ." Conservative Republicans had objected to this extreme claim with Browning of Illinois crossing swords with Sumner, insisting that the president had the war power under the authority of the commander in chief of the army. After the bill was passed, Browning privately advised Lincoln to veto it.

Senatorial attacks upon executive claim to the war power suggested a serious split between Lincoln and the radicals. The influential Fessenden, who had reluctantly voted for the measure but now feared that a veto would "dishearten the country," went to the White House. Lincoln had indeed prepared a veto, pointing out, among other matters, that the bill violated the attainder clause of the Constitution in providing forfeitures of real estate beyond the lives of guilty parties.

Congress, which at Lincoln's request had postponed adjournment to await his action, now passed a joint resolution explaining that the forfeiture of real estate was to be only during the lifetime of an offender, after which the landed property would be restored to his heirs. Lincoln thereupon signed the bill and the resolution "as substantially one," and emphasizing executive independence, he attached his contemplated veto to his message of approval.

This episode has often been told to dramatize conflict between Lincoln and radical Republicans. Yet in perspective it reveals not only intraparty tensions but also ultimate attainment of relative harmony. Techniques of select committees, conference committees, conciliatory leadership by Clark, liaison with the executive by Fessenden, and accommodation of presidential objection by joint resolution marked enactment of a complex and controversial law.

In softening the penalty against treason, Congress had set its face against wholesale executions. The war was not to witness a political blood bath. In the end the government did not execute any one for treason or in fact fully carry out a sentence of fine or imprisonment.

Congress had hoped, however, that under more moderate penalties the administration would proceed vigorously against persons in rebellion, confiscating land and slaves. But as the *National Intelligencer* observed, "The confiscation bill . . . is one the real import of which depends mainly upon the spirit in which it is interpreted, and the manner in which the wide discretion it gives to the Executive is used." Lincoln and Bates shrank from social revolution, proceeding cautiously and leniently. Few cases were pushed to completion. No slaves were freed under the act's terms.

Sometimes considered an ultraradical measure, the Second Confiscation Act refrained from mass execution of rebels and from permanent deprivation of landed estates and stipulated that proceedings against suspected property were to be instituted in civil courts. Extremism had been routed.

In addition to the previously mentioned sources of tension, sectionalism, deriving from divergence of economic interests between West and East, was often the cause of friction within the Republican party during the war.

The political marriage of the Northwest and the Northeast was very recent. Historically the agricultural Northwest and the agricultural South had been political bedfellows. Separation of these two had begun over the issue of federal aid to internal improvements, which the South opposed. Disengagement widened over the issue of excluding Negro slaves from the territories. And the severance was completed in 1860, when every free Western state swung its support to the antiextensionist Republican party, which promised not only to aid internal improvements but in addition to give land to the landless.

The new marriage of the young farm bride and the older commercial and industrial partner was often an uneasy one. The historian Frederick Jackson Turner long ago called attention to the significance of sections in American history. Sectionalism, derived from the localization of Black slavery in one part of the Union, as Lincoln observed, "was somehow the cause of the war." Antagonisms born of regional differences appeared markedly in this session.

Sectional issues of particular significance embraced taxes, especially direct and income, legal tender (in the House), tariff, and public lands, especially establishment of agricultural colleges. Sectional rivalry emerged in consideration of the Pacific railroad bill, of representation in the Federal judiciary, and of participation in the armed services. Blair of Missouri charged during debate over the railroad bill, "Why, sir, the eastern and sea-board portions of the Union have made money out of this rebellion. . . . The East has taken the entire profit of the labor of the West." In making appointments to the Supreme Court, Lincoln deferred to Iowa's insistence it have a member on the bench. General Grant recorded in his *Memoirs*, "The armies in the East and West acted independently and without concert, like a balky team, no two ever pulling together."

Sectionalism also contributed liberally to the Middle Western Democratic party's discontent with the waging of the war. Massachusetts, home of abolitionists, was the frequent butt of criticism in Congress from Westerners. We shall examine sectional sources of Copperheadism in another place; let it suffice, by way of illustration, to quote the sarcastic salutation once used by Ohio's S. S. Cox, "Oh! ye, honey-tongued humanitarians of New England, with your coffers filled from the rough hands of western toil . . . with your dividends rising higher and higher like waves under this storm of war. . . ."

A computerized study of senatorial voting on a variety of issues in the Thirty-seventh Congress discloses the relative importance of three determinants of voting: section, faction (that is, radicalism), and party. The investigation revealed that party was by far the most important determinant of voting, with factionalism second, and sectionalism third. Striking traits of the sectional patterns were the frequency of appearance on economic issues, the greater unity of Eastern Republicans than Western, and the larger proportion of radicals among Western Republicans. The sharpest sectional alignment arose over the agricultural college bill. It was one of the four "great western measures" enacted by this session, and to them we now turn.

"Agriculture, confessedly the largest interest of the nation," had only a clerkship in the government, Lincoln pointed out in his Annual Message of 1861. He suggested Congress organize an agricultural and statistical bureau for this interest. The House approved a bill to establish the agricultural division of the Patent Office as a separate department to be headed not by a cabinet officer but by a mere commissioner. No increase in appropriation beyond the $60 thousand a year already allocated to agriculture was recommended.

The Senate subjected the bill to a crossfire, as Democrats and Border Unionists sought to create an elaborate department of agriculture, while Republican leaders sought to reduce the agency to a mere bureau. "If the genius of agriculture could be impersonated and could come here today, its prayer to the American Congress would be, 'for God's sake, let us alone'," Hale proclaimed. Fessenden grumbled about enlarging the government and gloomily foresaw agency demands for money. The Senate passed the House bill, but both party and sectional lines were crossed, with eleven Republicans voting against the proposed department, six from the East and five from the West. The impetus from the president, who is sometimes said not to have shown interest in nonmilitary legislation, the leadership of Grow and Lovejoy in the House, and the support of Border and Democratic senators had made possible creation of a Department of Agriculture, a proposal discussed for two decades. The nation's primary economic interest had outgrown a clerkship. And as Fessenden forecast, governmental expenditures on agriculture rose. In his next Annual Message, Lincoln reported he had organized the department on a "liberal basis"; and in 1862 Congress appropriated for agriculture nearly twice as much as it had in any previous year.

Five days after he had signed this law, Lincoln gave his approval to a second bill enacted on behalf of farmers. For many years giving free land to homesteaders had been a subject of controversy. Opponents argued that the public domain should be retained for revenue purposes, keeping taxes —including the tariff—low; that it was unconstitutional to give away public land; that speculators would engross the land; and that military veterans should be given preference to the public domain. In the 1850s the strongest opposition to a homestead law had sprung from Southern fears that free land would spell the doom of slavery by fostering westward migration. Eastern apprehensions that homesteads would drain off a labor supply had sufficiently abated by 1860 that the Republican party could incorporate the homestead plank in its platform. In that year President Buchanan exacerbated party and sectional (North-South) conflict by vetoing a limited homestead bill.

Sectionalism on the homestead issue in the House of Representatives in 1862 is better revealed on a vote to postpone than on the final vote. With the congressional elections close, with the Republican party vulnerable in the Middle West, few Republicans dared vote against a major platform plank. A vote early in the session to postpone consideration until February broke party lines. Prevailing 88 to 50, it was distinctly sectional with strong Republican support in the East and strong Republican opposition in the Middle West. At this stage the proportion of Democratic support for homesteads was slightly greater than Republican.

When the House again took up the bill, the Speaker, in an unprecedented act, displayed the party whip. Galusha Grow, who had sponsored homestead measures in the House in the fifties and was now Speaker, left the chair and took the floor in behalf of a bill almost a replica of his bill of 1859. Thereafter no Republican sought postponement or even spoke against the measure. The House passed the bill, with only sixteen negative votes, and these almost entirely from Border states.

Hannibal Hamlin, who had denounced homestead measures in the Senate in the fifties, now was presiding officer of that body. He watched the new homestead bill brought to the floor by Wade, who back in 1859 had memorably phrased the sectional struggle over territorial expansion: "shall we give niggers to the niggerless or land to the landless?" Acting in concert with Grow, Wade pushed the bill through the Senate after brief debate. Republican adherence was one hundred percent, and some Democrats and Unionists supported the majority. The seven nay votes came largely from the Border.

This momentous measure was the culmination of a democratic aspiration that, as Lincoln said, "every poor man may have a home." It extended the right to a homestead, not exceeding 160 acres on the surveyed public domain, to loyal heads of families, who would use the entry "for the purpose of actual settlement and cultivation." Though abused by speculators, it helped to build the West and at the same time to build future political capital for the Republican party. A victory for free soil, it went into effect January 1, 1863—the same day as the Emancipation Proclamation.

Like the homestead bill, an agricultural college bill had been vetoed before the war. In 1859 James Mason, a Virginia senator, and now the Confederate minister to England, had asserted the pending bill was "misusing the property of the country." It is "an unconstitutional robbing of the Treasury for the purpose of bribing the States." Buchanan in his veto had said it was unconstitutional to give away land; and conceding that Congress in the past had granted land to states for educational purposes, he objected to the proposed principle of granting to states land in other states.

To this time higher education in the United States was largely classical in curriculum, church-related, and privately supported. The agricultural college movement contemplated an institution in every state, where the curriculum would be vocational, free from sectarian influence, and publicly supported. It promised a major shift in the structure of American education, with training of industrial classes, equality of access to higher learning, and acceptance of public responsibility for maintaining the colleges. Scientific and classical studies were not to be excluded and military tactics were to be offered.

Strikingly enough, Easterners were more ardent for the agricultural college measure than Westerners. The main reasons for Western opposition were: a belief the bill would benefit speculators who would buy from the states the rights to Western lands; realization that the grants, which were based on population, would benefit the older states at the expense of the new; and knowledge that the grants were to be carved from the public domain in the Western states. The main reasons for Eastern support were: in addition to exacting benefits from the West, to modernize their educational systems and to wring some benefit from the public domain before the homesteaders should occupy it.

Led by Wade again, the Senate overrode Western efforts to restrict the bill, and passed it, every nay vote coming from the West, several Westerners abstaining. "The land-grant college bill shattered party lines and provided the most striking illustration of the sectionalism of East against West in the voting of the Republican senators during the session," a historian of sectionalism has concluded. The House experienced a similar triumph of section over party, and on July 2, 1862, signed the Morrill Act.

Constitutional issues were unimportant in the enactment. Narrow construction, which previously had shackled the national government, had been dismissed. Yet it would be in error to say that states rights had been cast aside and nationalism had prevailed. What had been implemented was the principle of federalism, the division of authority between states and nation. The national government gave the land and specified the use, but the states established the colleges and operated them. A federal partnership had been made; and in the absence of national supervision of education, it may be said the states were the senior partners.

The last of the great Western measures passed by this session was the Pacific Railroad Act. Federal aid to railroads through land grants, though sometimes thought of as an Eastern Republican tactic to enrich financiers, was not new in 1862; it had begun with a Western Democrat. Stephen A. Douglas in 1850 had successfully secured a land grant for the Illinois Central Railroad; and he appears to have been motivated in part in 1854 to introduce the tragic Kansas-Nebraska bill by considerations of opening the territory to rail development. Federal aid to an East-West railroad had raised the question whether South or North was to have the transcontinental, and, like the homestead issue, the matter had antagonized these sections and failed of enactment.

The absence of Southerners from Congress and the needs of national defense now combined to make possible a Pacific railroad that would benefit the loyal states. "You have some seven hundred miles of coast to defend," pointed out a representative from Oregon, "and with no iron-clad steamers and no forts there, we are at the mercy of any foreign Power, and especially at the mercy of England." Private capital could not do the job of constructing a road through a vast uninhabited region. "The Government must come forward with a liberal hand, or the enterprise must be abandoned forever," exclaimed another congressman.

The contest in Congress in 1862 was in part the sectionalism of East versus West, but more importantly a scramble by Western interests for land grants to pet lines. Though the railroad was ostensibly to serve the public interest, private gain was pursued; and though the road was intended to be national in purpose, local groups pushed their own ends.

The House passed the Pacific Railroad bill through a partnership of the West and large commercial states of the Northeast. On the final roll call, some 27 Republicans, many of them Easterners, failed to answer, and 18 voted nay. New Englanders divided, 11-9 in favor, and Border men, 10-9 against. In the Senate sectional politics was more plain. A key vote came on the attempt to make the measure a special order. The attempt failed, 17-19, every nay vote but one Republican, and every New Englander (save two absentees) opposed. Though the bill expressed a platform commitment, few Eastern Republicans were eager to redeem the pledge. Subsequent to this vote, the measure made rough progress in the upper house. A band of fifteen Republicans, mostly Easterners, favored drastic revisions, most of which were defeated by a combination of Democrats, Border State men, and Western Republicans. The Senate lopped off one local branch, removed an advantage which St. Louis had won in the House, and approved the bill with only five nays.

By this act Congress incorporated the Pacific Railroad, granted it a right-of-way, ten alternate sections of land per mile of public domain, and bonds that constituted a first mortgage. Grants were extended to the Central Pacific of California and the Leavenworth, Pawnee, and Western Railroad of Kansas.

Though in this session sectionalism had eroded Republican unity, particularly over the agricultural college bill, it had not prevented the party from making a striking contribution to the development of the West and the promotion of commerce and industry. The "great Western measures" were a notable legislative achievement. Party loyalty and nationalism in the main had prevailed.

With great satisfaction, Lincoln, in reviewing for Congress the public land laws, remarked upon "a higher and more enduring interest in the early settlement and substantial cultivation of the public lands than in the amount of direct revenue to be derived from the sale of them." This opinion, he continued "has had a controlling influence in shaping legislation upon the subject of our national domain." Looking back on the Thirty-seventh Congress, one of its members observed, "It seems to have been possibly the first whose vision and grasp embraced the continent."

The Republican platform of 1860, except for the planks on slavery, had been substantially enacted with the passage of the homestead, railroad, and tariff measures. We must now turn to the politics of slavery in the early years of the war.

CHAPTER SIX

Slavery and Politics

"If all earthly power were given me, I should not know what to do" about slavery, said Abraham Lincoln in 1854. "My first impulse would be to free all the slaves, and send them to Liberia,—to their own native land. But . . . [this] is impossible. . . . What then? Free them, and make them politically and socially our equals? My own feelings will not admit of this; and if mine would, we well know that those of the great mass of white people will not."

Racial prejudice conditioned the politics of slavery, which the Civil War generation never forgot was slavery of *Negroes*. Together with economic and constitutional considerations, racial prejudice made impossible a major party in America based upon emancipation. These factors contributed to give the slavery issue in the United States its peculiar form: the question of extension into the territories.

Republican leaders had tried to make plain in 1860 that the party intended only to prohibit slavery in the territories, that it upheld slavery's right to exist in the states, that Republicans did not stand for racial equality.

The pervasiveness of racial prejudice in the free states was a harsh reality. Negroes were not numerous there, numbering only 225,000 as against 18,500,000 whites. Over half the Black population resided in the three Middle Atlantic states, Pennsylvania having the largest number—nearly 57,000. Elsewhere, Ohio, Indiana, Massachusetts, and Connecticut each had considerable concentrations.

Disfranchisement, discrimination, and segregation were the lot of the Northern Negro. Only in New England, except Connecticut, could Negroes vote on the same terms as white men. New York imposed a property test, requiring ownership of $250 worth of property, and Ohio a color test, allowing persons with a greater visible mixture of white than Negro blood the right to vote. In 1860, even though Lincoln carried the state of New York, voters defeated an amendment to abolish the property qualification for Negroes. Frederick Douglass, the Black abolitionist, bitterly complained that New York Republican leaders avoided the issue. The Radical Abolition party's presidential candidate polled so few votes in New York that there is no record of the number. His known total for all the states is 172 votes.

Several states prohibited Negroes from testifying against whites in court and from migrating into the states. Negroes were excluded from jury service in every state but Massachusetts. Segregated public schools were common, but not universal. Negro children frequently did not attend school. Separate and unequal was the prevailing principle of Northern race relations. Though it was true that Massachusetts, with equal suffrage and desegregated schools on the statute books, was the most advanced state in Negro rights, discrimination predominated over legal principle. The Black lawyer John Rock complained in 1862, "the position of the colored people in Massachusetts is far from an enviable one. . . . While colored men have many rights, they have few privileges. . . . We are colonized in Boston."

Hostility toward Negroes, amounting to Negrophobia, had a stronghold in the Northwest. There legal disabilities upon Blacks were cramping. The Indiana antislavery politician George W. Julian complained in 1858, "Our people hate the Negro with a perfect if not supreme hatred." Lincoln's

Illinois was notorious for its "Blacks Laws," which, among other matters, prohibited Negroes from testifying in court when a white man was a party to the suit and maintained all-white schools. The Black abolitionist H. Ford Douglass told in 1860 how he had gone about the state trying to find signers to a petition to repeal the "Testimony Law." "I went to prominent Republicans, and among others to Abraham Lincoln and Lyman Trumbull [U.S. Senator], and neither of them dared to sign that petition. . . ." Continuing his indictment of an antislavery party that wanted to make territories free but was indifferent to rights of Negroes, Douglass charged, "if we [Negroes] sent our children to school, Abraham Lincoln would kick them out, in the name of Republicanism and anti-slavery."

Besides the prevalence of anti-Negro prejudice in the free states, the intensity of the resolve to maintain white supremacy in the loyal slave states was an important determinant of administration policy. We have already seen how Kentucky's reaction to Frémont's emancipation effort influenced Lincoln. And we shall further see how Border State hostility to Negroes influenced the politics of emancipation.

Constitutionalism also hindered action against slavery. Almost everyone agreed that the Federal government had no authority to abolish slavery in the states. Endorsing that construction, Lincoln had said in his first inaugural address that he had no objection to its being "made express, and irrevocable" by a proposed thirteenth amendment. Three states—Ohio, Maryland, and Illinois—ratified this amendment, which, however, had come too late to deter secession and civil war. Former president John Quincy Adams had subscribed to the view that Congress had no authority to interfere with slavery in the states, but during the "gag rule" controversy in Congress back in 1836 he had gone on to say that in the event the slave states ever became the theater of war, "the war powers of Congress [would] extend to interference with the institution of slavery in every way." Few Americans accepted this extreme view. The belief that the Constitution protected slavery prompted some abolitionists to denounce it as "a covenant with death and an agreement with hell." The abolitionist William Lloyd Garrison for a time embraced disunionism, demanding that the North withdraw from the proslavery compact.

The Constitution protected slavery in the states not only as a social institution but also as property. The sanctity of private property stood high; and in the making of the confiscation bill, the moderate viewpoint that judicial proceedings were necessary for the confiscation of property had prevailed. Even the radical Wade acknowledged, "I do not wish to touch the property of the masses of the people."

Though protected by prejudice, the Constitution, and the sanctity of property, slavery ultimately succumbed to the assaults made upon it by a continuing war. What was to be done with slaves who escaped to refuge with Federal armies? What was to be done about slaves employed in labor or arms against the United States? What was to be done about slaves employed on plantations and in factories, thus sustaining the Confederacy, while their masters fought against the United States? Why not weaken the Confederate cause and strengthen the Union by enrolling Negroes in the Federal armies, promising enrolled slaves their freedom? And was not the time ripe for Congress to enact the planks of the 1860 Republican platform, prohibiting slavery in the territories and assuring suppression of the transoceanic slave trade?

The first assaults upon slavery came from the military. As early as May 1861, when slaves began to escape to Federal lines, General B. F. Butler refused to return the fugitives, calling them "contraband of war," and put them to work. The War Department sustained him. Later, as we have seen, when General John C. Frémont declared rebels' slaves free, Lincoln overruled him. When in December 1861 the Secretary of War tried to force the president on the question of arming the slaves, Lincoln required Cameron to change his statement.

At the end of the year 1861, the declared policy of the Lincoln administration continued to be that the government had no right to interfere with the institution of slavery in the states. This moderate view apparently had the approval of the great mass of Northerners. It allayed the fears of residents of the loyal slave states, surprised the fire-eaters in the seceded states, antagonized radical antislavery men, and dismayed liberals of Western Europe.

In Congress, however, the conviction was deepening among Republicans that slavery was the cause of the war; that the nation was fighting for its life and any measure of self-defense was justified; that in the words of Thomas Eliot of Massachusetts, in time of war "the safety of the state is the highest law, subordinates rights of property, and dominates over civil relations"; and that if slavery were not abolished, another war might result.

The moderate Fessenden remarked, "Possibly, we may ultimately be successful in this war without taking such measures as shall result in the abolition of slavery.... But in this event, we return from victory, as did the Thracian horse, still bearing a master on his back."

A series of antislavery measures was introduced with the opening of the second session of the Thirty-seventh Congress. Perhaps the least controversial proposal enacted, so far as Republicans were concerned, was an "additional article of war," prohibiting persons in the military or naval service from returning escaped fugitive slaves. The Fugitive Slave Act was further abridged by a law that forbade surrendering slaves of rebel owners coming into Union lines. Outright repeal of the Fugitive Slave Act, however, broke Republican unity, and repeal was tabled in the House when seventeen Republicans sided with Democrats and Unionists. Most of the Republican bolters came from New York, Pennsylvania, and Ohio. The Act, obnoxious as it was, fulfilled a constitutional obligation; and for the next two years loyal slave owners were allowed to recover their fugitives.

It was one thing for Congress partially to set aside the Fugitive Slave Act, but it was quite another for it to abolish slavery. The emancipation of slaves in the District of Columbia long had been an abolitionist aim. The slave *trade* in the District had been eliminated as a part of the Compromise of 1850. However, abolition of slavery in the District had seemed so radical, in 1860 it had not appeared in the Republican platform.

Slavery actually was waning in the District, the number of slaves dwindling by 1860 to fewer than at the beginning of the century. The census of 1860 reported 3185 slaves, 11,131 free Negroes, and 60,764 whites in the District. Antislavery men argued Congress had authority to end slavery in an area under its jurisdiction and not protected by states rights.

The Senate in mid-March opened debate on a bill to abolish slavery in the District. "Inexcusable and almost inexplicable," a measure of "downright madness," sputtered the Louisville *Daily Journal*. Garrett Davis of Kentucky proposed mandatory colonization out of the limits of the United States of all persons liberated by the law. He foresaw a war of the races, ending in the exile or extermination of one race or the other. The Senate, under the force of prejudice, amended the bill to provide for voluntary colonization together with compensation to slaveowners. Under Henry Wilson's leadership, the Senate approved the bill by a party vote.

In the House Crittenden of Kentucky gave the most temperate speech against the proposal, arguing that it would stiffen Confederate resistance, that it broke the implied pledge given to the states of Virginia and Maryland when they ceded the District, and that it was in effect a measure of confiscation. Stevens would not long brook discussion and brought the bill to a vote. By a margin of 92 to 39, nearly every Republican and five Democrats voting yea, the bill won approval, exactly one year after the war had begun.

The New York *Anglo-African*, perhaps the most important Negro newspaper, rejoiced: "It was a fitting celebration of the anniversary of Fort Sumter, that Congress should pass a bill to emancipate the Capital from the thrall of slavery forever." Whittier, who had despaired of seeing freedom at the capital, exulted:

> But now I see it! in the sun
>   A free flag floats from yonder dome,
>   And at the nation's hearth and home
> The justice long delayed is done.

Freedom for Blacks was not enough, some men saw. Equality before the law also was needed. The first Federal breakthrough in the realm of civil rights was made by this Congress. Municipal Black codes that had, among other matters, barred Blacks from various businesses, imposed a curfew, and consigned them to "nigger heaven" at the theater, were repealed. Separate schools for colored children in the District were established, but with inadequate tax support. Henceforth, Negroes might testify in judicial proceedings in District courts.

The struggle for civil equality was a brave beginning, but it was checked by Republican resistance to further measures and by popular prejudice. Efforts by the ardent Sumner to remove the disability of Negroes as witnesses in the courts of the United States and as carriers of mails failed in this session. And as early as July, just after the legal walls established by slavery had been torn down, a congressional committee reported, "the prejudice of caste becomes stronger and public opinion more intolerant to the negro" in the District.

Of vast importance for Africa as well as for the Americas was Senate ratification of a treaty with Great Britain to suppress the Atlantic slave trade. For half a century the United States had been prevented by sensitivities toward England from cooperating in stopping the traffic. Displaying the United States flag, and thus immune to search by the superior English slave patrol, slavers had continued to carry Africans to the New World. Though there had been a movement to reopen the slave trade, which incurred Republican censure in the 1860 platform, the Confederate constitution had prohibited the trade. Now a treaty, negotiated by Seward, to cooperate with England in searching and condemning vessels was ratified by the Senate without dissent. Sumner rushed to tell Seward of the Senate's unanimity. The Secretary of State, who had been sleeping, leaped from his lounge, exclaiming, "Good God! the Democrats have disappeared! This is the greatest act of the Administration." Within a short time the Black flow dwindled to a trickle.

That the Democrats had not disappeared became clear when Congress took up the question of diplomatic recognition of the Negro republics of Haiti and Liberia. The prospect of Black diplomats being received in Washington roused strong protest both in the Senate and in the House. Suggested by Lincoln, recognition prevailed by a partisan vote. The State Department shortly announced it could not receive a Black man as a diplomat, but Lincoln modified this, telling an agent for Haiti, "You can tell the President of Hayti that I shan't tear my shirt if he sends a nigger here."

The divisive political question of the 1850s had raged over slavery in the territories. Republicans had asserted it to be the right and duty of the Federal government to prohibit Negro slavery in the territories. The Supreme Court in the Dred Scott case had in effect ruled that the Republicans advocated a violation of the Constitution, because property in slaves was protected by the Fifth Amendment. In June the Republican-dominated Congress accomplished the distinctive purpose of the party. Without providing for compensation or colonization, as in the recent District bill, Congress prohibited slavery in the territories. It dropped a clause to prohibit slavery in all areas under Federal jurisdiction—for example, forts, arsenals, and dockyards—and restricted its action to the territories, where there were only sixty-three slaves. But a great principle had been achieved, that the nation had the power to abolish slavery in the territories; and the Republican party had fulfilled its original purpose. The negative vote was strongly partisan, the Border States almost solid in saying nay.

Antislavery men were cheered by so much lawmaking against slavery. James Russell Lowell, who had revived the dialect verse he so effectively employed during the Mexican War, now exhorted:

> It's Slavery that's the fangs an' thinkin' head,
> An' ef you want selvation, cresh it dead.

Two measures that became law on July 17—the last day of the session—climaxed Congress' assault on slavery. The basic militia law of the United States, enacted in 1792, restricted enrollment to white citizens. Apart from this, however, Negroes had served in the American Revolution and the War of 1812. When in 1861 many Northern Negroes volunteered their services, they were bluntly told, this was a "white man's war." In February 1862, while preparations were being made for the Peninsula campaign, Frederick Douglass, the leading spokesman for the Northern Negro, complained, "Colored men were good enough to fight under Washington. They are not good enough to fight under McClellan."

Racial prejudice played against acceptance of Blacks. "I am quite sure there is not one man in ten but would feel himself degraded as a volunteer if negro equality is to be the order in the field of battle," said a writer in the *New York Times*. The belief that Negroes were too servile and cowardly also worked against service by Blacks. Lincoln in 1862 acknowledged the force of white prejudice and shared the notion Blacks would make poor fighters. "To arm the negroes," he told an Indiana delegation in August that offered two Black regiments, "would turn 50,000 bayonets from the loyal Border States against us that were for us." Not long later he said, "if we were to arm [the Blacks], I fear that in a few weeks the arms would be in the hands of the rebels."

However, a combination of factors was inducing a change in policy: manpower needs, pressure from generals, a desire to weaken the enemy, and humanitarianism. As we have seen, the Union became desperate for soldiers in early July. Among generals, David Hunter made his special contribution to the congressional decision to authorize Black soldiers. Commanding the base established at Port Royal, South Carolina, Hunter, an old West Pointer of independent mind, on his own began to form the first Negro regiment in the Union Army. News of his experiment impelled Representative Charles Wickliffe of Kentucky to demand an explanation. Hunter returned a saucy reply, which was read to the House on July 2, "amid roars of laughter. . . ." At first flippant and finally serious, Hunter denied that he had organized a regiment of fugitive slaves and retorted that he had a regiment of fine persons whose late masters were "fugitive rebels." "The experiment of arming the blacks," he went on earnestly, "so far as I have made it, has been a complete and even marvelous success."

Increasingly in the first six months of 1862, the questions were being asked: Why should the Confederacy be allowed to have the benefit of slave labor? Why should white men do the work of building fortifications and digging ditches for which Blacks were available? Why should white men die in a war caused by Negro slavery and Blacks be spared? "Shall we love the Negro so much," asked a New York newspaper, "that we lay down our lives to save his?"

Further, friends of emancipation argued, Negro military service would lead to freedom. While the Senate was debating confiscation, Grimes of Iowa confided to his wife, "I regard the employment of colored persons in the Army and Navy as of vastly more importance in putting an end to slavery than all of the confiscation acts that could be devised by the ingenuity of man."

One of the legislative compromises in the making of the Second Confiscation Act was a sop to radical opinion that empowered the president "to employ as many persons of African descent as he may deem necessary and proper for the suppression of this rebellion." The act also declared that all slaves of rebels, following judicial proceedings, "shall be forever free." "The Blacks are to be employed and slaves are to be freed," rejoiced Sumner, stressing these two points of agreement between radicals and president.

Simultaneously, the Militia Act repealed the old bar to Black enrollment and authorized the president to receive "persons of African descent" into the service of the United States. The sanction was bitterly fought in the Senate by Border State men who sought in vain to restrict Blacks expressly to construction and camp service and to confine the provision to free Africans. Radicals fought to "direct" the president to receive Blacks and to free the mother, wife, and children of all Black soldiers, but the final phrasing merely "authorized" the president and freed these family members only if the owner was a rebel. The act decreed that when any Negro slave shall perform military service, he "shall forever thereafter be free."

The two laws of July 17 are legislative landmarks in the annals of Negro freedom, but they had their limits in attaining this goal. Confiscation procedure was not specified, and emancipation under this law was not enforced. As for Negro military service, the laws merely authorized the president to employ and receive Negroes, and Lincoln was loath to raise a Black military force. Months would elapse before he would bend his efforts toward that aim. Meanwhile, he was pressing his own plan for the future of American Negroes.

Known in history as the "great Emancipator," Abraham Lincoln might better be known as the "great Nationalist." For him the question of preserving the nation predominated over freeing the Negroes. Taunted by Horace Greeley with timidity in not executing the Confiscation Act to give freedom to rebels' slaves, he forthrightly replied in a public letter: "What I do about slavery, and the colored race, I do because I believe it helps to save the Union.... My paramount object in this struggle *is* to save the Union, and is *not* either to save or to destroy slavery. If I could save the Union without freeing *any* slave I would do it; and if I could save it by freeing some and leaving others alone I would also do that."

And yet he believed, as he had once said, that slavery was "the only one thing which ever endangers the Union." To retain slavery would be to keep the Union in peril; to remove slavery would be to assure perpetuity to the Union. But he further believed the Federal government had no constitutional authority to abolish slavery in the states. And beyond all this, to try to force emancipation would risk the loss of the loyal slave states and alienate Northern white conservatives, especially in the Northwest. Finally, Lincoln thought that if the Negroes were freed, the two races could not coexist in the United States.

In this light the problem for Lincoln the statesman was to devise the means of encouraging emancipation without jeopardy to the nationalist cause, without loss of the Border States or alienation of the conservatives, and without mixture of the two races in the same country. If he could find the means, he might, in addition to the avoidance of these political injuries, placate the radicals in the Congress and country, conciliate liberal opinion in Europe, and ease his own conscience which told him all men ought to be free.

Lincoln had given the main design of his plan for emancipation to Congress in his first Annual Message. In December he had (1) suggested the possibility that some states might legislate to free slaves, (2) recommended that Congress accept the freedmen in return for compensation to the states, and (3) recommended that Congress take steps for colonizing both freedmen and free Blacks of the North. Voluntary state action, Federal cooperation, compensation, colonization, and to these principles he would add gradualism—here were the five points of the Great Emancipator's plan for the future of American Negroes.

In early March, before Congress had taken any steps against slavery, Lincoln sent a special message asking Congress to adopt a joint resolution, stating "that the United States ought to cooperate with any State which may adopt gradual abolishment of slavery, giving to each State pecuniary aid. . . ." He hoped to initiate a conservative movement that by thus disposing of the Negro slavery issue would shorten the war. As to the cost, he pointed out to a Democratic senator, that eighty-seven days' cost of the war would pay for all the slaves held in the four loyal slave states and the District, at $400 per head.

Lincoln now commenced extraordinary efforts to secure adoption of his plan. Besides urging his case in private letters to Senator McDougal, a California Democrat, and to the editor of the *New York Times*, he invited the Border State congressmen to the White House. In placatory language, acknowledging that emancipation was exclusively under control of the states, he sought support. House and Senate approved the resolution by partisan votes. It was an announcement of policy, a mere resolution, leaving matters to the states. Stevens ridiculed it as "the most diluted, milk and water gruel proposition that was ever given to the American nation," and withheld his vote. Wadsworth of Kentucky objected, "I utterly spit at it and despise it."

The Border States did not take up the offer. In late May in language suggesting despondency, Lincoln said, "To the people of those States I now appeal—I do not argue—I beseech you to make the argument for yourselves—you cannot, if you would, be blind to the signs of the times. I beg of you. . . . The changes it contemplates would come gently as the dews of Heaven. . . ." The occasion was a presidential proclamation rescinding a military order by General Hunter that freed the slaves in three rebel states.

But the Border States remained blind to "the signs of the times." In July the president again called Border congressmen to the White House. He referred to Hunter's act, said the pressure was upon him, and begged their consideration of his plan before they went home for the summer. A majority of the members signed a statement rehearsing their objections and concluding that if the Congress, whose good faith they doubted, would first make available money for compensation and colonization, their states would consider the president's plan.

Two days later Lincoln in an irregular act sent a measure to Congress for distributing bonds to states enacting immediate or gradual emancipation, and he went over to the Capitol for further talks with Border men. That staunch antislavery senator, Grimes, objected to the direct introduction of a bill by the executive. "I do not recognize the right of the President to send a bill in here," he protested. Coming at the same time as Lincoln's contemplated veto of the confiscation bill, this measure further antagonized executive-legislative relations. Neither chamber acted upon it.

Congress in its lukewarmness to Lincoln's plan for compensated, gradual emancipation by the states had tossed aside a magnificent chance for statesmanship. The plan differed radically from the uncompensated, immediate emancipation by the Federal government which eventually became national policy. Though it of course is difficult to say what would have occurred had Congress been as much in earnest as the president, it seems probable that adoption of the plan at this time would have drawn the guidelines for a less convulsive solution of the problem of Negro slavery than the later policy.

Colonization had been close to Lincoln's heart. Like his idol Henry Clay, he ardently believed colonization held promise of solving a great race problem. In three acts Congress had cooperated with him to encourage colonization of free Negroes: in appropriating $100,000 to aid in colonizing District of Columbia Negroes; in appropriating a further $500,000 to carry out the act of Congress pertaining to the District and to colonize Negroes to be made free by the Confiscation Act; and, thirdly, in inserting a clause in the Confiscation Act that authorized the president to make arrangements for voluntary colonization.

In his desperate appeal to the Border State congressmen, Lincoln had held out the bait of colonization. Failing with them, Lincoln invited a committee of free Negroes to the White House. After greeting the men, Lincoln referred to the colonization appropriation, bluntly told them why he believed Blacks should leave the country, and asked the committee to organize a number of Black families to undertake a pilot project in Central America.

"Why should the people of your race be colonized?" he asked rhetorically. The two races were incompatible, he answered: the Negro presence had brought on civil war; and freedom would not bring racial equality. Lincoln spoke plainly but without harshness. What he had to say cut to the core of his ideas about the Negro and the cause of the Civil War. "You and we are different races. We have between us a broader difference than exists between almost any other two races. . . . Your race are suffering, in my judgment, the greatest wrong inflicted on any people. But even when you cease to be slaves, you are yet far removed from being placed on an equality with the white race. . . . But for your race among us there could not be war. . . . It is better for us both, therefore, to be separated." If the committee could give him only twenty-five able-bodied men with families, he could make a start. The committee chairman made a brief reply and the Blacks withdrew.

Outraged, Frederick Douglass denounced the president; "In this address Mr. Lincoln [shows] all his inconsistencies, his pride of race and blood, his contempt for negroes and his canting hypocrisy. . . ." Negro and abolitionist protests were numerous. Lincoln subsequently entered into an ill-considered contract to colonize Negroes on one of the islands of Haiti. The project was a disaster, and the government brought the survivors back to the United States. Lincoln made no further efforts to execute his policy of colonization, but there is reason to believe he never abandoned the idea. Congress in 1864 repealed its appropriations for colonization. A government report in March 1864 showed that only $33,000 had been spent of the $500,000 appropriated.

While Lincoln in the summer of 1862 was keeping his plan of compensated state emancipation and Federal colonization in the foreground, he was deliberating a drastically different—and more familiar—plan. Four major factors explain why he issued the Emancipation Proclamation. Of great importance was the failure of his three "earnest, and successive appeals" to the Border States. Second, he saw that a social revolution was occurring as increasing numbers of slaves were gaining freedom and increasing numbers of Northerners in Congress and out were demanding freedom for Blacks. With the fumbling progress of the Union armies (the collapse of the great Peninsula campaign, Second Bull Run, and stalemate in the West), the Union need for manpower became urgent. Emancipation and arming the Blacks would weaken the Confederacy and strengthen the Union. And finally, Lincoln was concerned about British and French intervention on behalf of Southern independence, a possibility that he thought might be prevented by proclaiming freedom.

But, withal, he was merely changing tactics to attain his invariable objective: "I issued the proclamation on purpose to aid you in saving the Union," he afterward wrote to a mass meeting held in his home city. The proclamation was on his mind from at least the middle of July. In a cabinet meeting Seward is said to have persuaded the president to wait until the Union Army had won a victory. The battle of Antietam (in Maryland) gave the Union a technical victory. Lee pulled back to Virginia, and on September 22 Lincoln issued his preliminary Emancipation Proclamation. It was a curious document. What it came down to was a warning of a future policy to extend freedom to slaves of rebels and a present invitation to rebels to return to the Union and be spared emancipation. The deadline was January 1, 1863.

One month before this date Lincoln in his second Annual Message refined his first plan of compensated emancipation. Where, earlier, he had asked Congress merely for a resolution stating policy and for a modest appropriation, he now asked Congress to approve three amendments to the Constitution and thus incorporate his plan in organic law. One amendment would provide financial compensation to any state which would abolish slavery before 1900. A second would compensate loyal slaveowners whose slaves had been freed by the chances of war. And the third would authorize Congress to appropriate money to colonize Negroes, with their own consent, outside the United States.

Growing in rhetorical power with his year and half a in high office, Lincoln made an eloquent plea for his proposal. These constitutional guarantees, he thought, "would end the struggle now, and save the Union forever." Freedom for white men was his concern; and in a nakedly ethnocentric entreaty he went on, "In *giving* freedom to the slave, we *assure* freedom to the free. . . . We shall nobly save, or meanly lose the last best hope of earth."

The amendments, as every schoolboy knows, never became American policy; and with the opening of the new year, Lincoln released his promised proclamation. He hurdled the constitutional barrier protecting slavery by invoking his power as commander in chief in time of actual armed rebellion; and he described emancipation as a "fit and necessary war measure." All slaves in areas in rebellion were declared free. Freedmen were urged to abstain from violence and to labor faithfully for reasonable wages. The president announced he would receive "persons of suitable condition" into the armed services for garrison duty and to man vessels.

The proclamation concluded with Lincoln's statement that he believed emancipation to be "an act of justice, warranted by the Constitution upon military necessity."

The great proclamation clearly was a weapon of war and not a torch of freedom. It was a piece of statecraft and not a program of social reform. Lacking in fervor, it left in servitude all slaves in loyal areas—some 832,000. Receiving freedmen into the armed services it assigned them to garrison duty and to manning vessels. Stressing emancipation for the purpose of suppressing the rebellion, it urged freedmen not to engage in violence. Less radical than commonly thought, it rested on an awareness of constitutional and political considerations and went about as far as Northern Democratic opposition would allow. Consistent with his fixed aim, Lincoln was using emancipation as an instrument of nationality.

Reduced to its political dimensions, the Emancipation Proclamation—controversial though it was—within a short time enlisted the support of a majority of the Northern public and disarmed European critics of the Union cause. The House of Representatives in December, over the impassioned outcries of a minority by a vote of 78 to 51 had endorsed a resolution saying that the Proclamation was "warranted by the Constitution; that the policy of emancipation, as indicated in the proclamation, is well adapted to hasten the restoration of peace, was well chosen as a war measure, and is an exercise of power, with proper regard for the rights of states, and the prosperity of free Government." From London the son of the United States Minister to Great Britain wrote, "The Emancipation Proclamation has done more for us here than all our former victories and all our diplomacy."

Blacks and abolitionists, with exceptions to be sure, rejoiced. "We shout for joy that we live to record this righteous decree," exulted Frederick Douglass. William Lloyd Garrison hailed the proclamation as "a great historic event, sublime in its magnitude, momentous and beneficent in its far-reaching consequences, and eminently just and right alike to the oppressor and the oppressed." Republican conservatives, Democrats, and Border State people had differing views—of particular importance for the congressional elections of 1862—and we shall examine these later.

The Emancipation Proclamation gave an impetus to using Negroes in the military. This was one of the most important reasons for issuing the proclamation, as we have seen, and one of its most important results. In the latter part of the year 1862, the administration was inching toward accepting Negroes in the army. The first authorization was made in late August to General Saxton, Hunter's successor in the Department of the South. Another demonstration of change showed in the annual report of the Secretary of War in December 1862, one year after his predecessor had been forced to expunge a proposal to arm slaves. Now without presidential contradiction, Stanton wrote that Southern Negroes could "aid in holding fortified positions" as well as "free the white soldier from the most unwholesome exposure of the South."

The long-standing white prejudice against Blacks in the army now revolved into a realization that Blacks would free whites from military service. Private Miles O'Reilly, a character invented by Charles G. Halpine, poet and editor, put into popular verse a preference for letting the Negro share in the fighting:

> Don't think I'm tipp' you chaff
> The right to be killed we'll divide wid him.
> And give him the largest half!

As the war persisted and volunteering waned, pressure to fill Union ranks with Negroes rose. Backers of vigorous prosecution of the fighting, abolitionists, Blacks, and businessmen who wanted the use of white labor or who wanted the war to end—all supported using Negroes. "Give them a chance," Douglass exhorted. In late January, Stanton authorized the governor of Massachusetts to raise two Negro regiments.

The month of March marked the turning point in administration policy. The War Department interpreted the phrase "all male citizens," in a new enrollment law, to include free Negroes. Late in the month the adjutant general of the United States was dispatched to the lower Mississippi to recruit Negroes. Here among the Southern Negroes lay the great reservoir of Black manpower, for there were only 45,000 Negroes of arms-bearing age in the free states. Adjutant General Thomas, now serving as recruiting sergeant, did his work well. By the end of the year, he had organized twenty Negro regiments; by the end of the war, he had been instrumental in organizing over forty percent of all Negro soldiers in the Union Army.

The day after Thomas was sent South, Lincoln, long reluctant to arm Negroes, wrote to Andrew Johnson, military governor of Tennessee and an "eminent citizen of a slave state and himself a slaveholder," encouraging him to raise a Negro military force. "The colored population," Lincoln said, "is the great available, and yet unavailed force for restoring the Union." Nothing came of this.

Not all Union generals favored arming Negroes. As late as February, U. S. Grant, engaged in the Vicksburg campaign, was turning away fugitive Negroes from his picket lines. In late July, having swung over to support the new policy and having taken Vicksburg with the help of Black soldiers, he was saying, "By arming the negro we have added a powerful ally." Employment of Negro soldiers swiftly went beyond the garrison duty contemplated in the Emancipation Proclamation. In August the judge advocate general was rejoicing, "The tenacious and brilliant valor displayed by troops of this race at Port Hudson, Millikens Bend, and Fort Wagner has sufficiently demonstrated to the President and to the country the character of the service of which they are capable."

Heartened by Thomas' reports of success in mustering Blacks, the War Department in May created the Bureau for Colored Troops under the adjutant general. Recruitment went forward. To those who said they would not fight to free Negroes, Lincoln retorted, "Some of them seem willing to fight to free you." To those who continued to complain as late as April 1864, he asked whether they would take away from the Union the 130,000 Blacks then in the military service.

Congress during the last two years of the war further strengthened the "sable arm." In February 1864 it provided for conscription of all male Negroes between twenty and forty-five, slave as well as free, with compensation to a loyal master and freedom for the slave.

Not until June did Congress right a grievous wrong it had committed in authorizing Negro soldiers under the Militia Act of 1862. That act, passed when menial rather than combat duty was anticipated for Negroes, stipulated unequal pay as between white and Black. This galling distinction, inciting strenuous protest from Blacks and some whites, was substantially removed in June. At about the same time, however, Congress unwisely agreed to a bucketshop operation by which Northern states could recruit Southern Negroes and credit them to their state quotas, thus relieving white men of military service. In March 1865, when the war was almost finished, Congress repealed this obnoxious authorization and took further steps to equalize pay.

The official records show that 179,000 Negroes served in the Union army, over one-tenth the total enlistments. Of these, 104,000 were recruited in Confederate territory. The policy of employing Blacks in the army obviously weakened the Confederacy and strengthened the Union. Despite considerable Northern white opposition and continuing discrimination while they wore the blue uniform, Negroes importantly contributed to winning the war and their own freedom.

Union use of Black soldiers at first provoked threats of Confederate retaliation. In August 1862 President Jefferson Davis branded two Union generals as outlaws, to be executed as felons if apprehended, because they used slaves in the armed service. However, in March 1865 he approved a limping law that authorized him to call out 300,000 additional troops, "irrespective of color," leaving within states rights the vital questions of furnishing Blacks and freeing them. The grudging enactment, of course, was too little and too late.

The year 1862 saw the start of a social revolution. In the exigency of war, the Republican party repudiated its platform with respect to Negro slavery. Congress and the president had each taken giant steps toward the emancipation of Negroes. They had called upon Negroes to help win the war, prove themselves in battle, and secure freedom.

Yet there existed real differences between the lawmakers and the chief executive over the mode of emancipation and the future of the Negro. Congress had declined to appropriate additional money for compensated emancipation and to pass the proposed constitutional amendment that would encourage colonization of Negroes freed by voluntary, gradual, compensated state action. The legislators had moved faster and farther than the president. They had given him powers to free slaves and arm Negroes that he was loath to use. They had helped prod him toward his September proclamation. They had taken the initiative in attaining civil rights for Negroes.

But much was yet to be done: the completion of emancipation, the winning of the war, and the formulation of a national policy on freedmen. Racial prejudice remained strong. A white backlash, hesitancy of policy, and uncertainty of outcome lay ahead.

CHAPTER SEVEN

A Crisis in Northern Unity

The last months of 1862 witnessed a crisis in Northern unity. The Democrats resolved to maintain their separate identity and to wage partisan war. Popular disaffection deepened over the threat of conscription, the unfolding of emancipation policy, and the dim prospect of peace. Citizen violence, a Black scare, and peace meetings marked the Union states. In the autumn elections the Democrats, exploiting these and other difficulties, made a comeback, gaining control of key states and growing in numbers in Congress. Through a gloomy December congressional Republicans quarreled with the president because they thought only a more vigorous war would bring victory. At the same time the Democratic threat increased Republican cohesion in Congress, and it pushed through a nationalistic program and cooperated with the president on crucial matters. The crisis reinvigorated the two-party system and led to a stronger prosecution of the war.

"Shall the Democratic Party be now abandoned?" demanded a Democratic party manifesto in the congressional election year of 1862. Appearing in early May, while Congress was still in session, it was an attempt to repudiate fusion with the Republicans and to define the issue for the fall campaign. The party should not be abandoned, the manifesto declared, and it should uphold its traditional principles of strict construction of the Constitution and non-interference by the Federal government with slavery. Though signed by only eighteen representatives, it apparently spoke for most Northern Democrats in affirming faith in the need to continue the party and to resist broad construction and emancipation.

Called "Copperheads," "Secesh" men, "Peace Democrats," and other epithets, the Democrats during the war acquired a reputation for obstructionism, subversion, defeatism, and even treason that was used against them by Republican politicians for nearly a generation after the war. The cooling of war passions and the research of scholars have gone far to rehabilitate the Northern Democrats.

A careful student of the Democrats in the Thirty-seventh Congress (1861-63), Professor Leonard Curry has concluded that they were a loyal opposition. In the Senate they refused to leave the body without a quorum by abstaining from voting. Analysis of roll calls reveals they avoided becoming a "fractious opposition" on military bills and had better voting records than Republicans on some of the "great Western" measures. Without an acknowledged leader and not holding any official caucuses, they nonetheless maintained a high degree of party unity. At the same time Senate Democrats strenuously disagreed with Republicans on the important issues of emancipation, raising Negro troops, confiscation, and confirmation of "illegal" presidential acts. Often bitter in their verbal assaults upon Republicans, they declined to resort to parliamentary delaying tactics.

In the House of Representatives, the pattern was similar. House Democrats had no acknowledged leader, did not hold regular caucuses, maintained a high degree of party unity, supported many war measures, and disagreed with Republicans on the same issues that Senate Democrats opposed. Faced with a more radical opposition than their party colleagues in the upper chamber, they were more obstructionist than the Senate Democrats, and they were less frequently a part of the House majority.

The philosophy of the Congressional Democrats, Professor Curry found, was to conserve the Constitution, restore the Union by compromise or concession following victory, uphold property rights including property in slaves, and restrict the area of action by the Federal government. Combining scholarship and sympathy, Curry evaluated this portion of the wartime Democratic party as loyal to the Union, steady in support of the war, and imbued with conservatism. This scholar was of course not concerned with party activity in the states, sectional differences among Democrats, and some of the more aberrant party members.

Historians have lavished attention upon the Democrats of the Middle West. This region—Ohio, Indiana, and Illinois, in particular—produced much of the party leadership. Possessing both Southern and Northern population strains, diverse in economic interests, dependent upon both South and East, the section was in travail.

Middle Western disaffection expressed itself in many ways. We have no convincing evidence to demonstrate the existence of a "Northwest Conspiracy," intent upon insurrection and alliance with the Confederacy. But acts of terrorism against individuals and communities, led to arbitrary arrests, military trials, and occasional suppression of the press. Historians have tended to relieve the Democratic party, which denounced the Republican administration's extraconstitutional counteraction, of complicity in the acts. One may give sympathetic recognition to the rival claims that Democrats and Republicans made, though they conflicted with one another. The Democrats, in denouncing curbs on liberty, were striving to save the Constitution; and the Republicans, in curbing liberty, were striving to save the Union.

Besides the constitutional base of Middle Western disaffection, five other contributing causes are worth noting. One important source was economic. Largely agricultural and heir to a frontier tradition, the Middle West often looked with mistrust upon the East with its commercial, industrial, and cultural differences. Sectionalism, as we have seen, figured in congressional voting. Party played a large role; the May manifesto, signed mainly by Middle Westerners, represented an effort to maintain the party, which could be accomplished only by opposing the Republicans. And maintenance of the Democratic party meant more than partisan politics; it meant as well maintenance of a medium to fight the economic and social changes that the Republicans favored. A third factor of great importance in assessing the nature of Middle Western disaffection was the greater degree of Negrophobia in the region and among the region's Democrats than was to be found elsewhere in the free states. The intensity of racism among Middle Western Democrats goes far to explain the region's resistance to Republican antislavery measures. And though—like party—not peculiarly a Middle Western trait, ethnic and religious loyalties formed a hard core of Democratic alienation from the "Republican war." Finally, one must endeavor to dissociate disaffection and party. The two have often been slurred together as though one. Much disaffection existed outside of party; and contemporary newspapers tell stories of violence, draft resistance, secret societies, and alleged collaboration with the enemy for which the party of Jefferson, Jackson, and Douglas was not responsible.

The most notorious Copperhead came out of the Middle West. Clement L. Vallandigham, representing the Dayton, Ohio, district in Congress, had established before the war a reputation as a foe of abolitionists and a friend of states rights and Western interests. In the special session of 1861, he had proclaimed, "I am for peace—speedy, immediate, honorable *peace*, with all its blessings," and had proposed sending peace commissioners along with the Federal armies. He had introduced resolutions to censure Lincoln for "a series of unconstitutional acts." He had voted for the volunteer army of 500,000, but against the bills to finance the war.

By 1862 he was the center of controversy. His admirers praised his stand for freedom of expression, for compromise, and for restoration of peace. His detractors called him a Copperhead and even a traitor. Declaring his own purposes were "to maintain the Constitution as it is, and to restore the Union as it was," he placed himself at the head of the Peace Democrats. On the Fourth of July 1862, the Ohio Democratic party enthusiastically listened to his attack upon abolition and violations of civil rights and renominated him for representative. An extremist, going beyond his fellow Ohioans S. S. Cox and George Pendleton, he was a discordant element in the Democratic party.

Credit for maintaining the national Democratic party goes in part to its national chairman, August Belmont. A native of Germany, the American agent for the Rothschilds, he had been made party chairman by Stephen A. Douglas in 1860; and he was to hold that post to 1872. With the coming of the war, he staunchly supported the Union as well as his party. Going abroad, he tried to find out whether a foreign loan could be floated for the Union. On his return in the early summer of 1862, he found widespread apathy and distrust in the North and disarray in the Democratic party. He advocated immediate conscription and reinforcement of existing regiments, "without reference to the states."

With views so different from those of Vallandigham, he set about filling the void left by the death of Douglas and the defection of Breckinridge by establishing a base in New York state on which to reconstruct the national Democratic party. In taking up the party battle, he first secured support of a major New York paper, lack of which he believed had conduced to Douglas' defeat. Together with other New York Democrats, he bought into the New York *World*, which had a circulation of 40,000 and a brilliant editorial staff headed by Manton Marble.

He next turned to the New York gubernatorial race, where the incumbent, Edwin D. Morgan, Republican national party chairman as well as governor, was not standing for a third term. No Democrat had been elected governor since 1852, when Horatio Seymour had carried the state. A moderate Democrat, a man of wealth and cultivation, Seymour in the summer of 1862 was helping Morgan by recruiting in his home county. Belmont attended the party's state convention and assisted in the nomination of Seymour. Accepting the party nod, Seymour took as his special target the radical Republicans.

Vallandigham and Seymour were the two principal leaders of the Democratic party in 1862 and stood respectively in the peace and conservative wings of their party. Seymour opposed emancipation, denounced arbitrary arrests, and believed the North could not subjugate the South. Vallandigham went beyond this in his advocacy of ceasing hostilities as a preliminary to restoration of the Union through negotiation. Eastern Democrats tended to look to Seymour for leadership, while Western Democrats in lesser degree looked to Vallandigham.

An important element in the campaign of 1862 was the unsatisfactory progress of the fighting. Nothing succeeds like success, and had the North been on the verge of military victory, there would have been no doubt of a Republican political victory. But a year and a half of war had left the Confederacy in control of most of the seceded states, had been enormously costly to the North in men and money, and was impelling the administration to adopt policies that departed from long-standing traditions of individualism, states rights, and racial attitudes. With the war as the background, four specific issues emerged as the focus of the campaign: the draft, constitutional liberties, the Emancipation Proclamation, and the Negro.

Conscription ran against the grain of Anglo-Saxons. As early as 1647 the "Agreement of the People" during the English Civil War had inveighed "that the matter of impressing or constraining any of us to serve in the wars is against our freedom." Though the Militia Act did not expressly sanction conscription, Lincoln, in another of his "dictatorial" acts, authorized a militia draft. The War Department on August 4 ordered the draft of 300,000 militia, adding ominously that if by August 15 any state had not met its quota of the 300,000 *volunteers* called for on July 2, the deficiency would also be met by a militia draft.

The War Department also issued orders to prevent draft evasion and to suppress disloyal practices. No one liable for the draft was allowed to leave the country, and provision was made for military arrest of evaders and denial of the writ of habeas corpus to disloyal persons. The long, bureaucratic arm of the Federal government was further extended by War Department appointment, on nomination by the state governor, of provost marshals to enforce the draft. As draft dodgers rushed to Canada, the epithet *skedaddler* was added to the term *Copperhead* in the lexicon of politics.

The extraordinary executive interpretation of the law, the unpopularity of the draft, and Federal intrusion into state recruiting combined to provoke widespread protest. Violence erupted in many places, a stampede to Canada set in, peace meetings were convoked, and states rights assertions challenged the authority of the national government.

Violent opposition to the draft flared in Maryland, Pennsylvania, Ohio, Indiana, Illinois, and especially Wisconsin. The governors of the first two states asked for Federal troops to maintain order. Ethnic tensions compounded draft resistance. In the Pennsylvania anthracite fields, where the antagonism of the Irish-born Molly Maguires was intense, the government avoided continuing conflict by accepting fictitious affidavits that the quota had been filled. In Ozaukee County, Wisconsin, where the antagonism of German Catholics created the most serious draft disturbance of the year 1862, state militia were used to quell a mob that attacked the draft commissioner and destroyed much property.

So serious was resistance to the draft as well as to volunteering, Lincoln on September 24, shortly before election day in several states, issued a blanket proclamation, which a distinguished constitutional historian called "a perfect platform for a military despotism." By fiat he extended martial rule throughout the entire United States. His previous suspensions of the ordinary processes of the law had been confined to designated localities. He now made "all persons discouraging volunteer enlistments, resisting militia drafts, or guilty of any disloyal practice" subject to martial law and without benefit of the writ.

Arrests were numerous, and Democratic orators rained criticism upon the administration. Professor Joel Parker of the Harvard Law School branded the president a monarch; Vallandigham urged voters to rebuke the administration for crushing liberty; Seymour made the issue a major one; and Marble's *World* angrily scored the arrests. A dramatic clash between state and nation took place in Wisconsin, where Nicholas Kemp heard with satisfaction a unanimous State Supreme Court rule that his arrest and detention had been without warrant; and for good measure, the draft was unconstitutional.

While the draft and arbitrary arrests were agitating the electorate, the Emancipation Proclamation contributed to political dissension. This half-way measure was hailed by Republicans and cursed by Democrats and on balance may have cost more votes than it gained. An astute contemporary, Senator John Sherman thought the proclamation ill timed with respect to the elections. A pamphlet "Executive Power," by former Supreme Court Justice Benjamin R. Curtis, argued that the president had no authority to issue the proclamation, adding to the idea that Lincoln was a despot. Marble remarked that the proclamation made every Southerner a zealot for the success of the rebellion.

The preliminary Emancipation Proclamation conjured up a "Black scare," especially in the Middle West. "I told you so!" cried Vallandigham in a vindicatory reproach when Lincoln made his announcement. Many Northerners feared a Negro exodus to the free states. They expected emancipated Blacks would swarm North, take white men's jobs, settle in white communities, expect equality, and inevitably Black males would want to marry white girls.

Republicans countered all this the best they could. As to the draft, they could point to the administration's suspension of deadlines in reponse to numerous requests from anguished governors. Local and state systems of bounties and substitutes diminished the need for drafting. The civil liberties issue was not easily handled, but Republicans kept up their claims that the Union stood in danger from conspirators. A sensational Indiana grand jury report that a subversive order, the Knights of the Golden Circle, had 15,000 members in the state fueled the fall election in the Hoosier state.

The Emancipation Proclamation was defended as a military expedient. The overriding issue, it was stressed, still was to save the Union. And for this the Republican party, or the party of the Union, was the only fit instrument. A party of peace and compromise could not restore national sovereignty.

Republicans countered the Black migration issue with plain talk that they did not want freedmen to come North, that the party had enacted measures to colonize Negroes out of the country, and that Negroes did not want to live in the North. As to the accusation that they favored racial equality, Republicans mainly ignored it or, in the words of the Indianapolis *Journal*, exclaimed, "What a monstrous and villainous lie."

Radical Republicans softened their radicalism in the face of reaction. The North's two most radical governors deferred to white racism. Governor Austin Blair of Michigan told an audience in Adrian: "Possibly some people might differ with me, but I am utterly unable to see why it is not proper to use a rebel's sacred nigger. . . . I am entirely unable to see, too, why Sambo shouldn't be permitted to carry a musket." Governor John Andrew of Massachusetts, asked by Union General John A. Dix to receive "loyal blacks" in his state, retorted they should be taken into the army in the South and the Northern climate was the worst possible one for "these poor people." Sumner, running scared for reelection to the Senate, defended the Emancipation Proclamation in a speech with the conservative title, "Emancipation! Its Policy and Necessity, as a War Measure for the Suppression of the Rebellion."

The October elections portended a Republican reversal. Democrats polled majorities in Pennsylvania, Ohio, and Indiana, all of which Lincoln had carried in 1860. In the Keystone State the Democrats won half of the congressional seats and just enough strength in the legislature to elect a Democratic senator. Speaker Grow was defeated as a result of a gerrymander. In the Buckeye State the Democrats won fourteen of nineteen congressional seats and Vallandigham was defeated as a result of a gerrymander. In the Hoosier State the Democrats won seven of eleven congressional seats and control of the legislature, which in time sent two Democrats to the Senate.

How low had Republican fortunes sunk? men were asking, as the

November polling approached. Illinois, the nation's fourth largest state as well as home of the president, had already given sign of defection. In April inveterately Republican Chicago had elected a Democrat as mayor; in June the anti-Negro provisions of the state constitution had been overwhelmingly sustained. Now in November the Democrats won nine of the fourteen congressional seats and control of the legislature, which later sent a Democrat to the Senate.

When the results from the Middle West were in, the Democrats had gained eighteen seats in the House and three in the Senate. The leading Peace Democrat (that is, one who favored peaceable restoration of the old Federal Union) had lost his seat. In the Middle Atlantic states, the Democrats won two important victories. New Jersey was inundated by a Democratic flood, the opposition party sweeping the governor's office, the state legislature and four of five congressional seats.

The Empire State, as Belmont knew, was a base for national power. Seymour snatched the governorship from a radical Republican nominee by a decisive majority. The national Democratic party gained a new leader, and the Lincoln administration a powerful antagonist. The Democrats won seventeen of thirty-one congressional seats, defeating the ardent Republican Roscoe Conkling and sending New York's ex-mayor Fernando Wood to Washington. The Republicans retained control of the legislature, which impressed by the voters' rebuke of radicalism, named the moderate ex-governor Edwin D. Morgan as U.S. Senator.

The elections of 1862, placed in perspective against those of 1860, meant a Republican reversal but not a rout. Though some states were yet to vote in early 1863, the Republicans would apparently still control Congress by a scanty majority, and the Senate was secure. To Republican advantage also was the fact that the Thirty-eighth Congress would not meet until December 1863, and by then the face of the future might be brighter.

The election had maintained the separate identity of the Democratic party. "Party spirit has resumed its sway over the people," Seward observed. The canvass had required both major parties to define the issues and had enabled the electorate to judge. Post mortems there were aplenty. Lincoln blamed the outcome upon the fact that most states did not allow absent soldiers ("our friends") the right to vote and the fact that the press vilified and disparaged the administration. Greeley thought that the polling showed a "popular repugnance" to the sacrifices of the war. He went on darkly to assert in his history of the great rebellion that an election held at any time during the year following July 4, 1862, on the issues of peace or emancipation would have yielded a majority for the first and a still larger majority against the second.

Off-year elections, lacking the luster of a presidential contest, often go against the party in power. Nearly every state showed a decline in voting from 1860, which can partly be attributed to failure to authorize soldiers in the field to vote. But beyond this, whether the balloting reflected ideology or indifference is difficult to determine. What is salient is the success of the Republicans in continuing to hold power and responsibility. And what seems clear is that a Republican resurgence would depend upon military progress.

Military progress in 1862 rested heavily upon the young Democrat Major General George B. McClellan. He had not gained victory in Virginia —prevented from winning the Peninsula campaign, his backers said, by Lincoln's interference. Reduced to a subordinate post, he had seen his splendidly trained troops assigned to the boastful General John Pope. After Pope's inglorious defeat at Second Bull Run, McClellan had been called upon to take charge of the retreating forces and engage Lee. On "the bloodiest single day of the war," September 17, McClellan frustrated Lee's invasion at Antietam Creek, near Sharpsburg, Maryland. He failed, however, to inflict a defeat upon the enemy and he allowed Lee a full day to organize a retreat. Antietam, "a defeat for both armies," was followed by Lee's escape and McClellan's failure to pursue.

Whatever the military merits of all this, in political terms the radical Republicans denounced McClellan, sometimes portraying him as a traitor, while conservative Democrats defended him, often seeing him as a victim of Republican intrigue. Lincoln at length lost patience with McClellan. On the day after the November election, McClellan received word he was to turn his army over to General Ambrose Burnside. McClellan's military career was over; his political carer lay in the future.

A little more than a month later, Burnside with incredible incompetence presented the Union cause with a bloody defeat. Commanding the overwhelmingly superior Army of the Potomac (113,000 Union troops— 75,000 Confederate), he had spectacularly failed at the Battle of Fredericksburg (Virginia) with a toll of 12,600 men as against Lee's loss of 5,300. If poor Burnside was nearly beside himself with grief, the North was nearly beside itself with indignation and despondency. "How long is such intolerable and wicked blundering to continue?" demanded the New York *Evening Post* under the heading, "The Late Massacre." Burnside unwittingly had precipitated a political and constitutional crisis.

With storm clouds gathering in the public mind, the Republican senators caucused. They were disheartened by the military reverses and the voters' verdict. The radicals disliked the president's continuing conservative espousal of compensated, voluntary emancipation and his modification of the Second Confiscation Act. Recalling from the previous session the tensions between the president and themselves over emancipation and confiscation, members believed the administration lacked unity and vigor, and they believed they must act to help restore public confidence in the Republican administration.

The senators held two caucuses on successive days, the second to cool off the first. They agreed to send a committee to visit the president and present their views. Though some historians have smelled a radical plot in these proceedings, it must be observed that the caucus vote was unanimous (with one abstention and two absences) and that the spokesman was the party's most conservative senator, the venerable Collamer of Vermont. The movement may more properly be seen as one by the Republican senators than by radical Republicans.

At seven in the evening of December 18, the committee met with Lincoln for three hours. The members urged a more vigorous prosecution of the war, declared the president should act upon important matters only after careful consultation with his cabinet, and the cabinet in turn ought to be made up of men who agreed with these principles. This last point was a thrust at Seward, who, the committee thought, was lukewarm in the conduct of the war and exercised undue influence over the president. They believed the president had good purposes, they said, but Seward contrived, as Lincoln later put it, to suck them out of him unperceived.

Seward had already gotten wind of the senatorial onslaught and had sent in his resignation. The senators in fact misapprehended the Seward-Lincoln relationship, in which the president was dominant. Seward had antagonized some of them, especially Sumner and other radicals, and Chase had fed them rumors and suspicions.

Much was at stake. To begin with, if Lincoln deferred to the committee, which spoke for his own party in the upper chamber, he would yield control of his cabinet and policy to the Senate. If he refused to comply with the committee's request, he might lose the support of Senate Republicans. Further, he was in a dilemma about the makeup of his cabinet. If he accepted Seward's resignation, he would sacrifice a valuable cabinet officer on the basis of what he knew to be "an absurd lie." If he kept Seward, he might have to dismiss Chase, another valuable cabinet member. To fire Seward would be to give in to the Senate Republicans; to fire Chase would be to antagonize them. And finally, there was the constitutional consideration. What the committee was asking for was the power, first, to dictate cabinet appointments, and next, to require the president to be bound by cabinet decisions. The episode could set a precedent for superseding the American system of separation of powers by a parliamentary form of government.

Lincoln the next day met twice with his cabinet. In the morning, Seward being absent, the president explained what had happened the night before. In the evening, Seward still absent, the cabinet met with the Senate Committee. Sumner and others sharply attacked Seward when Lincoln invited their views on Seward's withdrawal. Lincoln defended him and said the cabinet was not divided. Postmaster General Blair asserted the cabinet was in general harmony; and Attorney General Bates vigorously objected to the idea that every important measure and appointment should undergo cabinet scrutiny.

Chase, author of unfounded rumors now controverted by his colleagues, was embarrassed. The next morning he went to Lincoln and said he had written out his resignation.

"Where is it?" asked Lincoln, his eyes lighting up.

"I brought it with me," answered Chase.

"Let me have it," said Lincoln, reaching out his long arm and seizing the paper from the reluctant secretary. "I see my way clear," he exclaimed with delight to the perplexed Chase.

Lincoln was in the saddle. He said to a friend who came into his office soon after he had secured Chase's resignation, "Now I can ride; I have got a pumpkin in each end of the bag." If Chase's friends in the Senate still demanded Seward's head, they would lose Chase too. Holding the resignations of both men, Lincoln did not have to choose between them. He sent identical notes to each asking them to resume their duties. Lincoln had kept his executive independence, repulsed his Republican critics, maintained a coalition cabinet, and avoided a party split.

Nearly a year later he remarked with satisfaction: "I do not see how it could have been done better. I am sure it was right. If I had yielded to that storm and dismissed Seward the thing would all have slumped over one way, and we should have been left with a scanty handful of supporters. When Chase gave in his resignation I saw that the game was in my hands, and I put it through."

The attack upon Seward had another political dimension. There was bad blood between the secretary of state and the chairman of the Senate Foreign Relations Committee. Sumner had discovered in the diplomatic correspondence a dispatch linking abolitionists and extreme advocates of slavery as equal enemies of the Union. He referred to this and other offensive remarks by the jaunty secretary during the Collamer committee's confrontation with Lincoln.

Moreover, Sumner aspired to Seward's place at the president's right hand. "Many talk and write to me about going into the cabinet," he confided in December to the poet Longfellow. "Of course, I should not shrink from any duty required of me by my country at such a moment of peril." In the early months of the war, Sumner had appeared friendly to Seward, whom he privately distrusted. During the *Trent* crisis Sumner had supported the decision to release the two Confederate diplomats.

But by the winter of 1862-63, Sumner was suspicious of Seward's domestic and foreign policy, and he set out to assume control over Union foreign policy. Through the first two years of the fighting possibilities seemed to exist that England and France might side with the Confederacy. England depended upon the cotton states for three-quarters of her raw cotton supply; her statesmen, especially the sword-rattling Prime Minister Palmerston, appeared to favor weakening the power of the United States in the Western hemisphere; her aristocracy sympathized with the planters' cause; and her shipbuilders were constructing, under thin disguise, naval vessels for the Confederacy. France under Napoleon had similar cotton and shipbuilding interests; and as to United States power in the Western hemisphere, France went beyond England by invading Mexico with the purpose of placing a puppet on the Mexican throne.

Sumner's belief that the Union should not risk war with France was challenged by a Senate Democrat and by Seward. Resolutions condemning the French invasion of Mexico as hostile to the United States, introduced by the senator, seemed wantonly provocative to Sumner: and he succeeded in tabling them by a party vote.

At almost exactly the same time, Napoleon III proposed French mediation between the Union and the Confederacy. Ever the politician, Seward seized his chance to appeal to sagging American nationalism. In blunt language, which he deemed safe because the Emperor did not have the support of other European powers, he replied to Paris, "peace proposed at the cost of dissolution would be immediately unreservedly, and indignantly rejected by the American people."

Sumner both feared that Seward might provoke a war with France and hoped that Seward might be dismissed from the cabinet. Moreover, the wily secretary in his dispatch to Paris had introduced another danger. He had said that peace could be restored simply by return of Southern senators and representatives to Congress. To Sumner this sounded as though Seward might be willing, while Congress was not in session, to negotiate a peace without emancipation. He therefore thought it important that Congress should declare its convictions about pacification through foreign mediation.

He offered for adoption by both houses of Congress resolutions asserting that the rebellion lived on the hope of foreign support; that foreign governments should understand the rebel government reposed on the cornerstone of slavery, an institution "shocking to civilization"; and that Congress could not hesitate to regard every proposition of foreign interference "unreasonable and inadmissible." By large majorities both chambers endorsed these resolutions.

On a question of foreign policy regarding England, however, Seward bested Sumner. In the spring and summer of 1862, the C.S.S. *Florida* and the lethal *Alabama* had sailed from British yards to prey upon Union commerce. The menace was vast, for by the end of the war Confederate raiders had destroyed 257 ships and caused Union shipowners to transfer over 700 vessels to foreign registries. Seward threatened to resort to American privateers and had Senator Grimes of the Committee on Naval Affairs sponsor a bill authorizing privateers in both domestic and foreign wars. Privateers, it was clear, could be used against England or any power that built Confederate raiders.

Sumner pointed out that privateers were presumed to prey upon the commerce of an enemy and England was a neutral, and that licensed rovers might embroil the Union in war with England. By a vote that crossed party lines, Sumner in the minority, the Senate approved privateering; and the House sanctioned this vast power to be used at executive discretion without a division. Apparently intended merely as a diplomatic weapon to influence the English government to halt the building of Confederate raiders, the authority was never used.

Seward had scored a personal triumph over Sumner and he soon would gain his objective of having the British government crack down on the shipbuilders. In September Sumner made yet another attempt to seize control of American policy. In Cooper Union, where Lincoln had won fame, he delivered a turgid address, lecturing England upon her duties with respect to intervention in a foreign war and slavery. Two days before this severe, schoolmasterish lecture, the British government had ordered detention of the powerful ironclad rams designed to break the blockade. Sumner of course had not known of the order, and when the news did reach American shores, he was subjected to a good deal of criticism.

Seward had prevailed again. He wrote Sumner a patronizing note of congratulations, and at the same time sent out word the speech should not be circulated abroad. Sumner had failed to grasp control of foreign policy as well as to find a cabinet post.

The Thirty-seventh Congress, in review, had supported administration foreign policy, leaving, as Lincoln did, the conduct of foreign relations in the hands of an astute politician, who grew in sagacity as he continued to hold his high office. Seward could be rash, but he usually calculated the limits of his rashness, and he could turn difficult situations to good American account.

A number of perils to Northern and Republican unity had successfully been met. The Republicans, though assured of continuing in power, were faced with a greater proportion of Democrats in the next Congress and with a states rights insistence by a number of states under Democratic control. One source of dissension between executive and legislative had been the Republican congressmen's drive for a more vigorous conduct of the war. The ironic outcome of the crisis in unity was to foster passage in Congress by the Republican majority of a series of nationalistic measures to which we should now turn.

CHAPTER EIGHT

"The National Spirit Is Growing Stronger"

The cabinet crisis and the duel between Seward and Sumner occurred while the Thirty-seventh Congress was holding its third and last session. The months from December 1862 to July 1863 were perhaps the darkest the Northern cause knew during the war. The decline of administration strength shown at the polls, differences within the Republican party, and defeat in the field seemed to embolden peace Democrats like Vallandigham, augment popular disaffection, encourage desertion, foment antidraft riots, and stiffen states rights protagonists like Seymour.

After Fredericksburg, the Army of the Potomac was turned over to Major General Joseph Hooker, who estimated that in 1863 some 85,000 officers and men deserted this army. In the spring Lee, with the aid of Stonewall Jackson, outgeneraled Hooker at Chancellorsville and gave the Confederacy another victory, though at a heavy cost in casualties. In the West Grant through the first six months of the year 1863 failed to take the river fortress of Vicksburg.

This darkness at noon, before the sun broke through at Gettysburg and Vicksburg, was relieved by congressional enactment of a series of laws which amply justified Stanton's exultant, "The national spirit is growing stronger and stronger." In addition to sharing in the conduct of foreign relations, as already seen, Congress strengthened the central government by enacting a national banking measure, a conscription law, and a habeas corpus act. It faltered in the realm of compensated emancipation, the policy for which Lincoln had, as we have noted, long labored.

Congress by joint resolution had endorsed the policy of compensated emancipation. At its opening the Congress had been reminded by the president in his Annual Message of his anxiety to secure the advantages of his policy. The three constitutional amendments which he suggested were a long-range plan; more immediate opportunities to apply compensated emancipation were available to the Congress in measures pertaining to the proposed new state of West Virginia and to the state of Missouri.

The admission of West Virginia, along with the question of policy toward slavery, encompassed vital constitutional questions. It will be remembered that in the year 1861 the western area of Virginia declared itself a new Virginia government. It won recognition from the Federal government as the true government of the Old Dominion, and in time gave its solemn consent to the separation of various western counties to form the state of West Virginia. The Federal Constitution, however, offered a barrier, requiring that no new state shall be formed within a state without the consent of the legislatures of the states concerned.

The Senate quickly saw that the partition of the Old Dominion and the addition of another loyal border state to the Union would aid in suppressing the rebellion. In the summer of 1862, it set aside scruples about consent of Virginia and debated a bill favorable to admission. The West Virginia constitution, ratified by an overwhelming majority, said nothing about abolishing slavery. Wade's Senate Committee on Territories inserted a requirement that the provisional government, before admission of the state, provide for gradual emancipation. Again a constitutional question was raised, whether Congress may impose an unequal condition upon a state (Kentucky and other Border States legally maintained slavery), and again Congress set aside scruples. Emancipation was ordered; but was it to be gradual or immediate? Sumner insisted upon immediate freedom, but could find support among only ten other senators. Fourteen Republicans, including some of the strongest antislavery men, voted against him. The bill passed the Senate July 14 with only one Democrat in favor and seven Republicans in opposition.

The House withheld approval until December. The scheme fell under sharp attack, Crittenden contending, "The Constitution gives us no power to do what we are asked to do." Stevens airily dismissed the "delusion" of constitutionality: "We may admit West Virginia as a new State, not by virtue of any provision of the Constitution but under our absolute power which the laws of war give us in the circumstances." The bill passed by a virtual party vote, a few Republicans adhering to the opposition.

Lincoln now was in distress about approving the bill. "We have great fears that the President will veto the new State bill," Senator Willey of "Virginia" wrote the "Governor of Virginia." Lincoln addressed two questions to his cabinet: Was the bill constitutional? Was it expedient? The cabinet split evenly in returning written answers. The president formed his own opinion, swallowing the fiction of constitutionality, avowing the admission was expedient, and ignoring the matter of compensation. He made the bill law, requiring West Virginia to accept emancipation. Oddly enough, the next day in issuing his Emancipation Proclamation, he excepted West Virginia as a part of the Union left with slavery "as if this proclamation were not issued."

West Virginia bowed to the will of Washington, establishing an interesting system of gradual emancipation. Slaves under the age of ten were to become free by arrival at the age of twenty-one; those between ten and twenty-one by arrival at the age of twenty-five; and children born after July 4, 1863, at birth. No slave was to come into the state for permanent residence. Later developments swept away this experiment in progressive emancipation.

As to the constitutional questions, the forthright Stevens probably occupied the firmest ground—admission under the laws of war. As to the compensation question, the anticipated willingness of West Virginia— whose 48 counties in 1860 held only 12,771 slaves as against 334,921 whites—to emancipate without demanding payment seemed to resolve the matter. Admission of West Virginia augmented the political strength of the North and advanced the cause of emancipation. In 1864 the state cast five electoral votes for Lincoln; and the following year its legislature unanimously ratified the Thirteenth Amendment.

Lincoln's policy of compensated emancipation came closest to realization in Missouri, where the issue was put before the people in the election of 1862. The outcome was choice of a legislature with a majority for emancipation; and of nine members of Congress six were emancipationists. The emancipationists elected the speaker of the Missouri House; and the governor recommended adoption of compensated gradual emancipation.

Accordingly, members from Missouri took up the president's plan in Congress. The House approved an offer of $10 million in bonds if the Missouri legislature should provide for immediate emancipation. There was little debate; the bill was rammed through on the day the committee reported with a vote of 83-50—mainly on party lines. The Senate deliberated a month, divided over the issue of immediate or gradual emancipation. At length it agreed to offer $10 million for gradual emancipation (by July 4, 1876) or $20 million for emancipation of all slaves by July 4, 1865. The vote was 23-18, with five Republicans in opposition.

Returned to the House, the bill fell victim to Border Democratic opponents. It became impossible to unearth it from a mound of parliamentary rules under which it was buried, and Congress adjourned without coming to accord. Democrats assume a good part of the blame for the bill's failure, but the Republicans had not made the extraordinary exertions which were required for passage. Failure in the case of Missouri encouraged filibuster in the case of Maryland. Before the new Congress could meet in December, the swift rush of national affairs had made impossible adoption of Lincoln's plan. Lincoln had warned Crittenden, "You Southern men will soon reach the point where bonds will be a more valuable possession than bondsmen." That point had been reached by the time the Thirty-eighth Congress convened.

"Volunteers we cannot have," the chairman of its military committee told the Senate in February 1863. The war's bitter duration, defeats in the field, and lucrative employment opportunities made enlistment languish. Regimental strengths eroded under the forces of battle, disease, discharges for disability, and desertions, while terms of men earlier accepted were expiring.

The Confederacy, after only one year of war, had instituted a draft and, unlike the Union, was using it to fill out existing regiments, wisely mingling recruits with veterans. The United States had never drafted men; legislation looking to a draft in the War of 1812 had failed. By early 1863 resistance to national conscription was being worn down. Step by step the national government had been outpacing the tradition of local reliance: from Lincoln's arbitrary increase of the army and navy, through his contrived call for 300,000 more men in the summer of 1862, on through the attempted draft under the Militia Act, and beyond this to Federal enrollment of Negro troops. The next step in the advance of nationalism was a law to supersede the draft of state militia under supervision of the governors with the draft of national forces under direct supervision of the Federal government.

Herein lay the bold thrust of the conscription law that Wilson presented to the Senate February 16 with his statement the government could not get volunteers. Apparently worked out in cooperation with the administration, the bill, avowing the necessity to maintain the Constitution and the Union, defined the "national forces" (not the militia) as all able-bodied male citizens and all aliens who had declared on oath their intention of becoming citizens, who were between the ages of 20 and 45. These persons were liable to military duty on call of the president. The bill's phrasing eschewed the word "state."

Federal draft machinery, starting with the Provost Marshal General, who was made head of a separate bureau in the War Department, extended down into districts that largely corresponded with congressional districts, each of which had a draft board which included a representative of the Provost Marshal General.

Provision was made for exemptions, and priority in being called was given to men between twenty and thirty-five and all unmarried men. There was written into the bill the old custom of substitution, under which a man who furnished a substitute could be excused. The insertion of substitution then led to the notorious provision for paying a sum of money in place of serving. "A rich man's war and a poor man's fight!" cried the critics of commuting military obligation by money. Yet, once the principle of substitution had been accepted, the possibility of buying a substitute was opened up. A fixed money payment, it was argued, would place a ceiling on substitute prices, and thereby eliminate the advantage accorded wealthy men by the substitute system.

Insisting passage was necessary to prevent the death of the nation, Wilson drove the bill through the Senate without a recorded vote. In the House, with but a few days left before the Congress would expire, Republican managers took a firm hand, meaning to ride roughshod over the opposition. But the bill's foes persisted, wanting to voice their beliefs that the draft was unconstitutional, that white men should not be conscripted to free Negroes, and that the bill yielded broadly coercive powers to the military. Vallandigham made his valedictory, charging the bill would make Lincoln "the master dictator of the United States. And for what?" he demanded, answering, "The abolition of negro slavery by force." Crittenden also made his last speech, claiming the remedy for the falling off of volunteering was repeal of the abolition measures, thus "making this again a national war." Democrats who in the future would lead the House asserted their objections. Cox tried in vain to limit the draft to white men, Holman of Indiana in vain to eliminate substitution and commutation, and Voorhees, "Tall Sycamore of the Wabash," in his reverberant tones decried Republican tactics. The bill passed by a partisan vote, 115-49, and was returned to the Senate for final action. There, opposition took the shape of a motion to postpone, which failed 11-35. On March 3 Lincoln signed the nation's first draft law.

Child of necessity, approved by substantial majorities, the law nonetheless promptly incurred strong criticism. To meet this, Lincoln prepared an elaborate address, which, in fact, he never released to the public. But it reveals his thinking. "We must somehow obtain more [men] , or relinquish the original object of the rebellion." As to constitutionality, Congress' authority "to raise and support armies" was unconditional. As to the provision for commutation, the real discrimination came from substitution, "an old and well-known practice," to which there would have been "great objection," if omitted. The money provision, he wrote, really modifies the inequality which substitution introduces, preventing substitution from being possible only for the wealthy. Strange as this last argument may ring today, investigation of commutation in portions of Ohio and New York suggests that draftees from lower economic groups could pay commutation at $300, but would have been unable to buy substitutes at prices above that ceiling.

A clash in constitutional principle between president and chief justice was avoided. Taney prepared an opinion which he never delivered and which for many years was unknown. His "Thoughts on the Conscription Law of the U.S." pronounced the law unconstitutional. With characteristic stress on federalism, he upheld the rights of the states to maintain their own militia; but under this law he feared the national government might destroy the militia. Moreover, under the law, civil officers of states, governors excepted, might be drafted, and the state governments might be virtually destroyed. The vexed question never reached the High Court during the war, but, as we shall see, had a mixed reception in lower courts.

Historians have passed varying judgments on this law, the judicious J. G. Randall calling it "drastic," the sharp-tongued F. A. Shannon branding it "a grotesque shadow of a conscription act," the temperate Allan Nevins describing it as a "stunning disappointment." Yet it is worthwhile remembering that this act, now hurriedly passed, was later several times amended. The Provost Marshal General thought the law as improved established "a military system adequate to any emergency...." This opinion is perhaps too lofty, but the careful scholar J. F. Leach came to a similar conclusion. The effect of the draft was not actually to conscript men. Only 170,000 men were drafted, and of these, 120,000 were substitutes. But the law appears to have spurred volunteering, indirectly attaining its purpose. Beyond this, the law helped to put down the pretension that the United States had no power to draft for its military service. A breakthrough in nationalism, it afforded a useful precedent for the World Wars of the twentieth century.

"Our financial troubles are thickening every day," Fessenden in mid-January confided to a correspondent. Tax receipts were low, bonds not selling, currency chaotic, and soldiers and sailors were going unpaid. Congress authorized a third—and final—issue of $150 million in greenbacks and abrogated the privilege of converting them into bonds—a thoughtless change which later made return to specie payments difficult. Lincoln regretfully approved the inflationary measure, reminding the legislators that in his Annual Message of only the previous month he had urged Congress to provide a uniform currency through banking associations organized under a general act of Congress.

The need for a uniform national currency was both immediate and of long standing. Currency largely was issued by state banks. State bank currency could not legally be accepted in payments to the Federal government; and the issue of many Western banks was based upon questionable securities. Greenbacks were unsecured by specie.

A model, however, could be found in New York where a law followed successfully since 1838 required banks to secure their note issues by deposit with the state of approved securities and, secondly, to keep specie reserve against the notes. From this model, Secretary of the Treasury Chase drew his proposal to create a national currency, issued by banks organized under a national banking law, with security of the currency assured by U.S. bonds and a specie reserve.

In this historical light, the notion held by some historians of a radical conspiracy to fasten a national banking system upon a reluctant nation appears ludicrous. The leading advocate of the system was Chase, whose concern was a uniform national currency, not banks and their profits. During the exigency of a costly war, he ardently wished to end the fluctuation in currency and at the same time sell bonds, not to aid bankers and capitalists. His interest lay with the government, not with the private sector, with the winning of the war, not with the making of peacetime profits. He repeatedly urged such legislation upon the Republican-dominated Congress until March 1863. By that date, as we have seen, Lincoln, upon whom, legend runs, the radicals were endeavoring to impose their ideas, twice had appealed to Congress to authorize a sound national circulation.

The true political context in which the famous National Bank Act was passed may further be clarified by the fact that Thaddeus Stevens, presumed archradical as well as chairman of the House Ways and Means Committee, opposed the measure because he thought it would aid moneylenders. Fessenden, Senate Finance chairman, abdicated leadership of the bill because of his reluctance to imperil state banks and only grudgingly voted for it. As to bankers, many New York City bankers opposed the bill, and there existed little enthusiasm except in Western states which had suffered from wildcat banking. Few bankers availed themselves of the 1863 law, or of the 1864 amendment. Not until the Federal government imposed a prohibitive tax on state bank notes did many banks convert to the national system. In the Senate the bill passed by the margin of one vote, made possible by the shift of one senator. Nine Republicans voted nay. In the House the margin was unusually close, 78-64, with 22 Republicans in opposition. The bill split the party and the radicals. Republican defectors, who included Conkling and Morrill, were centered in New York, New Jersey, and New England; only four of the party's nays came from states west of the Alleghenies.

Amended in 1864, the National Banking system authorized national banks to issue notes up to ninety percent of their U.S. bond holdings. The banks were required to invest at least one-third of their capital in U.S. securities. The system lasted until it was superseded by the Federal Reserve. It avoided the perils of the former Bank of the United States—a giant, consolidated institution in which the government owned an interest but did not control—and failed to attain the benefits of decentralization, elasticity, and public control that were written into the Federal Reserve Act.

Like the Pacific Railroad Act and the draft law, this measure required amendment. In all three instances Congress, pioneering in lawmaking effected improvements. As early as December 1863, Lincoln judged the national banking law had proved "a valuable support of the public credit." And a year later he declared the system "is proving to be acceptable to capitalists and to the people."

Welling up from the depths of adversity, the surge of nationalism that had borne before it the opposition to a national banking system and conscription now swept over the resistance to authorizing executive suspension of the writ of habeas corpus. Congress in previous sessions, as we have observed, clinging to the view that only Congress could suspend the writ, declined either to sanction or to censure Lincoln's continuing denial of that view.

As in the case of conscription, the Confederate Congress had acted before the Union Congress. In the Confederacy, executive suspension was authorized in a series of laws that greatly limited as to time and place the president's power to suspend. Admirable as these restraints upon arbitrary power may seem, they nonetheless were attended with strenuous states rights opposition. Vice-President A. H. Stephens, virtually a deserter from his post, in March 1864 in a widely circulated speech attacked the government's "despotic" suspension of the writ; and from July through the end of the war President Davis was refused the power. Liberty turned into license, as state judges freely issued writs to deserters and draft dodgers. General R. E. Lee complained that the resulting drain on the army was "more than it can bear."

The safety of the state in wartime, whether North or South, posed the ancient problem, liberty versus authority. Lincoln's arbitrary rule caused the Englishman James Bryce to conclude, "Abraham Lincoln wielded more authority than any single Englishman has done since Oliver Cromwell." On the other hand, Attorney General Bates, fearing the Supreme Court might rule adversely on the president's suspending power, on January 31, 1863, confided to Stanton that such a decision would "do more to paralyze the Executive . . . than the worst defeat our armies have yet sustained."

Congress could no longer escape the issue. On the opening day in

December, Democrats, heartened by the recent elections, assailed arbitrary arrests. Lincoln's blanket suspension in September had caused concern to Democrats and Republicans. After his victory Governor-elect Seymour wrote Manton Marble of the *World*, "I am glad to see that you follow up the subject of illegal arrests. It must be made the issue." For some time responsible Republicans like Trumbull had believed there was a need to regularize the matters of suspension and arbitrary arrests. There were the supplementary problems of protecting Federal enforcement officers against law suits and of removing cases from the jurisdiction of states rights judges—this last, as suggested earlier, a problem that plagued the Confederacy. To secure their ends, Republicans in Congress resorted to extraordinary parliamentary tactics.

One week after the session began, Stevens introduced a bill to indemnify the president and other Federal officers against law suits and authorize the president to suspend. He asked special consideration for early passage, and when Vallandigham vehemently objected, the masterly Stevens "with an obedient majority at his command," in Voorhees' angry phrase, moved the previous question and rammed the bill through within an hour by a vote of 90 to 45. Thirty-six outraged Democrats sought to enter a protest on the House journal, but this was not permitted, and Stevens laid their protest on the table.

The Senate enacted its own habeas corpus bill; and the two chambers thereupon named a joint committee to harmonize the indemnity and habeas corpus bills. The House, as expected, agreed to the committee version, but a fight broke out in the Senate. Opposition senators resorted to a filibuster, delaying action until five in the morning of the last night of the session. After failure of a motion to adjourn, the presiding officer, Pomeroy of Kansas, arbitrarily declared, "The question is on concurring in the report of the committee of conference. Those in favor of concurring in the report will say 'aye,' those opposed 'no.' The ayes have it. It is a vote."

Democrats protested the chair's ruling; and a motion to reconsider measured the strength of the opposition, 13-25, and finished the matter. The unusual tactics employed on both sides demonstrated the sensitivy of the issue. The filibuster was the only attempt by the Democrats in this session to use this parliamentary delaying tactic. The highhanded ruling by Pomeroy was more in keeping with the character of the man who was the inspiration for Senator Dilworthy in Mark Twain's *The Gilded Age* than with the normal character of Republican parliamentarianism.

The Habeas Corpus Act of 1863, as passed, had four important provisions. In carefully worded language, it authorized the president to suspend the privilege of the writ of habeas corpus. The language straddled the vexed constitutional issue, leaving unclear whether the president was "authorized" by the act or, as Lincoln claimed, by the Constitution. It provided that any order made by the president should be a defense in courts, thus protecting Federal officers, including the president, against law suits. Beyond these two provisions the act sought to curb infringement upon civil liberties and to curb state resistance to national authority. The secretaries of state and war were required to furnish lists of political prisoners to Federal judges. If after adjournment of a grand jury, a prisoner had not been indicted, the judge was to discharge him on his taking an oath of allegiance. Indicted persons were to be admitted to bail pending trial.

Of far-reaching significance was the final provision that allowed removal of suits from state to Federal courts. In the short view the provision gave protection in Federal courts to Federal enforcement officers, but in the long view it extended judicial authority over the states, effecting, as one scholar has put it, a reconstruction of Federal judicial authority.

Lincoln and his lieutenants inclined to ignore the new law. Arrests went forward, and not until September did the president clothe himself with the authority of the statute. By 1864-65 some of the most ardent Republicans were sharply criticizing executive noncompliance with congressional law. The Supreme Court refused to take up the question of political prisoners until after the war. Yet tales of an American Bastille were exaggerated. It was once believed that the number of political prisoners soared to 38,000. Careful research has reduced this figure to less than 14,000. No doubt injustices were done; though offsetting factors were the exceptional circumstances of an internal war and the fact that no lasting damage to democratic institutions resulted.

Under the threat of Confederate successes, of the Democrats' resurgence at the polls, and finessed by the astute president in the challenge over his cabinet, Congress had subsequently gone far to cooperate with the executive. Not only had it at last swallowed its reluctance to enact a habeas corpus law, but it had also handed him a victory of potentially great moment. The House in early February had seated two representatives from Louisiana, elected under the authority of a military governor appointed by Lincoln. We must reserve for later treatment the great divisive issue of reconstruction, but what is to be stressed here is congressional acquiescence to an executive course of reconstruction.

If this short and last session of the Thirty-seventh Congress had been marked by a high degree of cooperation between legislature and executive, sources of tension remained. Republican lawmakers had been more extreme than Lincoln about admitting West Virginia. They had failed to make the requisite effort to secure compensated emancipation in Missouri. And in passing the Habeas Corpus Act, they had papered over real differences between the two branches.

The Thirty-seventh Congress closed March 4, 1863, two years after Lincoln's inauguration and twenty months after it first had met. In its three sessions it had acted with a high degree of responsibility toward the unexampled emergency, and at the same time it had enacted a momentous program for the peacetime future. With respect to the war, it had provided sword and purse beyond the dreams of any antebellum generation. It had blighted the institution of Negro slavery, generally thought to be the root of the war.

In nearly all essential respects, Congress had cooperated with the president, giving Lincoln the means of war—men, equipment, money, letters of marque and reprisal, and control of foreign affairs; deferring to his scruples about confiscation; agreeing in principle with his compensated emancipation scheme (though failing to provide the means); and at length authorizing him to suspend the writ of habeas corpus. Lincoln was intent upon winning the war to save the Union, and though on occasion executive and legislature significantly differed on means, Congress cannot fairly be charged with obstructing him. Some radicals wanted him to go faster than he was willing to go, but, often imperceptive of the political needs of Northern unity, they were perhaps wrong about timing.

With respect to peacetime needs, Congress had restructured American institutions: banking and currency, taxation, including the tariff, public lands, higher education, and transcontinental railroads. Its legacy to the postwar generation was great, and if the Gilded Age failed to husband its legacy, the fault lies most of all with the heir.

One intangible bequeathed by the Thirty-seventh Congress was an enhanced nationalism. In this regard the last session in particular had been historic. It had overridden state sovereignty to authorize the draft by Federal officials of the "national forces," to create a national banking system, and to give jurisdiction to Federal courts in matters pertaining to the habeas corpus law.

In championing the national banking system, Senator John Sherman had argued, "It will promote a sentiment of nationality." It is, he went on, the "bad sentiment that has elevated State authority above the great national authority that has been the main instrument by which our Government is sought to be overthrown." On the day Congress closed, the German-born Professor Francis Lieber wrote to General Halleck: "We must conquer the South, not for a crown, as a province, but for the *country* and the *National* constitution." Many persons besides Lincoln believed the war was for the Union—a Union which could endure only if it was superior to the states.

Within a week of congressional adjournment, the Supreme Court in its most important decision during the war, upheld national power and also defended the administration. The high tribunal, once pro-Southern and still presided over by the author of the 1857 Dred Scott decision, had been remade by Republican appointments. Lincoln had named three Republicans to vacancies, all of whom sustained him in the important Prize cases. However, it was an aged Democrat, Robert Grier, born in Pennsylvania in 1794 and named to the court by Polk in 1846, who wrote the majority opinion. Enlargement of the court to ten members by a law passed March 3, appears not, as sometimes said, a court-packing attempt but a move to bring California and Oregon within the Federal judicial system by creating the new justiceship and the Tenth Circuit for the area.

The Prize cases, involving ships taken as prize for violating the blockade, posed delicate constitutional questions. Were Lincoln's war measures undertaken before Congress met, including proclamation of the blockade, illegal? A blockade in international law is an incident of war, but Congress had never declared war, contending that the conflict was an insurrection. If the court should follow the view that the conflict was a mere insurrection, then the blockade, comprehending seizure of ships and sealing off foreign trade, was illegal. If the court should rule the blockade was legal, it would be saying that war, not insurrection, existed, and foreign governments might recognize the Confederacy.

In a marginal 5-4 decision, Grier sustained both Lincoln and the "double status" theory of the legal nature of the war. On the first point, Grier upheld the legality of the blockade, even though there had been no congressional declaration of war. "A civil war," he said, "is never solemnly declared; it becomes such by its accidents. . . ." The President was bound to meet the war in the shape it presented itself "without waiting for Congress to baptize it with a name."

As to the legal nature of the conflict, Grier held as a basic fact that it had a dual nature: the United States sustained the double character of a belligerent and a sovereign and had the rights of both. That the conflict was both a war and an insurrection was a view which Lincoln and many members of Congress found convenient. Significantly, the Supreme Court now seemed on the side of the Republican party. The three branches of government after years of controversy had reached relative harmony. On the same "momentous day," the last day of the term, the tribunal furthered Unionism in two cases, striking down state taxation of U.S. bonds and ruling in favor of the U.S. government in a California mining case.

The progress of nationality in the North in the early months of 1863 was further evidenced by a unanimous decision of the Wisconsin state supreme court, by the start of recruiting Negro troops, by the success in selling U.S. bonds, and by the spring elections. The Wisconsin high court was persuaded to reverse its states rights ruling against the draft and suspension of the writ of habeas corpus.

In circumstances that will probably never be known, Senator T. O. Howe of Wisconsin, a staunch nationalist who in the 1850s had opposed his state's defiance of the national fugitive slave law, prevailed upon the court to uphold the national cause. Exultantly, Howe wired Stanton, "The supreme court has just decided unanimously the draft of last fall to be valid, and has denied the writ of habeas corpus."

Stanton answered, "I thank you with exceeding great joy. . . . It will do much to correct the evil occasioned by the action of your supreme court last fall. Accounts from all parts of the country show that the national spirit is growing stronger and stronger."

Under the aegis of the national government, state after state altered its policy concerning Negro soldiers. Within months there were fifty-eight regiments of Negro troops in the Union Army, drawn from eight Northern states, seven Confederate states, and the District of Columbia. Remarking upon the advance of the national cause, Lincoln said some of his most successful generals "believe the emancipation policy, and the use of colored troops, constitute the heaviest blow yet dealt to the rebellion."

In addition, the working of the national spirit was visible in public purchase of government bonds. The financial legislation enacted by Congress strengthened confidence in the government. Secretary Chase, in cooperation with the Philadelphia banker Jay Cooke, using sales and advertising methods that anticipated the twentieth century, sold bonds directly to the public, bypassing the bankers. By May, subscriptions were averaging over $3 million a day.

The spring elections in New England sustained the Union cause, though by narrow margins. The only general elections held in the loyal states during the first half of 1863 saw the Republicans scrape by in New Hampshire, with the loss of a House seat; retain Rhode Island; and in the key contest, in Connecticut, defeat the vigorous peace candidate for governor.

Walt Whitman maintained his robust faith in the success of the national cause, in spite of the Union's worst naval loss of the war at Charleston. "And even if we fail for a while elsewhere," he said in late April, "I believe this Union will conquer in the end, as sure as there's a God in heaven. This country can't be broken up by Jeff Davis, & all his damned crew."

Amid these swells of nationalism, however, powerful crosscurrents were at work. States rights had not died among the Democrats, especially in the Middle West and the Middle Atlantic states; vigorous antinational leadership was given by Vallandigham and Seymour; resistance to the draft had not yet attained its crest; and public acquiescence in the Lincolnian course of restoring the Union, using the means of military coercion, arbitrary arrest, conscription, emancipation, and heavy spending, had not been wholesale.

CHAPTER NINE

Dissidence and Decision

Dissent in the North, of little significance in 1861, rose in 1862, gathered strength in the autumn elections of that year, and attained a new peak in early 1863. In the last part of that year, it waned, only to crest in the presidential election of 1864.

Dissent in 1863 had many dimensions: congressional Democrats, state governors, sectionalism, and secret societies. Congressional Democrats, as we have seen, were always in the minority and usually disinclined to employ tactics of obstruction. They lacked a recognized leader, and they were divided in their views. Those Democrats who espoused a negotiated peace and opposed emancipation in principle were wrong: they would have done better to have thrown their weight on the side of clemency for Southerners and compensation for slaveholders. As members of the loyal opposition, all congressional Democrats would have done well to uphold civil liberties in the North, economy and honesty in public affairs, and vigorous prosecution of the war accompanied by insistence upon a just reconstruction of the Union.

In Horatio Seymour, governor of New York, the Democratic party found its ablest wartime leader. On taking office in January, Seymour essayed to place himself at the head of the national party. He emphasized strict construction of the Constitution as a means of reuniting the nation at a time when Vallandigham was crying, "Stop fighting." He customarily employed merely firm language while the Westerner was becoming increasingly violent, proclaiming the choice lay between armistice and anarchy. Seymour bore himself with dignity, perhaps with an eye on the presidency, while the Ohioan, leader of the peace Democrats, conducted himself in a dramatic manner that invited criticism and martyrdom.

More than two-thirds of Seymour's annual message to the legislature dwelt on national affairs. He declared that slavery was not the cause but the occasion of the war. With penetrating argument he attacked arbitrary arrests and martial law for civilians. He declined to believe that emancipation and conscription were required to win the war. We can never consent, he said, to the breakup of the Union, but war alone will not preserve it. We will hold out every inducement to Southerners to return to their old allegiance with every constitutional right guaranteed to them. These principles won hearty endorsement from the Democratic legislature of Indiana, which refused to receive its own Republican governor's message while passing a joint resolution of thanks to Governor Seymour.

Seymour's tone disturbed Lincoln, who penned an anxious letter to "the head of the greatest State of [the] nation." "The cooperation of your state . . . is indispensable," the president told him. After an interval of three weeks, Seymour, disclaiming any superior wisdom, replied, "I am confident the opinions I hold are entertained by one-half of the population of the Northern States." He had marked out his own pathway for the preservation of the Union, he flatly announced. Here relations between the president and the governor hung until the crises over Vallandigham and the draft brought their clashing principles into the open.

The Democrats displayed considerable regional variety. They were weakest in New England where they lost their best chance of capturing a state with Connecticut's repulse of their peace candidate for governor. The party had won governorships of two Middle Atlantic states in 1862, New

Jersey as well as New York. Joel Parker, governor of the state of New Jersey, in his inaugural address opposed "the sudden liberation of . . . millions of beings without property . . . without education . . . or enterprise." The assembly passed a Negro exclusion bill, and both chambers endorsed peace resolutions. In Pennsylvania the test of Democratic strength in 1863 would come in the fall elections.

If the New York Democrats had Seymour, they also had Fernando Wood, a divisive Democrat tilting with Tammany Hall, and now a member of Congress, and brother to the publisher of the scurrilous New York *Daily News*. The term *Copperhead*, whether derived from the patriotic practice of wearing the head of Liberty cut out of a copper penny, or from a comparison to the poisonous snake, was widely applied to Democrats like Wood and Brooks.

The word *Butternut* was commonly applied to Democrats in the Middle West. Derived from the method of home-dyeing the clothing of rural folk of Southern origin, the term was proudly accepted by Democrats who liked to believe their party represented the common man and understood the Southern people. In the Middle West the Democrats enjoyed power with their majorities in the Illinois and Indiana legislatures; and they aspired to capture the Ohio governorship.

In the Middle West ties of kinship, commerce, party, and geography bound the area south of a line drawn from Columbus through Quincy to the South, while a common dependence upon agriculture and an aversion to Negroes reenforced Southern sympathies. Lodged between the Northeast and the South, the Northwest had swung its support to the Republican party in 1860 and had given the nation its president. Under the weight of war-weariness and of Republican plans to emancipate Negroes, centralize the government, and establish an economy benefiting the Northeast, the region had begun to seethe with discontent. Illinois in 1862 had in effect voted against Lincoln, to his mortification.

As the new year opened, Lincoln divulged he feared "the fire in the rear"—meaning the Northwestern Democrats. It was not only that the Democrats controlled the Illinois and Indiana legislatures, but also alarming reports of treasonable, secret political activities there were being reported to Washington.

On the eve of the legislatures' opening, Governor Morton of Indiana wired Stanton: "I am advised that it is contemplated when the Legislature meets in this State to pass a joint resolution acknowledging the Southern

Confederacy, and urging the States of the Northwest to dissolve all constitutional relations with the New England States. The same thing is on foot in Illinois," Morton frantically added.

What was afoot in Illinois became clear when the legislature met in Springfield in early January. The lower house adopted a resolution condemning the Emancipation Proclamation as unconstitutional and an invitation to racial war. The house denounced secession and recognition of Confederate independence, while urging an armistice and a national peace convention, for which they named commissioners. Approval in the upper chamber was frustrated by withdrawal of the Republican minority. After a recess until June, the legislators took up bills to tighten the Negro exclusion law, prevent illegal arrests, and protest the growth of Federal power.

Governor Yates seized on a constitutional quirk to prorogue the legislature. Outraged, some 40,000 antiadministration Democrats gathered in Springfield. Along with calling Yates' act a usurpation, they affirmed the supremacy of the Constitution in war as well as in peace, condemned violations of the Bill of Rights, and in the notorious "twenty-third resolution" proposed a national peace convention to work out terms of peace on the basis of restoration of the Union.

This political amalgam of myopia and constructive opposition could be almost duplicated in Indiana. Indianapolis differed from Springfield in doing without a legislature from adjournment in 1863 to 1865. The party struggle suspended constitutional government when Republicans broke the quorum. Attempts by Democrats to assert states rights had cost Indiana her sovereignty. In one sense Morton became a dictator without a legislature to check him. But in another sense he became a puppet, dependent upon private and Federal money to keep his state in the war for the Union. In neither Illinois or Indiana had the Democratic alternative to Republican policies shown responsibility or wisdom.

In the borderland extending from Delaware to Missouri, it is difficult to determine party allegiance, distinguishing between Democrat and Unionist. Suffice it to say that the loyal slave region maintained an outlook of guarded Unionism. Troops had supervised the 1862 elections in Delaware and Missouri. Lincoln had carefully nursed Kentucky out of her neutrality, and in 1862 he named a Kentucky Democrat as the Judge Advocate General. In this state, where opposition to the Lincoln administration was most prevalent, peace Democrats were girding to win the governorship from Union Democrats.

In the story of Northern opposition to the war, somewhere beyond the dissidence of the Democrats murkily lies the Knights of the Golden Circle. Organized in the South during the 1850s, this secret order agitated to extend slavery. The order spread into the southern portion of the Northwest and by 1863 had become a vehicle of the peace Democrats—that minor faction which worked for a negotiated peace with slavery. Republicans in Illinois and Indiana exploited the existence of the Knights in an effort to tar the Democrats with treason.

Alarmed contemporaries and the Judge Advocate General viewed the Knights as traitors. Disloyal deeds attributed to the order ranged from circulating seditious literature to distributing guns to rebel raiders in the North. A more balanced judgment by historians sees the order concerned in agitating against Republican rule and in holding mass meetings to demand peace negotiations for reunion.

Outside of legitimate opposition through party and of elusive activities through a secret order, dissent through violence was alarmingly frequent and epidemic throughout the Civil War. We have already noticed evidence of popular fury and lawlessness: in Baltimore at the beginning of the war, in mob action against presses and editors, and in resistance to the militia. There is an ongoing story of turbulence directed against soldiers, conscientious objectors, Negroes, Irish, editors, abolitionists, and Southern sympathizers. The spring of 1863 was no exception, though the incidents were overshadowed by the New York City draft riots of July, which we shall presently examine.

In a battle for men's minds, Democrats systematically circulated pamphlets. Some of the most responsible New York Democrats met at Delmonico's, February 6, to organize the Society for the Diffusion of Political Knowledge, a propaganda agency. The inventor S. F. B. Morse took the presidency; and the constitutional historian George T. Curtis spoke. Supported by millionaires, the Society published and diffused pamphlets attacking emancipation and abrogation of civil liberties and upholding states rights. Morse soon was urging men to quit fighting so long as emancipation was a war aim; and Curtis was confidentially urging Seymour to issue a proclamation defining the duties of state officers to limit the pending habeas corpus bill.

Republicans, rallying war Democrats to their side, countered this activity with societies of their own. Well-born leaders organized Union Leagues—ultimately to become elitist social clubs—with a national headquarters in Washington, and the Loyal Publication Society. These and similar societies became a useful arm of the Republican party, distributing documents and journals. Pamphleteers defended the draft law, tax measures, and executive suspension of the writ of habeas corpus. One of the most widely circulated pamphlets was Francis Lieber's *No Party Now but All for Our Country* calling on all good men to come to the aid of administration efforts to defeat the Confederacy, free the slaves, enforce the draft, and resist European meddling. On the whole, Union propaganda rose to a higher level than Democratic, as the rival organizations defined the political options open to voters.

During the year 1863 the North's two leading Democrats challenged the Lincoln administration in confrontations famous in the political annals of the American Civil War. Vallandigham, to whom many Western Democrats looked for leadership, demanded that the war be halted and "King Lincoln" be voted from his throne. He became the center of a civil liberties struggle that brought the Lincoln administration its most severe criticism on this score. Seymour, to whom many Eastern Democrats looked for leadership, demanded that the draft be halted and the radicals be voted from power.

Defeated for reelection to Congress, Vallandigham appears to have sought the Ohio governorship by way of martyrdom. Upon the expiration of Congress in March, he made a journey into the Northeast, urging, "Stop this war," and attacking the administration. Vallandigham visited Seymour and other Democratic leaders in Albany. They discussed the recently enacted draft and habeas corpus laws, to which Vallandigham had made vociferous objection, and means to unite Eastern and Western Democrats.

Back in Ohio, with the state Democratic convention in the offing, Vallandigham kept up his onslaught against the Lincoln government. His course was eyed with suspicion by General Burnside, reassigned after defeat at Fredericksburg, to command of the Department of Ohio. This bluff, imperceptive general issued an order against "the enemies of our country" in his department, and sent officers in civilian clothing to report on a speech Vallandigham delivered on May 1.

Standing among a crowd of Butternuts and Copperheads, the officers recorded a diatribe against administration despotism, emancipation, and the war. Decrying Burnside's order, the orator said he could spit on it and stamp it under foot. Three days later Union soldiers took Vallandigham from his home at night and clapped him into military prison.

Over his protest that it had no authority to try him, a military commission found him guilty of violating Burnside's order and sentenced him to close confinement in some fortress of the United States for the rest of the war. His prompt appeal to a United States Circuit Court for a writ of habeas corpus was denied. (The U.S. Supreme Court in the following year refused to review the case.)

Arrest and trial by the military of a civilian, who was a prominent spokesman of the opposition to the Lincoln administration, occasioned an outpouring of protest. Bidding for martyrdom and the gubernatorial nomination, Vallandigham marshalled partisan support. On the day he was arrested, he issued an address "To the Democracy of Ohio." A prisoner, he solicited help from Manton Marble and Horatio Seymour; the editor wrote "noble articles" and the governor publicly denounced "the whole transaction as cowardly, brutal, and infamous."

Vallandigham won martyrdom not in a Union bastille but in exile. Lincoln, embarrassed by Burnside's act but concluding to accept it, commuted the sentence to banishment within Confederate lines. The plight of the Ohio Copperhead was immortalized by publication in the *Atlantic Monthly* in December of the story "The Man without a Country."

Of all the partisan protests, that of the Albany Democrats was notable because it drew from Lincoln his view of the case. It was a difficult argument to make, for, as the historian Rhodes judged, Lincoln should have released Vallandigham after rescinding sentence, and, as the historian Nevins observed, there had been "an indefensible invasion of fundamental civil liberties."

In his reply to the Albany Democrats, Lincoln admitted he did not know whether he would have ordered the arrest and asserted he was pained to learn of the necessity. But he assumed responsibility and sought to extenuate the arrest. He claimed he had been slow to adopt the strong measures he regarded as indispensable to the public safety. The time might come, he said, when he would be blamed for having made too few arrests rather than too many. And then he phrased his dilemma in a way to make it understood at Northern hearthsides: "Must I shoot a simple-minded soldier boy who deserts, while I must not touch a hair of a wily agitator who induces him to desert?"

Eloquent, and even moving, as this may be, it advances the bad tendency doctrine—men may be punished for the tendency of their words—which courts later held to be an infringement on free speech. The other main argument Lincoln used was that Vallandigham was damaging the army. There is no proof of this assertion, and on the whole Lincoln might have done better to overrule Burnside on this rash act against civil liberties, just as he had overruled other generals in their unauthorized acts against slavery.

Vallandigham won the Democratic gubernatorial nomination, the Ohio Democrats thereby transmuting the issue to "peace or war." The nominating convention sent Lincoln a copy of the platform and a demand for the recall from exile of their nominee. Lincoln in reply asked the Ohio Democratic Committee to sign a pledge of full support of military suppression of the rebellion, saying he would then revoke the sentence. The committee refused to comply, and the political resolution of the struggle between Vallandigham and Lincoln went over to the Ohio voters in the fall elections.

Unrebuked by the president, Burnside further infringed on free speech by suppressing a Copperhead newspaper. The Chicago *Times* was a voice of the peace Democrats of the Northwest. Long critical of Republican war measures, it now took as its main theme, "Vallandigham vs. Lincoln," until at three in the morning of June 3, Burnside's troops took possession of its office. Two days earlier the bumptious general had issued a military order to suppress the *Times* and circulation of the New York *World*.

Indignation among Illinoisans was immediate, vocal, and bipartisan. At noon Chicagoans of both parties at a meeting presided over by the recently chosen Democratic mayor asked the president to rescind the order; and the Illinois Republican leaders Senator Trumbull and I. N. Arnold reinforced the request by joint telegram. That night 20,000 citizens gathered to resolve that freedom of the press should be upheld. The Illinois house denounced the order. Regretting Burnside's fresh blunder, Lincoln, reluctant to weaken military authority but influenced by the Republican's telegram, the following day revoked the order.

Famous in history for his muttonchop whiskers, Burnside, apparently at last subdued, soon issued orders freeing all political prisoners in his department who could be released with safety; and he advised his subordinates to exercise restraint in making future arrests. The Chicago *Times* resumed its attacks upon the Lincoln government. The revocation and release did not go far to soften Democratic criticism of arbitrary government.

A week after the draft law had been passed, Lincoln by proclamation called on all patriotic citizens to aid in restoring to their regiments all soldiers absent without leave and to assist in the execution of the draft. To supervise the nation's first conscription, he appointed Colonel James B. Fry of Illinois as Provost Marshal General.

Fry, soon to be enveloped in controversy systematically set about his duties of registering and drafting and punishing enemies of the government. With military precision and some political skill, he created the draft machinery. The law provided only for national and local authorities—himself and the district draft boards—thus bypassing the states. Fry wisely created an additional office—assistant provost marshal general—for each state (providing three for huge New York). Intended to coordinate national and local activities, the assistant provost marshal generals were named by Fry after consultation with members of Congress. They served to reduce the abruptness of the shift from state to national recruiting and are an important illustration of Federal-state cooperation during the Civil War. Different from twentieth-century practice, the district draft boards had a military member (the provost marshal) as well as two local citizens, one of whom was a doctor. There was no national lottery, each board running its own wheel of chance.

The great experiment in conscription, for which the militia draft of the previous year had been an ominous prelude, was undertaken in a climate of tensions. Forced military service, by a remote government in Washington, under a law that allowed money payment in lieu of service, in a war whose aim had gone astray to pull down the barriers protecting whites from Blacks—all this augured ill for placid acceptance of the new law.

"Niggers and poor men must hereafter constitute the national forces," remarked a Wisconsin editor. "Drafting is an anomaly in a free State; it oppresses the masses," fumed Greeley. A Pittsburgh paper observed, "A certain class of men in this community have been taught to despise and disregard the conscription act, as a tyrannical and unconstitutional measure. . . ."

With tensions mounting, the war faltering, soldiers deserting, and rumors spreading of secret organizations intent on obstructing the law, Fry took up the task of enrollment—the first inventory of the nation's military manpower. New York, with its states rights governor and Democratic metropolis, was a special case. Seymour insisted the draft was unconstitutional as well as unnecessary. Fernando Wood's Mozart Hall Democrats held monthly meetings to protest against the war and the draft.

In late April Fry informed Seymour about the naming of assistant provost marshal generals, expressed the hope they were agreeable, and asked the governor's cooperation. The enrollment went forward, peacefully enough in New York, but with violence in the Middle West. Fry later reported there had been no district in which the enrolling boards were free from annoyance by persons hostile to the government.

While preparations were being made to draft from the enrolled manpower, the military outlook darkened. The mighty Lee, at the head of the Army of Northern Virginia, was advancing, obviously with the purpose of invading the North. On June 15, Lincoln and Stanton called for troops; and saying, "I will spare no effort," Seymour on the eve of the draft sent a substantial part of the New York militia.

An aroused North contributed to the defeat of the seemingly invincible Lee at Gettysburg (July 1-3). The next day—the Fourth of July—was memorable. Lee began to retreat and Vicksburg fell—the war had passed a major turning point. "The signs look better," Lincoln soon rejoiced. But on that day Seymour delivered an unfortunately timed, partisan, and myopic speech, in which he accused the Lincoln administration of broken promises of victory, despotism, and deserving the whole blame for the war.

As drafting began in New York one week later, trouble simmered, especially in the Ninth District. Economic and ethnic tensions between immigrant Irish Catholics and Negroes were strained to the breaking point. The celebrated New York City draft riots were about equal parts antidraft and anti-Negro. The district was heavily Democratic, and its Irish voters were fearful that emancipation would bring a stream of Blacks from the South who would take away their jobs. In confirmation of this fear, when New York City longshoremen went on strike in the first half of 1863, Blacks were hired in their place, working for less money under police protection.

On the second day of the drawing, while a partisan press and agitators fanned resentments, rioting started. A mob, largely Irish, with longshoremen in the lead, began a campaign of pillaging, burning, and Negro-lynching that raged nearly four days. The draft headquarters was destroyed, the Republican mayor's house attacked, the Colored Orphan Asylum set fire, the office of Greeley's antislavery, anti-Catholic, and pro-draft newspaper gutted.

Seymour arrived in the burning city from nearby New Jersey, where he had been visiting, on the second day of the rioting. Hoping to quell the riot, he addressed a crowd, opening his remarks with a salutation that scarred his reputation—"My friends." Later in the day he issued proclamations against the riot and declared the city in a state of insurrection. That night a combination of Federal, state, and city forces began to subdue the populace. On the third day notice was published that the draft was suspended. Meanwhile, militia regiments were returning from Gettysburg, and on the fourth day the mobs were dispersed. The July days had taken many lives, about whose number estimates have wildly varied, inflicted many injuries, and cost an estimated two million dollars in property losses.

"The ugliest turbulence that ever disgraced the republic," the historian Allan Nevins pronounced in judgment on the New York riots. The violence in New York City was the most famous disruption, but there was violence in many other places. "The whole North is volcanic," wrote Garrison, the abolitionist, with characteristic exaggeration as on July 14 he prepared to leave town. A Boston mob that day had tried to take possession of an armory and had been prevented by Federal troops who shot and killed many persons. In New Jersey, as in New York, the draft had to be suspended in the face of popular resistance. Federal troops stood by in the coal fields of Pennsylvania where the Molly Maguires had organized to resist the draft. In Illinois some 2000 draft resisters were arrested over a period of four and a half months. In another form of resistance, young men went west and to Canada, where the Toronto *Globe* observed, "our towns and villages . . . are crowded with motley groups of fugitives from the draft."

Many communities and states tried to avoid explosions by paying bounties to men who would volunteer. Badly abused by "bounty jumpers," the practice only worsened operation of the draft. One of the most important outcomes of the disturbances was a developing conviction that the commutation clause of the draft law ought to be repealed. Secretary of War Stanton told Senator E. D. Morgan of New York, a member of the Military Affairs Committee, "The $300 exemption clause was always, in my judgment, a highly objectionable feature. . . ."

Judges disagreed about the draft law's constitutionality. The most notable disagreement over whether nation or states had ultimate authority to draft men occurred in Pennsylvania. In November the Pennsylvania Supreme Court by a vote of three (Democrats) to two (Republicans) declared the national draft law unconstitutional. The chief justice found that Congress had authority only to provide for a voluntary standing army and to call forth the state militia. Congress had no warrant to draft "national forces." Further, the law subjected the civil, social, and military organizations of the states to the Federal power. An important concurring opinion was written by Justice George W. Woodward, the Democratic candidate for governor of Pennsylvania in 1863.

The United States District Court in Philadelphia two months earlier had upheld the law, finding, "The constitutional authority to enact the law . . . was derived exclusively from the power to raise armies." In making his ruling to confirm national authority, the Federal judge won endorsement from Supreme Court Justice Grier, the Pennsylvanian who, it will be recalled, had sustained the national cause in the Prize cases. Like the Vallandigham case in Ohio, the draft cases in Pennsylvania became issues in the political contests of 1863.

Through the summer the state courts were issuing writs of habeas corpus for soldiers and military prisoners. The Federal judge who had upheld congressional power to raise national armies independently of the state militias had at the same time suggested that the ordinary tribunals might review decisions of draft boards under a writ of habeas corpus. On the morning of September 14, five days after the decision, Lincoln called his cabinet into special session. He spoke of the difficulties arising out of frequent and increasing issue of writs of habeas corpus. "The Prest. was greatly moved—more angry than I ever saw him," Attorney General Bates recorded in his diary. Lincoln "declared that it was a formed plan of the democratic copperheads, deliberately acted out to defeat the Govt., and aid the enemy. That no honest man did or could believe that the State Judges have any such power, &C."

The upshot of two successive days of spirited discussions was a sweeping executive proclamation. Invoking for the first time the authority of the Habeas Corpus Act, the president suspended the privilege of the writ of habeas corpus throughout the United States. Cases in which suspension were applicable were specified, concluding with the catchall category, any offense against the military or naval service. All judges and other civil and military officers were required to give full effect to the suspension, and all citizens to govern themselves accordingly. That the president issued his blanket suspension three weeks before the crucial October state elections was a measure of the judicial resistance to the national draft law.

States rights resistance to the draft was the subject of correspondence between Seymour and Lincoln in the early half of August. Seymour earnestly requested that the draft be suspended until the law's constitutionality be determined. One-half the people of the loyal states, he believed, thought the law unconstitutional. Moreover, the quotas assigned to New York were unfair.

Lincoln answered he was willing to abide by a decision of the United States Supreme Court, but he could not consent to lose the time while it was being obtained. Meanwhile the enemy was drafting every able-bodied man he could reach, "very much as a butcher drives bullocks into a slaughter pen." Further correspondence resulted in an adjustment of New York's quotas. But on August 19, with 10,000 veteran troops from the Army of the Potomac present in New York, and with a proclamation from Governor Seymour admonishing New Yorkers to submit to the draft, the national authority prevailed; and drafting was peacefully resumed.

Secretary of War Stanton, supervising the draft, pointed up the states rights conflict: "If the national Executive must negotiate with state executives in relation to the execution of an Act of Congress, then the problem which the rebellion desired to solve is already determined. . . . The governor of New York stands to-day on the platform of Slidell, Davis, and Benjamin [Confederate leaders] ; and if he is to be the judge whether the Conscription Act is constitutional and may be enforced or resisted as he or other state authorities may decide, then the rebellion is consummated and the national government abolished."

The Lincoln administration made strenuous efforts to influence voting in the 1863 elections. Lincoln wielded the patronage as well as his pen, and Stanton furloughed home soldiers and clerks. The Ordnance Bureau advised Connecticut munitions manufacturers to encourage their workers to vote for the administration candidate for governor; and in Maryland provost marshals guarded the polls. For the important Ohio election, government clerks were handed free railroad passes to go home to vote. The War Department repeatedly threw its immense weight on the side of administration candidates. Politicians for their part urged men to vote for the Union, and Republicans campaigned for office under the name of the National Union party.

Administration policies were to be tested in the autumn elections. Peace, emancipation, the draft, and civil liberties were foremost issues. In Lincoln's home state, where disaffection was strong, a meeting of unconditional Union men was planned to be held at the capital. Lincoln sent a long public letter to be read at the meeting, using this means to answer his critics. In language that often rose to eloquence he made three important points. "You desire peace," he observed. Of the ways to attain peace—compromise, dissolution of the Union, and suppression of the rebellion—only the last could bring peace and the restoration of the Union.

"You are dissatisfied with me about the negro," he acknowledged. But his measures respecting the Negro, he contended, were designed to save the Union. He preferred compensated emancipation, but his critics would not consent to be taxed to buy Negroes. He rejected the argument that his Emancipation Proclamation was unconstitutional, justifying himself under the war power. Finally, his decision to arm the Negroes "leaves just so much less for white soldiers to do, in saving the Union."

Union victories on land and sea—at Vicksburg, Gettysburg, and elsewhere—gave promise that, "Peace does not appear so distant as it did." War, emancipation, Negro soldiers—"Let us diligently apply the means, never doubting that a just God, in his own time, will give us the rightful result," he summed up.

The contest in the reluctantly loyal state of Kentucky lay between the Union Democrats and the Peace Democrats. The presence of the Federal government was everywhere, preventing the States Rights party from meeting and supervising the elections. "The order of the day now in *Ky* is to denounce the measures of the administration," a correspondent wrote Judge Advocate General Holt. Would Kentucky cease to support the war? With the military discouraging voting for the Peace Democratic ticket and with a light vote, the Union Democrats handily won the governorship and the legislature and could claim three of the four new members of Congress.

Across the river in Ohio, the most important state election of the year was held. Vallandigham, running for chief magistrate of the state, symbolized Middle Western Copperheadism. In *An Address to the People*, which he issued from exile, he stressed civil liberties and his arrest; asserted the Confederacy could not be conquered; and claimed only the Democratic party could reunite the nation. His Ohio supporters, in addition to the issues of peace and military despotism, appealed to prejudices against Negroes, Puritanical reformers, and Eastern capitalists. John Brough, running on a Union ticket, was an ex-Democrat, ardent in his support of the war. The Secretary of War, a native Ohioan, made sure the soldiers voted; and nearly 40,000 voted solidly against Vallandigham.

"Glory to God in the highest, Ohio has saved the nation," Lincoln rejoiced when he learned Brough had won a majority of 100,000 votes. Ohio's rejection of Vallandigham was complete. Unionists swept the state legislature, and even traditionally Democratic Steubenville's "Bloody Fourth Ward" went Union.

On the same day Pennsylvania chose a governor. The Democrats had defined the issues clearly in nominating for governor George W. Woodward. Justice of the state supreme court, a states righter, he had condoned secession, did not believe that bayonets could keep a state in the Union, opposed the Emancipation Proclamation, asserted both the Legal Tender Act and the draft law were unconstitutional. The Republican incumbent, Andrew Curtin, called the "Soldiers' Friend," was running for reelection; and Stanton furloughed Pennsylvania regiments to vote. Republican national chairman E. D. Morgan sent money. General McClellan endorsed Woodward. The turnout was huge; and by a narrow margin Curtin kept his office, the Unionists won both houses of the state legislature, and, importantly, defeated the chief justice of the state supreme court, who shortly would rule the national draft law invalid.

These great administration victories in the Buckeye and Keystone states were followed within a few days by another of Lincoln's calls for troops. Apparently having waited for the election returns, he now called for 300,000 volunteers to serve for three years. In those states failing to furnish their quotas, he would impose a draft in early January. By first appealing for volunteers, despite existence of the draft law, he was recognizing the difficulties of recruiting; and further he gave recognition to states rights and popular resistance in adding, "In issuing this proclamation, I address myself not only to the Governors of the several States, but also to the good and loyal people thereof," invoking their aid.

Before the draft would be imposed, other significant elections were to be held in November, the most important in Seymour's New York, where shortly after Lincoln's call for 300,000 men, the Democrats attacked the draft law and the new call. Only minor offices were to be filled, but the issue was national: Seymour's states rights stand. At the Democratic state convention, Seymour stated defiantly, "We are ready to mark out a policy now . . . that the States shall return with all their rights as marked down in the Constitution."

The Union ticket won with a comfortable majority, and Democratic totals as compared with the preceding year declined. Seymour was rebuked at the polls. Everywhere the outcome in the fall elections evidenced a Republican resurgence. The upswing of military fortune had promoted an upswing of Republicanism. The army, with victory in the field and with bayonet and ballot at the polls, had sustained the Lincoln administration. Only little New Jersey insisted on being the exception that proved the rule. The state elections were the "political Gettysburgs of the North."

Of special interest for the future was Seward's declaration for Lincoln's renomination in a speech given on the eve of voting. The New Yorker, who had lost the nomination to Lincoln in 1860, now publicly affirmed his faith in his chief. A second portent of the future was the verdict in Maryland. Scene of pro-Southern sentiment early in the war, the state in 1863 had offered an Unconditional Union or emancipation ticket. With provost marshals guarding the polls and prospective voters swearing a required loyalty oath, the election gave emancipationists control of both houses of the state legislature with authority to provide for electing a state constitutional convention that would outlaw slavery in Maryland. At the same time the voters chose four of the five representatives in Congress from the emancipationist party. One of these was the fiery evangelist of the emancipation movement—Henry Winter Davis.

The turbulent year 1863 had begun in dissidence and ended in decision. Soldiers and voters, president and Congress had contributed to the outcome. "The signs look better," Lincoln had said. By the end of the year, the prospect of peace with reunion and emancipation had brightened. The next Congress would have to take up some work left unfinished by the old, but it would also face new issues. Constitutional emancipation for the whole of the slave-holding states and reconstruction of the nation would engage its attention. The president would be up for reelection. About these matters Winter Davis would have much to say. The Democrats in 1863 had not presented their best face, calling for a negotiated peace and opposing the draft and emancipation. In 1864 they would need to search for their identity as a party of the loyal opposition.

CHAPTER TEN

The Sharp Advance of Union Policy

In early December 1863 the bronze figure of freedom was raised to the top of the cupola above the newly finished dome of the Capitol. From every nearby fort cannon boomed. As the Thirty-eighth Congress was about to assemble, the meaning was plain: the ascendancy of emancipation and the assurance of success in waging the war for the Union.

In Philadelphia, city of Brotherly Love and Independence, the American Anti-Slavery Society held its thirtieth anniversary. Meeting in Philadelphia's largest hall, it celebrated emancipation. Veteran abolitionists and Black soldiers shared the platform, delivering self-congratulatory speeches about the progress of the Negro since the first convention in 1833. Perhaps the most notable discourse came from Frederick Douglass, recently disappointed by his failure to get a military commission. Looking forward to the Negro's future, not backward to the slave's past, he exclaimed, "Our Work is Not Done." Freedom was not enough. Restoration of the Union was not enough.

A reconstructed nation that recognized full citizenship everywhere for Negroes was the new goal. "We are fighting for unity . . . in which there shall be no North, no South, no East, no West, no black, no white, but a solidarity of the nation, making every slave free, and every free man a voter." The applause was scattered. Douglass was far ahead of his time. Meanwhile members of Congress were gathering in Washington under the new Capitol dome to take up these and other issues.

The Republican majority, to begin with, had to put down a challenge from the Democrats for control of the new House. It then had to grapple with increasingly complex questions of slavery and rights for Negroes, and of legislating for the military and for a changing economy. In all these matters the Republican party triumphantly made its way. The outcome was a sharp advance of Union policy.

Their strength thinned by the elections of 1862-63, House Republicans faced a parliamentary crisis. At stake was Republican control of the House, to be secured by electing a Republican Speaker. Beyond this lay the embarrassment of a Democratic House confronting a Republican Senate and president, weakening war legislation, undermining the emancipation movement, and strengthening peace sentiment. Moreover, the coalition of Democrats and Border State Unionists required to gain control of the House might look to the realignment of political parties in the United States, giving the nation a two-party system divided between conservative and radical-moderates.

The House, not institutionalized in its procedures as it would be in the twentieth century, had by a recent law left the former clerk of the House master of the situation through making up the roll of regularly elected members. The former clerk was a Tennessee Unionist, Emerson Etheridge, given his post in 1861 as a reward for defending Unionism in his state. By 1863 he was embittered by the apparent shift in Republican policy, particularly over emancipation. He entered into a conspiracy with S. S. Cox to elect the Ohio Democrat Speaker by excluding some Republican members-elect.

The Etheridge conspiracy was an open secret; and Lincoln and Republican leaders took a strong hand in preventing a Democratic coup. On Sunday, December 6—the day before Congress was to assemble—an administration caucus decided strategy. If Etheridge should try to exclude Republican members-elect, Stevens would move that the member of the House with the longest consecutive service, Republican E. B. Washburne of Illinois, be named Speaker *pro tempore*. With Washburne presiding, credentials of Republicans would be accepted, the caucus nominee for permanent Speaker elected, and the House organized by the Republicans.

Lincoln, for some time concerned about the plot, told the caucus nominee: "The main thing . . . is to be sure to have all our men there. Then if Mr. Etheridge undertakes revolutionary proceedings, let him be carried out on a chip [log], and let our men organize the House."

Lincoln's willingness to resort to force to organize the House for his party was shared by the caucus, to be invoked as a remote contingency. Meantime, efforts to dissuade Etheridge from executing his scheme were not successful. On opening day, playing to packed galleries, the clerk defiantly excluded from his calling of the roll the names of sixteen Republicans and included the names of three Louisiana conservatives.

The crisis had come. A Republican challenged Etheridge by moving that the names of the Maryland members be added to the roll. The vote was a test of the strength of Cox's coalition of Democrats and Border State Unionists, which had a majority of two. To the dismay of Etheridge and Cox, five Democrats and six Unionists sided with the administration, defeating an effort to table the challenge, 74-94. Acting swiftly now, the victorious Republicans assured themselves of control of the House for the next two years.

The attempted coup had disclosed the essential unity of the Republican party and the closeness of cooperation between party and president when pressed by the opposition party. The episode gave an impetus to emancipation, divided the opposition, and sent Etheridge and other conservatives to the support of McClellan for president. And it also revealed Republican readiness, if prodded, to resort to unorthodox procedures to maintain the party in power.

Backed unanimously by the Republicans, who gave him 101 votes as against only 40 for Cox, Schuyler Colfax of Indiana became the new Speaker. Though only forty years old, he brought eight years of congressional experience to his post. A former journalist and Whig, he had so successfully overcome a quick temper as to be called "Smiler" Colfax.

Genial, popular, enjoying the good will of both sides of the House, he would twice be reelected speaker and in 1868 rise to the vice-presidency under Grant.

His small features and frail-looking body belied the vitality and industry he possessed. A master of parliamentary procedure, he made his rulings promptly and fairly. Adept in the chair, on one spectacular occasion he left it to propose an unsuccessful expulsion of a Democrat who had spoken in favor of Confederate independence. His receptions were popular in spite of his refusal to serve wine or liquor. James G. Blaine, his colleague and successor as Speaker, heaped praise upon Colfax's conduct as presiding officer of the House. Lincoln, on the other hand, called him "a little intriguer"; and though he later came under a cloud for implication in the Crédit Mobilier scandal, he was exonerated.

With great trouble and care, sometimes revising his list twenty times, Colfax appointed his committees. The Republicans had suffered severe losses, especially in the finance and military committees. There were troublesome Democrats whom he put, as he confided to a correspondent, on "respectable committees but where they could not embarrass the War or the Administration." He named Cox, his Democratic rival, to the key Rules Committee. In selecting committees, the Speaker, observed the Democratic Chicago *Times*, "knows how to recognize ability, and the committees in the House are as well selected as the rules of the party will allow."

The new head of the committee on Military Affairs was the freshly elected Robert C. Schenck of Ohio. He brought both legislative and military experience to his appointment, having entered Congress as a Whig in 1843 and having resigned his commission as a major general only days before this session started. As commander of the difficult Department of Maryland, he had exercised a firm hand, causing the author John Pendleton Kennedy to write: "He even forbids the birds to sing 'My Maryland' . . ." The shrewd choice of his party, he had defeated Vallandigham in 1862. A talented parliamentarian, he would in time succeed Stevens as leader of the lower chamber. "On his feet," Blaine recalled, "he had no equal in the House. In the five-minute discussion in Committee of the Whole, he was an intellectual marvel."

Another vigorous new figure who shared power with Stevens was Henry Winter Davis of Maryland. An ardent Unionist, former American party congressman, and magical orator, he had helped hold Maryland in the Union and guide his state toward self-emancipation. Immediately made chairman of the committee on Foreign Relations, he ranged himself against Seward's foreign policy, Lincoln's reconstruction policy, and military arrests, all the while waging a fierce feud with Postmaster General Montgomery Blair for political control of Maryland. He was "the most gifted in eloquence and logic" in Congress that the veteran S. S. Cox had known.

In the Senate the Republicans gained E. D. Morgan, who had just stepped down as governor of New York and still held the reins of national chairman. On the opposition side the Democrats acquired a major leader, suave, handsome Thomas A. Hendricks of Indiana, future vice-president of the United States. Twice elected to the House, he now was sent to the Senate by a Democratic legislature; and he became an acute critic of administration policies, especially the draft, emancipation, and heavy taxation. The venerable constitutional lawyer from Maryland, Reverdy Johnson, former Attorney General of the United States, a Clay Whig turned Democrat, added to the opposition ability and learning presented with orotund tones. In the new Congress the Democrats had advanced in distinction as well as in numbers; the Border States had advanced in Unionism in their representation, and the House as a whole was less friendly, politically, than its predecessor.

"Another year of health" had passed, the newly organized Congress heard from the president, as he began his Annual Message. Lincoln contrasted conditions a year ago with those of late 1863, stressing the blue invaders' advance in the South, the brightening foreign outlook, and most especially the energizing policies of emancipation and employing Black soldiers. The proclamation had been accepted, several states seemed moving toward emancipation, "full one hundred thousand" Blacks were successfully bearing arms, "supplying the places which otherwise must be filled with white men." With relief, he remarked, "The crisis which threatened to divide the friends of the Union is past."

Lincoln suggested a series of legislative measures pertaining to aliens and the draft, homesteads for veterans, naval training, national banks, encouragement of immigrants, and a transatlantic telegraph—all of which were adopted. The concluding part of his message dealt with reconstruction of the nation, a subject we shall reserve for later treatment. In closing he reminded Congress that until the military had defeated the enemy, little could be done about reconstruction.

The Union's experience with the draft in 1863 pointed up the need for revision. Extremists demanded outright repeal. Cox introduced a resolution calling for a return to state militia, which failed. Governor Seymour denounced drafting as contrary to the genius of American political institutions and advocated volunteering, bounties, and militia. The respected Fessenden on the Senate floor criticized the administration for its policies of liberal exemptions and bounties.

Revision not repeal was the outcome of laws enacted in February and July. Conscription squarely contradicted the religious principles of Quakers and others who for reason of conscience objected to war. Religious scruples against war now for the first time were recognized, as Congress provided that conscientious objectors might be considered noncombatants when drafted, or should pay $300 to the benefit of sick and wounded soldiers.

Consolidated enrollment of young and middle-aged, single and married men superseded the previous two-class system. Aliens who had voted in any election were made liable to the draft. Negroes were specifically brought into the national forces and made liable to the draft. Whenever the slave of a loyal master was drafted, the slave was freed and the master given the bounty of $100 normally paid to drafted men. Hendricks vigorously opposed the enlistment of Negro troops, mainly because he thought them so objectionable to white soldiers that their presence would weaken the army. Fernando Wood, former mayor of New York, fumed: "This is a government of white men made by white men for . . . the protection of the states and the white people thereof." The section concerning Negroes passed the House without a single Democratic assent.

Substitution was retained, indeed encouraged. Both houses witnessed spirited fights to repeal commutation of military service by money payment—the most disliked aspect of the draft. Senator Henry Lane of Indiana offered figures showing enrollment had produced one million eligible men, of whom four-sevenths paid commutation, and another two-sevenths furnished substitutes. Provost Marshal General Fry, who supplied the figures, ironically summed up, "After our year's work we will have exempted the Nation from military duty . . ." Henry Wilson, chairman of the Senate Military Affairs Committee, alone in his committee favored keeping commutation. He prevailed in February in the Senate, but would fail in July.

While these revisions were being incorporated in the act of February 24, preparations for the spring military campaign were being made. For three years the Union had searched for a general who could accept overall responsibility and who could win the war.

A bill to revive the grade of lieutenant general, previously conferred only on George Washington, came forward in Congress. The three stars were intended for U. S. Grant, who since Vicksburg had added victory at the rail gateway of Chattanooga to his laurels. Opponents of the bill voiced alarm for the liberties of the republic, should the high rank be recreated. Privately, a number of radical Republicans feared the Democrats might nominate Grant for president. In the House Stevens, Winter Davis, Julian, James A. Garfield and other influential Republicans opposed the measure; but Schenck and Washburne pushed it through by a vote that crossed parties. In the Senate prominent Republicans, including Fessenden and Grimes, expressed doubts, but on the last day of February the bill became law.

Lincoln promptly nominated Grant to the post; and within a few days the western conqueror, a "scrubby-looking man," with clear blue eyes, straight nose, and look of resolution, appeared in Washington. He took his place in the newly improved command system formed by Lincoln as commander in chief, Major General Halleck as general in chief, and Grant as lieutenant general.

Primitive by twentieth-century standards, resting heavily upon the interdependence of personalities, the new command system proved an adequate vehicle for bringing victory. Both Lincoln and Stanton had faith in Grant. Lincoln relaxed his supervision over war aims and civil-military relationships. Halleck, schooled in military rules and customs, at his desk translated other men's decisions into precise military orders. The industrious, forthright Stanton devoted himself to administering the expanding bureaucracy of the War Department.

Simple in character, one of the plain people, Grant had an intuitive understanding of the art of war. He set to work. "I arranged," he tells us in his *Personal Memoirs*, "for a simultaneous movement all along the line." The Union would take the initiative, work all parts of the army together, and advance toward a common center.

More troops and more military laws were in order. The draft law did not exempt seamen, and by the hundreds they were being drafted. Informed by the Secretary of the Navy that thirty ships could not sail for want of crews, Congress authorized the transfer of experienced seamen from the army to the navy.

Lincoln on February 1 had ordered a draft for the army and on March 14 another for the navy and for a reserve force—each to be imposed on states that did not fill their quotas. Congress in late March offered a homestead bonus to soldiers with two years' service. A clash of principles between those House members who favored an outright bounty and those who favored the homestead idea was resolved by requiring one year's residence.

The grand advance of the armies in the East began in May, and so did drafting. Exemption from military service by payment of $300 continued to be a nagging political concern and a debilitating drain on manpower resources. Fry reported in early June that of 14,741 drafted men examined, 5050 paid commutation money. Secretary Stanton sent the report to Lincoln, with a strong recommendation for repealing a law that furnished money insted of men.

Wilson refused to repeal the law, and Senator Morgan, with memories of the New York City draft riots still vivid, reported it from the Military Committee. Lane assumed the lead in the Senate and Schenck and Colfax in the House to impose repeal upon a reluctant Congress, with various Republican leaders voting to retain pecuniary exemption. No House Democrat voted to repeal. An apparent triumph of democratic principle, repeal should have included the practice of substitution. The end of commutation destroyed the ceiling price on substitutes; and bounties soared as high as $1000.

Simultaneously, the burden of the draft was lightened in ways congenial to Wilson. The president in making his calls for men was authorized to shorten the term of drafted service from three years to one or two. Second, an extraordinary concession was made, partly to industrial Massachusetts whose war-booming factories were hard pressed for workers. Northern states were allowed to recruit Negroes in the Confederacy and receive credit on their quotas. Further, as a rather special concession to Wilson, states were allowed to credit naval enlistments to their draft quotas. An estimated eighty percent of New England's sailors had enlisted in Charleston, Massachusetts.

Sense and folly mingled in the making of this law of July 4. Strenuous disagreement in Congress resulted in sending the bill to a committee of conference, whose report was accepted by the narrow margins of 66 to 55 in the House and 18 to 17 in the Senate.

Two weeks later, after "Grant the Butcher" had incurred severe losses in his Virginia operations and Confederate general Jubal A. Early had been driven back from the outskirts of Washington, Lincoln under the new law called for 500,000 men, unfilled quotas to be drafted after September 5. Military service now was even less attractive than in the preceding year. Casualty lists lengthened; lucrative jobs were available in a flourishing economy; and exemption could no longer be bought from the government.

Violence, widespread in 1863, was avoided in 1864. It was only partly because, as Fry said, the people had "learned to look upon the draft as a necessity." Bounties for volunteering were prodigally offered by Federal, state, and local governments. The hiring of substitutes for as much as $1000 brought into notoriety a number of substitute brokers and an even more notorious class of bounty jumpers, who repeatedly enlisted and collected bounties. Canadians and European immigrants were recruited. It was apparent with what little wisdom Congress had acted in preserving substitution.

Congress in this session strengthened the financial base for a Union victory. By mid-1863 the national debt had soared over a billion dollars. Taxation was woefully short of paying for a war that was consuming over $2 million a day. Further issuance of legal tender notes seemed unwise as inflation intensified. Borrowing—the main reliance of the Treasury—again had become difficult, with Chase resorting to short-term loans. War profiteers were growing rich. Few banks were taking out national charters under which they must buy bonds to issue national bank notes.

In his third annual report, Secretary Chase urged the Congress to check the increase in debt, impose heavier internal taxes, and pass "proper measures" to induce conversion of state banks into national banks. The key measures were enacted nearly seven months after Chase made his recommendations. In the interim, Congress passed a new loan act under which long-term borrowing was unsuccessful and Chase fell back on hand-to-mouth short loans.

Chase had allowed another fiscal crisis to develop. Money was short and capacity to borrow low. Unpaid requisitions, many of them to pay for the army, on July 1 ran to nearly $72 million; the cash balance in the Treasury sank to less than $19 million. The Treasury's credit was unfavorable, as withdrawal of a bond issue on July 2 for lack of acceptable bids would vividly demonstrate. "Chase learns no wisdom," his cabinet colleague Welles on June 28 wrote in his huge diary. "We are hurrying onward into a financial abyss."

Just before the session expired, Congress mended fiscal matters in three vital areas. It enacted a comprehensive internal revenue law that contemplated an annual expenditure of $100 million and for interest and a sinking fund for $3 billion of debt. Every negative vote was cast by a Democrat, with many members not voting. Controversy centered on raising taxes on income, with Stevens, chairman of Ways and Means, decrying a higher tax as "a punishment of the rich man because he is rich." A committee of conference drove the tax upward, starting at five percent on incomes of $600 and taking ten percent on incomes over $10,000. Approved by both houses without a division, the victory was of greater moment to principles of progressive taxation in the future than to production of money for the war. With satisfaction the conservative Republican *New York Times* remarked on the Spartan tax measure, "Every man's income, should be, and we trust, will be taxed."

The critical need for revenue spurred an increase in tariff rates. While the internal revenue bill was still pending, Morrill whipped the House into approving an increase in import duties. "Every day's delay in the passage of this and the Internal Revenue Bill costs the Treasury not less than $500,000," he exhorted. Only two days were allowed for debate and amendment, and the bill passed the House, 88-28, every nay a Democrat, with many members not voting. In the Senate Fessenden took command, and reminding critics, "This is war," he drove the bill through to passage in two days.

The tariff of 1864 pushed levels to record heights, with a general average of forty-seven percent. The event is famous in the annals of American historical writing because some historians have taken the high Morrill tariff as the heart of a radical Republican design to fasten a capitalistic order on postwar America. A more accurate appraisal might note the circumstances in which the tariff law was enacted. It was first a revenue measure, and next compensatory to the increase in domestic duties. Moreover, it provided the means to secure revenue in gold to meet interest obligations on the national debt. Hastily passed, it was not primarily a protectionist device. Almost no historian seems to have noticed that the bill was approved with many members not voting, and that in the Senate absentees included some of the most famous radicals: Chandler, Lane of Kansas, Morrill of Maine, Pomeroy, and Wade. There were only five nay votes; the abstainers, who included Sherman, and opponents, who were all Democrats, came mainly from the West, disclosing a sectional, not factional pattern. The tariff, in perspective, essentially denoted war needs, and it also carried out old Whig principles and the Republican platform. What postwar Congresses did about protectionism, when the financial pinch was past, is another matter.

The Internal Revenue Act, the tariff, and a third measure—a loan act— all became law on the same day, June 30, comprising together "probably the greatest measure of taxation which the world has seen," Professor Taussig judged. The Loan Act, successfully implemented within the next half year by Chase's successor, did several things. It authorized the Secretary of the Treasury to borrow $400 million in six percent bonds or, in lieu of one-half that figure, sell interest-bearing legal-tender treasury notes. The aversion to more greenbacks, that is, *non*-interest-bearing legal tender notes, was further expressed by placing a permanent ceiling of $450 million on them. The act gave the secretary much discretion in fixing terms in order that he might cope with the precarious condition of the Union's credit.

Nudged by Lincoln and prodded by Chase, Congress improved the National Banking Law. In the first nine months, only 134 banks had been organized under the 1863 law. Noteworthy in the congressional debate was the antagonism between nationalism and states rights. Stevens moved to "withdraw these national banks from State taxation." Beyond the historic controversy lay the practical question whether a national banking system, exposed to state taxation, could live. The outcome was a compromise, allowing the states a limited right of taxation.

A Republican measure, it commanded not one Democratic vote in either chamber. In the House two Republicans, each from Border States, voted no; and in the Senate three Republicans voted against their party. The turning away from the banking heritage of Jacksonian Democracy was not yet completed with the enactment of this law, but the substantial revision stimulated conversion to national charters and sales of bonds.

Just as the national banking legislation required amendment, so also the transcontinental railroad legislation required revision. The transcontinental project was breathtaking, and it should not surprise us that seven years elapsed between the charter of 1862 and the laying of the last rail. Capitalists had been timid about investing, and congressmen in the early portion of the new session were timid about passing additional legislation. The sentiment of nationalism, ascendant in the first half of 1862, had ebbed; the nation's resources were being drained by protracted war; the audacity of lobbyists seeking more aid to the Union Pacific indicated that something more than the public interest was to be served.

Three alternatives were considered by Congress: more help, direct government construction, and postponement. Attempts to follow the third and second courses failed, and in the end—amid extraordinary legislative scenes—the first prevailed. The two chambers disagreed and sent separate bills to a committee of conference, which reported July 1. As Representative E. B. Washburne, who vainly had sought postponement, related the history of House passage: The committee report "was gagged through; the opponents of the measure were not permitted to have it postponed, so that they could see what it was. I struggled in vain . . . but the gentleman from Pennsylvania [Stevens] demanded the previous question . . . and it would seem incredible that in a matter of legislation involving interests so vast . . . even the yeas and nays were refused." The next day the bill, with munificent terms that formed the target of criticism, became law. The government had doubled the land grant and had accepted a second in place of a first mortgage on the railroad.

Under Stevens' leadership Congress also extended support to the Northern Pacific Railroad, running between Lake Superior and Puget Sound. Similar in terms to the Union Pacific measure, the grant passed both houses with little or no debate. When one member asked Stevens, who was a heavy investor in iron manufacturing, "whether he has taken care to provide that this road shall be built with American iron?" the House laughed, and Stevens replied, "Yes."

Congressional and public expectation of beneficent results from the transcontinentals was high. Lincoln, in his Annual Message in December, remarked with gratification that the "great enterprise" had been "entered upon with a vigor which gives assurance of success, notwithstanding the embarrassments arising from the prevailing high prices of materials and labor." The corrupt practices of the Union Pacific's construction came into the open in 1867, but even so it was a proud day in the spring of 1869 when the golden spike was driven into place at Promontory, Utah. Both Gilded Age politics and golden dreams of national progress were blended in the building of the great transcontinentals.

Development of the West, to which the transcontinentals would contribute, was the theme of other legislation. Liberal land policies, high prices for Western products, and the promise of a railroad fostered population growth in the West during the war. Moved by a variety of considerations, Congress provided for making new states in regions where minerals and fertile soil were attracting settlers. In the preceding year Congress had arranged for a temporary government for the Territory of Idaho, and in May 1864 made a similar enactment for Montana. Against Sumner's strenuous protests, both bills restricted suffrage to white men. With an eye to adding to the Republican muster, Congress in March passed acts to enable Nevada, Colorado, and Nebraska to become states. Failure at this time to require Negro suffrage later delayed admission of Nebraska. Colorado with a sparse population during this period gained statehood in 1876. Of the three territories authorized to form state governments, only Nevada was admitted before the presidential election in the autumn.

Congress during the war had gone far in shaping the nation's economy. The Republican platform and the war's necessities combined to make for a revulsion from the relative laissez-faire of antebellum Democratic administrations. By domestic revenue measures, including the income tax, high tariff, borrowing, spending, authorizing greenbacks, national banks, railroad subsidies, and land laws, Congress had changed the contours and stimulated the growth of the economy.

Along with all this, the war itself wrought economic changes which now engaged the attention of the lawmakers. A recession at the start of hostilities had yielded to a boom well before 1864. Wages lagged as prices soared. An irredeemable paper currency together with government insistence on gold for customs duties and interest on bonds encouraged inflation. Speculators were frenziedly active in Wall Street and elsewhere, dealing in securities, whiskey and other commodities, and trading with the enemy. Skilled and semiskilled tradesmen were organizing unions and striking for higher pay, while unskilled workers were in short supply.

For government intervention in economic matters like these, precedent was sparse. Nonetheless, Congress in 1864 took steps, which though too little and too late, were notable. Soldiers' pay, raised to thirteen dollars a month for privates in 1861, was increased to sixteen dollars in May. The raise was not in proportion to the change in the cost of living; and payable in depreciated currency, it offered little relief, leaving the soldier fighting for less than eight dollars a month.

"Gold was rising" had been for two years the faith of speculators and hoarders as Secretary Chase rather helplessly looked on. The gold market in New York engrossed the attention of various unscrupulous men. A minor crisis in May advertised the need for government action. Two gold speculators placed a false Lincoln proclamation in two Democratic New York newspapers. The document spoke of the dire condition of the Federal armies, announced a day of prayer, and called for 400,000 more troops. The secretary of war suppressed publication of the papers—the *Journal of Commerce* and the *World*. The perpetrators of the forged proclamation were soon arrested; and the newspapers innocent victims of the speculators, resumed publication.

The episode had many implications: for freedom of the press, for states rights, and for partisan politics. A cabinet member, Welles, acknowledged that the government's act was "arbitrary and oppressive." Governor Seymour brought the commander of the Department of the East to trial in a New York court, which ruled that the general, a Union Democrat, should be "subject to the action of the grand jury of the city and county," but no further step was taken.

To check gambling in gold, Congress on June 17 passed a law prohibiting contracts for future delivery and providing penalties. By June 30 gold rose from about 200 (that is, $200 in greenbacks would buy $100 in gold) to 250. New York bankers demanded repeal, exclaiming the law actually encouraged speculators in their desire to monopolize gold. Congress on July 2 repealed its brief-lived law. Gold soon attained its highest figure, 285, and then with the improved outlook of the war declined.

Historians have suggested that the Republican party began life as an idealistic crusader against slavery and once in power increasingly became soiled with materialism. The attitude of many congressional Republicans toward the whiskey tax in 1864 offers some corroboration of Republican complacency toward speculators. The whiskey duty posed the question whether to tax spirits distilled after passage of the law or spirits on hand. Stevens proposed the first course of action, imposing a future tax on distillers, while the Democrat Fernando Wood proposed an amendment, adding a tax on speculators, who had bought up most of the stock. Amid extensive charges of corruption, Congress with a mixture of motives twice enacted whiskey excises that yielded little revenue. The chairman of the Internal Revenue Commission, David A. Wells, later complained: "Congress . . . virtually legislated for the benefit of distillers rather than for the treasury and the government."

"The demoralising effect of this civil war," Attorney General Bates in March recorded in his diary, "is plainly visible in every department of life. The abuse of official powers and the thirst for dishonest gain are now so common that they cease to shock." A series of laws and executive decrees had sanctioned a certain amount of trade with states declared in insurrection. In particular cotton was wanted in the North. Under executive license as well as illicitly, the scope of trading with rebellious states widened and the appetites of traders sharpened. There was enough fraud in the cotton traffic "to destroy any administration at any other time," Senator Morgan confided to a friend.

By June Congress was aware that the Southern trade had grown fraudulent, implicating Treasury agents and army and navy officers, and had swollen to proportions that were signally helpful to the enemy. A Republican senator remarked that if the testimony taken by his committee were known, "the cheeks of every American senator" would "tingle with shame." Divided between complete prohibition of the trade and further restriction, the senate Committee on Commerce brought in a bill that resulted in a law of July 2 aimed at curtailing illicit trade. Congress had done its work well enough, but Lincoln by executive order in September facilitated the trade. He believed it better to have cotton come North than run through the blockade in exchange for guns and ammunition; and he further justified his order by arguing that Northern export of cotton would sustain the dollar by diminishing the flow of gold to Europe.

In the last months of the war, cotton rings flourished, and Northern profiteering was great. Between November 4, 1864, and January 24, 1865, the Treasury Department approved the purchase of about two million bales of cotton. General Grant strenuously and repeatedly opposed any commercial intercourse with the enemy; and in early February 1865 he finally won full authority to "disregard and annul" all trading permits. By that time many highly placed Republicans had filled their pockets through the cotton trade.

There is "a great deficiency of laborers in every field of industry," Lincoln told Congress in his Annual Message, while American consulates abroad were thronged with thousands of destitute persons yearning to emigrate. Congress, he suggested, should consider a system to encourage immigration. The president spoke not of filling the armies with foreigners but of placing them especially in agriculture and in mines, iron and coal as well as precious metals.

The idea of government aid to immigration, though congenial to many manufacturers and industrial capitalists, won advocacy mainly from the influential economist Henry Carey of Philadelphia and a labor-recruiting agency which aspired to profits from importation of labor. Carey embraced the idea as part of an economic program to industrialize the nation. The American Emigrant Company was organized in early 1864 as a means to make money through procuring foreign labor for the iron interests and through selling Western lands to immigrants.

In response to various requests, but in the absence of a general pressure from industrialists which some historians have alleged as the background of the measure, Congress passed a contract labor law. By its terms the law legalized contracts for the importation of labor, created the office of Commissioner of Immigration in the State Department, and established a United States Immigrant Office in New York City, the principal debarkation point. Efforts to recruit skilled labor through the new Federal bureau were futile. From July 1864 to the end of the year, only 165 contracts were registered. Assailed by organized labor, the law was repealed in 1868 and contract labor was outlawed in 1885. Not until 1907 did the Federal government seek again to aid in job distribution of immigrant workers.

To guarantee freedom to all Negroes became the concern of this session. Radical Republicans in House and Senate offered amendments to the Constitution. The American Anti-Slavery Society, in what has been called the first public movement for the Thirteenth Amendment, adopted a petition for amendment. Early in February two tall Negroes bore large bundles of petitions to Sumner's desk in the Senate. Rising, Sumner said to his colleagues: "This petition is signed by one hundred thousand men and women, who unite in this unparalleled manner to support its prayer" for national emancipation.

The Senate was the first chamber to act. Lyman Trumbull, chairman of the Judiciary Committee, cogently explained why a constitutional amendment was needed. True, Congress had passed many acts against slavery and the president had issued his proclamation. But these, Trumbull said, were "ineffectual to the destruction of slavery," having left no inconsiderable number in slavery. Moreover, the proclamation provoked doubts among its opponents about the constitutional power of the president to free any slave. Nor would it be satisfactory for Congress under the war power to abolish slavery throughout the states by mere law, leaving open the possibility of reestablishing it in peacetime.

"In my judgment, the only effectual way of ridding the country of slavery, and so that it cannot be resuscitated, is by an amendment of the Constitution forever prohibiting it within the jurisdiction of the United States," Trumbull declared. Reverdy Johnson, who, he was tartly reminded by Sumner, had argued the case against Dred Scott before the Supreme Court, now gave it as his opinion that if the war ended, those slaves not under United States military control would be slaves still. The learned Maryland Unionist favored an emancipation amendment.

In vain Senators Saulsbury and Hendricks appealed to the wisdom of the Founding Fathers, who, Saulsbury said, had not intended to abolish slavery; and for Congress now to do so would be in fraud of the original agreement. Hendricks questioned the fate of the freedmen: "Are they to remain among us?" He answered: "They never will associate with the white people of this country upon terms of equality.... There is that difference between the two races that renders it impossible." With six Democrats voting no and all Republicans and two Democrats voting yes, the Senate on April 8 approved a joint resolution proposing the Thirteenth Amendment.

The question was a party one, and in the House every nay vote was cast by Democrats. Twenty members did not vote, including seven Republicans and Unionists; and the tally of 95 to 66 failed to attain the requisite two-thirds majority.

Constitutionalism, racism, and reconciliation with the South loomed large in Democratic arguments against the amendment. State sovereignty made it impossible to abolish slavery by constitutional amendment, argued Pruyn of New York in what Lieber described as "hyper-Calhounistic remarks." "The irrepressible conflict is not between slavery and freedom, but between black and white," warned S. S. Cox. All Democrats are for "closing this war the moment it can be done with honor, irrespective of the fate of the negro," affirmed Herrick of New York.

The issue of amending the Constitution to abolish slavery carried over to the presidential election. A little more than a week before the House vote, the Republican party in national convention at Lincoln's urging had adopted a plank in favor of the amendment. Favorable reconsideration by the House at some future time was made possible by Ashley of Ohio, who, after rejection of the amendment, changed his vote, enabling him under the House rules to call up the joint resolution.

Equality as well as freedom was the aspiration of some Republican leaders like Sumner and Wilson. In the struggle for equality, this session made advances in the realms of schools, courtroom justice, equal pay, and rendition of fugitive slaves.

The law of 1862 requiring public schools for Negro children in the District of Columbia had relied upon taxes paid by Negroes. Though Blacks composed perhaps fifty percent of the potential school population, their taxes amounted to about two percent of whites' taxes. Against indignant outcries from voteless District white taxpayers, Congress without a division enacted a new law that distributed the total school fund in proportion to numbers of Black to white school children of school age. Fines and forfeitures paid to the Federal courts in the District were directed into the school fund to ease the strain; and the schools were to be segregated. The victory was more of the ideal than of the real, for at the end of the war, the historian of the District's Black community has written, Negro schools "still existed only on paper."

Building further on the precedents of 1862, when Congress had prohibited exclusion of Negro witnesses from District of Columbia courts, it now extended the ban to all Federal courts. In Senate debate over the ban sponsored by Sumner, Saulsbury coldly observed he did not wish "to say any thing about the 'nigger' aspect of the case. It is here every day; and I suppose it will be here every day for years to come, till the Democratic party comes into power, and wipes out all legislation on the statute-book of this character, which I trust in God they will soon do." With only one Democrat in the two chambers voting yea, the measure became law.

The glaring inequity of Negro soldiers' pay was partially alleviated. The white private received thirteen dollars a month plus a three dollar clothing allowance; the Black private ten dollars minus the clothing allowance, making the inequality nearly two to one. In his annual report for 1863, Secretary of War Stanton put the matter to Congress. Lincoln withheld his support even though his attorney general ruled that the law providing for unequal pay applied only to Negroes performing "the humble offices of labor and service."

"The fact is," the Chicago *Tribune* observed, "the chief disability of the black race, lies in prejudice and not in law." Not until mid-June could the two houses of Congress agree on a trifling compromise that granted equal pay to Negro soldiers retroactive to January 1, 1864, and arrears to all Negroes who were free on April 19, 1861. The law left under discrimination the large number of former slaves who had served prior to the first of the year. In view of the small financial cost to the Union of full equality, especially when set against the heavy cost of the war and the substantial contribution of Black soldiers, no economic justification of this parsimony seems possible. The voting was divided almost exclusively along party lines.

The Fugitive Slave Law, poorly drafted in its terms during the crisis atmosphere of 1850, long irritated many Northerners. Sumner, brought into public life by its passage, undertook to repeal both the law of 1850 and the one of 1793. Since the Constitution itself required the return of escaped slaves to rightful owners, his effort incurred opposition in the Senate. The House, however, which had failed to repeal the fugitive law in 1862, now in a party vote, with only two exceptions, repealed both laws. Sumner then pushed the bill in the Senate, which with a number of abstentions passed the bill, every aye vote coming from the Republican side. Repeal was another blow at the legal underpinnings of slavery, but in the light of the fact that slavery itself was still legal in the Border States and the Constitution decreed delivery of fugitives to owners, repeal appears to have been a denial of constitutional obligation.

We shall reserve for later this session's work on reconstruction of the Union and aid to freedmen. Congress had passed a measure on the first subject that wrangled Republican politics and it had failed to enact a bill to establish a bureau for freedmen. Historians engrossed in the developing party friction have failed to recognize the constructive work of this session. Historians engrossed in the Progressive Era critique of industrial capitalism have failed to recognize the wartime relevance of legislation.

Congress in this session had gone far in meeting the war's legislative needs. It had refined earlier laws on conscription, acknowledging conscientious objection as a basis for exemption from combat and abolishing commutation; had made the new national banking system operable; had made generous provision for the popular but faltering transcontinentals; and had enacted its most realistic tax program of the war. Congress had built for the future by providing for new states. And it had advanced the progress of civil rights by a series of pro-Negro measures while pointing in the direction of a constitutional security of freedom for all Negroes.

Considerations of winning the war, maintaining party ascendancy, and retaining the presidency had combined to achieve these results. The last of these—the presidential campaign of 1864—as we are about to see, had begun during the session and had waywardly spun out through the summer and early autumn of 1864.

CHAPTER ELEVEN

The Referendum of 1864

"It is a fact that the Democratic Party has opposed the Administration of Mr. Lincoln since the 22d day of September, 1862," observed the Chicago *Times* in September 1864. The *Times* referred of course to the Emancipation Proclamation, pointing to a major issue that had made impossible the dream of bipartisan support of the Lincoln administration.

As the presidential election loomed on the horizon in 1864, no thought seems to have been given to dispensing with it during war, as the United Kingdom has twice done in the twentieth century. The democratic process was to be exposed to the passions and hysteria of an internal war. Public attention fastened upon the presidency, even though a new Congress was also to be chosen.

The election of 1864 was a referendum: on Lincoln himself, on party unity, on peace or war, and on emancipation. On these issues hung American nationality—the continuing life of a nation that could be reunited only by war and kept united only by emancipation. Sometimes minimized by historians, the election of 1864 was a turning point in the history of the Civil War.

Odd as it may appear to twentieth-century observers, the reelection of Abraham Lincoln—today considered the greatest American president—was opposed by many members of his party. Early in the year 1864, the disaffection centered in the radical antislavery element. Lincoln's deliberation in dealing with slavery, together with dissatisfaction over the faltering progress of military operations, encouraged radicals to look elsewhere for a candidate.

A man whose antislavery ardor was equalled only by his ambition, Salmon P. Chase, became the first focal point of radical attempts to displace Lincoln. The Chase boom was short-lived. Begun by Senator Pomeroy of Kansas, who issued a circular in early February in Chase's favor, it collapsed within a few days when the Republican members of the legislature in Chase's home state nominated Lincoln for reelection. Chase, embarrassed, asked that no further consideration be given his name.

A second radical alternative arose in the movement that made General John C. Frémont its standard bearer. A convention attended largely by delegates from St. Louis and New York City adopted a platform favoring a constitutional amendment to abolish slavery, urging confiscation of rebel lands and distribution among soldiers and actual settlers, and asserting that the question of reconstruction belonged to Congress and not to the president. General Frémont, "whose first act was to use the freedom of the negro as his weapon," and General John Cochrane of New York for vice-president formed the ticket of the Radical Democracy. In accepting the nomination, on the eve of the Republican convention, Frémont announced that if the convention nominated any man faithful to his faction's principles, there need be no party division, but the renomination of Lincoln "would be fatal to the country."

"Mr. Lincoln is already renominated," wrote a Philadelphia editor the day before the convention. There was in fact no doubt about the choice; and after Missouri had changed its first ballot from Grant to Lincoln, the renomination was unanimous. In circumstances still somewhat murky, the delegates dropped Hamlin and nominated Andrew Johnson for vice-president. Lincoln, asked about his preference, tersely wrote, "Wish not to interfere about V.P."; but he doubtless shared the delegates' conviction that naming a Southern war Democrat buttressed the party that during the campaign took the name Union party.

The shift in name, neither a sudden development nor a clever mask to disguise an old party, was the climax to a party transformation that had been going on since the start of the war. The exigency of internal war impelled numerous Democratic leaders into the Union party fold: Andrew Johnson, John A. Dix, Ben Butler, and others. The pattern of change varied from state to state. In one-party New England states, the new name represented little more than that. In Ohio there was a real regrouping. There the Republican organization as early as the fall of 1861 merged into the Union party, which elected a war Democrat, David Tod, governor. Lincoln in 1864 tendered the treasury portfolio to Tod, who declined; and the president then offered it to Tod's successor, Governor John Brough, the war Democrat elected in 1863 on the Union ticket, who also declined.

In Pennsylvania Governor Curtin at the head of a Unionist ticket had won reelection in 1863 in a traditionally Democratic state. Fusionist efforts of varying degrees of success were carried out elsewhere. Maryland in 1863, for example, had elected four of five Congressmen on the Unionist ticket.

By the early part of 1864, the process of creating a broader wartime Union party was well advanced. Lincoln, Weed, and various state chieftains had cooperated to this end. The party convention in 1864 was called by the Republican National Executive Committee, but thereafter the old name was abandoned. Baltimore, in a loyal slaveholding state, was designated as the convention city. The temporary chairman was the former Kentucky Democrat Robert J. Breckinridge, who had sons in both the Union and Confederate armies.

On taking the chair Breckinridge said, "I see before me not only primitive Republicans and primitive Abolitionists, but I see also primitive Democrats and primitive Whigs. . . . As a Union party I will follow you to the ends of the earth. . . . But as a Republican party . . . I will not follow you one foot. . . ."

The permanent chairman similarly intoned, "In no sense do we meet as members or representatives of either of the old parties. . . ." The first plank of the platform spoke of "laying aside all differences of political opinion," and pledging "ourselves as Union men. . . ." The nomination was formally tendered to Lincoln by a committee of the National Union Committee, and he accepted in a letter addressed to that committee.

The platform emphasized restoration of the Union through vigorous prosecution of the war without compromise and through a constitutional amendment abolishing slavery throughout the nation. Suggested by Lincoln and presented to the convention by the party's national chairman, E. D. Morgan, the proposed amendment, strikingly reversing the party's 1860 stand, evoked prolonged applause, followed by three cheers.

Besides union and freedom the platform iterated the party's interest in favoring foreign immigration and a Pacific railroad. With an eye to votes in the future as well as in the present campaign, the platform spoke of permanent recognition of veterans and their survivors, and it pledged redemption of the public debt. Inner strains in the party were hinted at by two planks that called for harmony in national councils (a disguised thrust at conservative Postmaster General Blair) and declared against efforts of any European power to obtain new footholds for monarchical governments, sustained by foreign military force, in near proximity to the United States (a disguised thrust at the patient neutrality displayed by Seward and Lincoln in dealing with the French occupation of Mexico).

Moderation prevailed in the convention. Union Democrats could take heart in the choice of Johnson and the rechristening of the party as the Union party. Radicals could take heart in the commitment to universal abolition by constitutional amendment and in the criticism of conservatives by platform indirection. Centrists could take heart in the renomination of Lincoln and the reaffirmation of purpose to redeem American nationality. No mention was made of the tariff, which was not an issue in the canvass, nor of reconstruction, which was factiously to erupt a month later. Above all, the proceedings were a victory for Lincoln and the course he was steering. The convention had concluded, Lincoln in rustic metaphor remarked, "it is not best to swap horses while crossing the river."

> We are tired of the war on the old camp ground:
>   Many are dead and gone,
> Of the brave and the true who've left their homes;
>   Others been wounded long.

War-weariness, the Confederacy's bloody frustration of Grant in Virginia, and Frémont's defection from the Republicans combined to cause the Democrats to defer their convention. The events of a summer of discontent gave encouragement to the Democrats that they might capture the government.

Pacifism in the North and factionalism among Republicans darkened the outlook for the reelection of Lincoln and the restoration of the Union. Pacifism, strong among Democrats, now spread among Republicans. "The people are wild for peace," the experienced politician Thurlow Weed observed; and he told the president his reelection was an impossibility.

The influential, if often irresponsible, Republican editor Horace Greeley took up the peace movement, directing national attention to it. The National Executive Committee of the Republican party urged Lincoln to offer peace to the Confederacy on the sole basis of acknowledging the supremacy of the Union. The committee chairman dropped this notion after consulting with Lincoln and some members of the cabinet.

By this time the political balance in the cabinet had shifted with the departure of the radical Chase. Engaging in a patronage struggle with Senator E. D. Morgan of New York, Chase had offered his resignation, which to his surprise Lincoln accepted. Lincoln replaced him with the sagacious moderate W. P. Fessenden.

Factionalism divided the party after Lincoln pocket vetoed a congressional reconstruction bill. We shall have more to say later about reconstruction; let it suffice now to note the impact of the bill upon the presidential election. Radical Republican Senators Wade and Davis, the bill's authors, proceeded to publish in Greeley's paper an intemperate manifesto, "the most vigorous in attack that was ever directed against the President from his own party during his term," wrote his secretaries.

The angry Republican authors called the veto a "studied outrage" on the authority of Congress, and warned the president, "If he wishes our support he must . . . leave political reorganization to Congress." Other Republican malcontents, including the governor of Massachusetts and Sumner as well as Wade, Davis, and Greeley, arranged for a new convention for late September to nominate a new presidential candidate—possibly Chase. Lincoln despaired of reelection.

The powerful yearning for peace and the seemingly futile shedding of blood drained Northern confidence in the prospect of reunion through the sword. The darkest month of the war fell in August, following Grant's costly losses, the "stupendous failure" of a mine explosion to take Petersburg, the daring raid by Jubal A. Early that brought Confederate forces to the outskirts of Washington, and Lincoln's call for 500,000 troops. The premium on gold rose to its highest point: $2.85 in greenbacks for a gold dollar.

Amid this gloom the Democrats gathered in Chicago, where four years earlier Republicans had nominated Lincoln. The peace movement was well matured in the party. On Washington's birthday of this year, there had been formed the Sons of Liberty, a secret society headed by the exiled Vallandigham, carrying a strong suggestion of efforts to contrive a negotiated peace and to sympathize with the Confederacy, as well as defeat the Republican party. In June Vallandigham returned from exile, without hindrance from the administration, and placed himself at the head of the peace forces.

In opening the Democratic national convention, August Belmont, the dapper and smooth national chairman, urged party unity. He faced, his biographer has pointed out, a "conglomeration of Peace Democrats, War Democrats, old-line Whigs, Know Nothings, so-called Conservatives, States' Rights extremists, and pacifists. . . ." Though the Republican party has been described as "the party divided" in 1864, actually the Democrats were more seriously split. At the very least, three factions existed. The followers of Alexander Long's view, expressed in the House of Representatives on April 8, that the North should recognize the independence of the Confederacy, stood at one extreme. Censured by the House but not expelled for his speech, Long spoke for the smallest faction. Next in strength, perhaps, were Vallandigham and his followers, favoring an armistice and peace negotiations. And finally there were the adherents of Governor Seymour.

Made permanent chairman of the convention, Seymour from his dais charged that the Republicans could not save the Union, but "*we can*." His formula for the restoration of the Union was "the full recognition of the rights of the States." This of course meant immunity from national action against slavery. Seymour's formula for peace seems senseless since President Davis had recently said it was useless to approach the Confederacy with peace proposals on any basis but independence. Moreover, the chances of maintaining a postwar Union with slavery seem dubious. With some justification Blaine said of Seymour's speech, it was "able, adroit, and mischievous."

The Democratic leaders appear to have struck a bargain—and a fatal one—at the convention. They papered over their differences in a jerry-built construction that later came tumbling down. The platform condemned the war as a "failure," and demanded "immediate efforts be made for a cessation of hostilities, with a view to an ultimate convention of the States, or other peaceable means, to the end that at the earliest practicable moment peace may be restored on the basis of the Federal Union of the States." Armistice, negotiation for reunion on the basis of maintaining slavery—this was the Democratic stand. A victory for Vallandigham, the plank bore the naive belief that an unconquered Confederacy would negotiate a settlement on the basis of reunion. It assumed that hostilities having once ceased could be renewed after the collapse of peace negotiations. And it completely dodged the issue that had rent the Union—Negro slavery.

After adopting a peace platform, the convention blithely nominated a war hero for the presidency and a peace Democrat for the vice-presidency. Presidential nominee George B. McClellan, removed from command by Lincoln for his failures to wage aggressive warfare, had disfavored emancipation, conscription, confiscation, military arrests outside fighting areas, and territorialization of the Southern states (reducing them to territories, subject to the Federal government). Vice-presidential nominee George Pendleton, Ohio Copperhead and favorite of the peace men, as a member of Congress had voted against war revenue and draft measures.

A new wind blew from the South immediately after the Democrats adjourned. Atlanta, long under siege by Sherman, fell to her besiegers; and following upon the taking of Mobile in late August, Atlanta gave the lie to the charge the war was a failure. Lincoln proclaimed a day of thanksgiving. McClellan, unhappy about the "war failure" plank, weakly vacillated over his acceptance letter. After shifting his ground twice, he declared he "could not look in the face of my gallant comrades of the army and navy . . . and tell them that their labors . . . had been in vain . . . " He accompanied his disclaimer of the failure plank with the assertion, "The Union is the one condition of peace—we ask no more." The Southern states should have for the future a full guarantee of their constitutional rights, and though he did not mention the word "slavery"—as, astonishingly in this war, the platform did not either—it was plain he meant perpetuation of the right to maintain the peculiar institution.

"The Chicago surrender" did lasting harm to the Democrats, which McClellan's letter could not overcome. General Sheridan's victories in the Valley of Virginia brightened the military outlook in September and

October. Republican unity grew as disgruntled politicians and newspaper editors saw the Chicago alternative to a Lincoln victory. In rapid order the radical Frémont withdrew his candidacy and Lincoln dismissed the conservative Blair from his cabinet. Because Blair's ouster closely followed Frémont's withdrawal it has been suggested a bargain was struck: Frémont's retirement for Blair's head. Whatever the circumstances, Unionists by the end of September joined in supporting Lincoln.

"McClellan or Lincoln?" asked Lowell in the *Atlantic* for October, going on to support Lincoln as a practical statesman. Voters in state elections in Indiana and Pennsylvania—traditionally bellwether states—voted Republican, and in Ohio—home of Pendleton and Vallandigham—reduced the Democratic delegation in Congress from 14 to 2. The day after these triumphs of the Union cause, a triumph of emancipation was realized in Maryland. Prodded by Lincoln, who in a public letter urged state emancipation, and aided by ballots from soldiers in the field, Maryland voters by a margin of only about 270 out of nearly 30,000 votes adopted a new constitution abolishing slavery. On the same day, ironically, the state's distinguished bulwark of slavery and divided sovereignty, Chief Justice Taney, died.

It was a scurrilous presidential campaign, with much ugliness showing through the seams of a war-swollen democracy. Beyond the normal assaults upon candidates' characters, there were charges of "nigger-loving" against Republicans and treason against Democrats. Fears of conspiratorial uprisings in the Middle West and in the great cities, especially New York, hung like a pall over the last weeks of the canvass. The War Department learned that Confederate agents in Canada were planning raids into the northernmost states. Secretary Stanton employed the influence of his department to reelect Lincoln, facilitating soldier voting and dispatching iron-fisted General Butler with a detachment to police restless New York City.

Warily, Lincoln watched the returns on election day. Butler telegraphed, "The quietest city ever seen." From Philadelphia came word of a Union majority. From Maryland, which in 1860 had voted for Breckinridge, came the wire, "All Hail, Free Maryland." The trend was set: an orderly decision at the polls for union and emancipation. Lincoln spent the evening in the telegraph office of the War Department. By midnight sure of reelection, he ate supper; at half past two he responded to serenaders and then went home.

The voters seemed to have spoken plainly. McClellan carried only three states, Lincoln twenty-two. The electoral vote, 21-212, was extremely lopsided. The popular percentage was clear: fifty-five percent for Lincoln. No one could claim uncertainty about the naming of the next president.

Lincoln saw the outcome in philosophical terms. It had been a victory for free government, demonstrating to the world for the first time "that a people's government can sustain a national election, in the midst of a great civil war." It had shown how sound and strong the United States was, revealing "the purpose of the people, within the loyal states, to maintain the integrity of the Union." It had shown an increase in numbers of voters, despite war losses; "we are *gaining* strength, and may, if need be, maintain the contest indefinitely." And finally, it had been "the voice of the people now, for the first time, heard upon the question" of emancipation. Democracy, the Union, vigorous prosecution of the war, and abolition—this was the verdict of the election.

New York had been a special concern to Lincoln and his party. In the largest Northern state, scene of draft resistance the year before, Lincoln's most redoubtable Democratic critic Horatio Seymour was running for re-election. Though the margins were small, the radical Republican Reuben Fenton defeated Seymour and Lincoln defeated McClellan. The Democrats swept New York City, but in the sweep William Marcy Tweed's Tammany Hall prevailed over Fernando Wood's Mozart Hall. Republicans gained five seats in the next Congress, returning Roscoe Conkling and defeating both Wood brothers.

Kentucky, the most intransigent of the loyal states, was continually a problem to Lincoln and his party. In July Lincoln placed the entire state under martial law; and still under surveillance in November, Kentucky gave the Democratic party the largest majority of any state—seven of ten voters preferring McClellan to Lincoln in a light vote. Of states reporting a soldier vote, it alone had a Democratic plurality.

Only about one-half of the states had authorized soldiers in the field to vote. Taken in the aggregate the army voted for Lincoln in a three to one proportion—much larger than that for the civilian vote. Similarly, the urban county vote was overwhelmingly for Lincoln. In 1860 he had carried but eight of the nineteen largest counties; in 1864 he won twelve. For the twenty-two states that voted in both 1860 and 1864, the voter turnout showed an increase of 140,000.

Impressive as Lincoln's triumph appears, McClellan nonetheless polled forty-five percent of the popular vote and had no votes in the eleven seceded states. He doubtless suffered from those Northern counties which made no returns and from those polls guarded by Federal troops and open only to oath takers. Lincoln benefited from three new states admitted since 1860, all voting for him. Duress and fraud marred the returns. The Democratic party was perhaps equal in popular strength to the victor; a shift of 38,111 votes (less than one percent) in certain states would have elected McClellan.

Of vast import for the future—for finishing the war, completing emancipation, planning reconstruction, and maintaining Republican policies—was the Union upsurge in Congress. Unionist majorities in the Thirty-ninth Congress would be three to one in the House and four to one in the Senate.

The old Congress—the Thirty-eighth—still held power, however, and it met less than a month after the election, with purpose renewed, to see what it could do in its brief span to win the war, free the slaves, provide for the freedmen, and reunite the nation.

CHAPTER TWELVE

The Union Saved but not Restored

"The war continues," the president intoned in his fourth Annual Message. Distinguished not for its felicity of style nor for its elevation of thought, this state paper afforded a wide-ranging, nationalistic view of the Union's progress, needs, and prospects after nearly four years of civil strife. Lincoln and, in turn, Congress addressed themselves to refining the war state and preparing for the peacetime republic.

"The condition of our foreign affairs," which he judged as "reasonably satisfactory," was Lincoln's first theme. Toward the French-supported civil war in Mexico—long a nagging concern—the administration still maintained a strict neutrality. To accomplish final extinction of the African slave trade, he recommended two measures: authority to furnish the Black republic of Liberia a gunboat and provision for preventing foreign slave traders from using the United States as a base for slaving. Confederate depredations from Canada had occasioned the State Department to give notice that after six months the long-standing disarmament agreement, which since 1818 had provided for demilitarizing the border, would end. The decade-old tariff reciprocity agreement with Canada would be reviewed in the light of the outbreak of border troubles.

Success in the nation's finances had marked the year. Lincoln supported the secretary of the treasury's recommendation that taxes pay a heavier proportion of war expenses. With respect to war bonds, he suggested a wider distribution among all the people of this form of national property. Congress might induce buyers by exempting bonds from both taxation and seizure for debt. The great advantage of making citizens creditors of their government lay in the axiom, "Men readily perceive that they cannot be much oppressed by a debt which they owe to themselves." The new banking system he believed was serving the same ends: waging a people's war and forwarding the national interest.

"The maintenance of the Union"—Lincoln's eternal theme—might be assisted through emancipation. State abolition, notably by Maryland, molded, as he said, "society for durability in the Union." He recommended that this Congress reconsider its failure to approve the constitutional amendment abolishing slavery. The voice of the people upon the question had been heard in the last election. National abolition was a means to maintain the Union for all the future.

That election had itself been "of vast value to the national cause." No candidate in either party solicited votes on the basis of disunion. Never was the people's purpose to preserve the integrity of the Union more firm and unanimous. The election returns also exhibited the Union's strength in men; despite the casualties of war, the number of votes had increased by 145,000 since 1860.

With a mandate from the people and with resources more abundant than ever, the Union government would press on to peace and reunion. Peace by negotiation he thought impossible; by military power attainable; but he dwelt on peace by means of simply laying down arms. If the Southern people would stop fighting, accepting as the single condition the freedom of all persons freed by the Emancipation Proclamation and acts of Congress, "the war will cease." The door to reunion was open.

Dry, concise, and unconciliatory on reuniting the nation, the message largely was a statement of ways and means to win the war and maintain the Union in the future. Lincoln had directed his message to Congress, the North, and to the Southern people. Congress in the main cooperated with him, writing into statutory law most of his suggestions. The famous disagreement over reconstruction, itself misunderstood by many historians, has obscured the relative harmony between the two branches.

In the field of foreign affairs, the most critical issue was maintenance of neutrality toward the strife in Mexico. On this issue the House reflected popular emotion, and the Senate, constitutionally empowered to advise and consent to executive conduct of foreign relations, sided with the president.

A resolution, expressing hostility to the French threat to establish a monarchy in Mexico had won in April a unanimous vote from the House, inspired by the over-ardent Henry Winter Davis, chairman of the Committee on Foreign Affairs. Seward was obliged to explain to the French minister that, although the resolution spoke the unanimous sentiment of the American people, only the president could recognize a new government.

To the accompaniment of long-continued applause, a similar statement had gone into the national platform; but Lincoln candidly announced he would continue *his* policy of neutrality.

"Mr. Davis is a bold man. Having turned Radical for a purpose, he seems to . . . stake his all on the struggle for the leadership of his faction," observed the attorney general in his diary. In December Davis renewed his challenge to executive authority in foreign affairs. With eight dissenting votes he pushed through a resolution claiming for Congress an authoritative voice in declaring and prescribing the foreign policy of the United States. But both in April and December, the Senate declined to act upon the potentially dangerous Davis resolutions.

Lincoln and Seward were sustained in their wise policy of watchful waiting toward Mexico. One war at a time was all that the Union could cope with. Forbearance bore fruit in 1867, after the United States had been reunited and its armies freed of fighting a domestic war, when the French troops retired and the Emperor Maximilian faced a firing squad. The Monroe Doctrine had been maintained with a minimum of bellicosity and no bloodshed.

On the Northern border of the United States, the Civil War permanently altered Canadian-American relationships. By threatening abrogation of the 1818 Rush-Bagot disarmament agreement, Seward skilfully won a diplomatic victory. Canada tightened her neutrality law, ending the Confederate raids into the United States, intended to annoy the Union as well as to embroil it with John Bull. With the border quiet, Seward rescinded the notice of abrogation.

Though the landmark agreement, providing for the longest unfortified frontier in the world, survived the war, the reciprocity treaty was a casualty. Negotiated by the Democrats, who were disposed toward free trade, the treaty of 1854 had incurred Republican antipathies for a number of years. Encouraged by Lincoln, the House, led by the protectionist Morrill, passed a resolution calling for unconditional abrogation. Belief that the treaty injured United States economic interests joined with resentments against Canada and Great Britain in effecting Senate concurrence with only eight dissenting votes. In March the United States gave notice that twelve months later a tariff wall would rise along the border. The treaty's termination was an omen of future dominance of the protectionist philosophy in the Republican era.

When William Pitt Fessenden succeeded Chase as secretary of the treasury, he found the nation's finances in "serious confusion." Greenbacks dropped to an all-time low on July 11, 1864. The war was devouring two and a quarter million dollars each day, but the treasury cash balance on July 1 held less than nineteen million. Short-term obligations of the government, short-sighted and unstable, stood in vast disproportion to long-term debt. The national debt had soared to one and three-quarter billions from ninety millions on July 1, 1861. Chase had forfeited the respect of the banking community.

Fessenden in contrast was the respected, experienced former chairman of the wartime Senate Finance Committee. An early advocate of the income tax, he favored sound money and broad sales of bonds among the public. His annual report, reinforced by Lincoln's views, recommended more stringent income and internal revenue taxes.

Congress' response, here at the war's end, brought a high degree of rationality into war finance. Financial anarchy had prevailed at the beginning of hostilities: no national currency, no income tax, no workable precedent for internal taxation even with representation, no national banking system, no experience in dealing with fiscal problems of great scope.

Congress now tithed incomes over $5000, making for the highest income tax of the war. It gave the secretary latitude in borrowing $600 million, enabling him to pay both interest and principal in currency, instead of gold, but banning further legal tender. At the same time it struck a heavy blow at state sovereignty by a prohibitory tax on state bank notes.

By 1865 the income tax produced nearly twenty percent of the treasury's receipts; manufacturers' and sales taxes another twenty-three percent. The public debt peaked in August at $2,846,000,000; and in 1866 for the first time in a decade, the treasury enjoyed a surplus. The war, moreover, had made a foundation for banking and currency that, though strained in depressions, stood until Woodrow Wilson's New Freedom. The fiscal record of the Union, sometimes unfavorably compared with twentieth-century practice, stands in happier comparison with the Confederacy, which raised only one percent of its revenue by taxes.

Just as this last Civil War Congress refined the nation's fiscal system, so, too, it improved the military establishment. In a much-praised report Secretary of the Navy Welles noted that the blockade of the Confederacy, "greater in extent than the whole coast of Europe from Cape Trafalgar to Cape North, is an undertaking without precedent in history." The navy had taken nearly 1400 prizes and had grown from 42 ships on active duty in March 1861 to 671. Welles urged Congress to create the office of vice admiral, corresponding with the army grade of lieutenant general. Made aware of frauds in the Philadelphia Navy Yard, he later recommended a second important new office—naval judge advocate general.

Congress complied with both recommendations. David Farragut became the first vice admiral in United States History; when he appeared in the Senate following his promotion, it recessed to pay respects to him. William E. Chandler, later secretary of the navy under President Arthur, assumed the post of judge advocate general, continuing work he had already begun, uncovering numerous defalcations in Philadelphia.

In a radical attempt to bring the Navy Department under legislative control, Henry Winter Davis moved establishment of a board of admiralty, which would govern administration of the cabinet post. A majority in the House opposed the effort; and when Wade moved the same proposal in the Senate, he could obtain but two votes. The department emerged from the legislative session elevated in dignity and unscathed by the radical assault. The disgrace of Hale, charged with accepting a bribe, and his demotion from the chairmanship of the Senate Naval Affairs Committee removed "a constant and vindictive opponent of the Department," Welles joyfully noted.

As for the army Congress made minor changes that left the nation with a draft system that failed to draft and that pointed out lessons for the future. In a law enacted March 3, Congress did repeal that grotesquerie of national authority which had allowed Northern states to recruit Southern Negroes and count them in their quotas. No fewer than 1405 agents had swarmed South, recruiting less than four Negroes each. One-quarter of the recruits were credited to labor-deficient Massachusetts.

Against the protests of Massachusetts politicians and businessmen, Congress ended the recruitment provision, which had further underscored the inadequacy of the states to recruit men. In the last two years of the war, the Federal government recruited 100,000 Negroes, the states only 55,000. A second provision of the March enrollment law encouraged associations of individuals subject to draft to provide substitutes, thereby giving members immunity to the draft at low cost. The associations organized pools of substitutes, who served in place of drafted members.

These strange gyrations of the national legislature revealed a republic reluctant to conscript its citizens. Not surprisingly, the number of soldiers actually drafted into the Union Army during the Civil War was small, about 50,000. If one adds to these the number of substitutes, the total is but six percent of the Union forces. The Civil War draft, it is generally conceded, served more as a spur to volunteering than a source of manpower. In all, it would appear, Union enlistments, reduced to three-years service equivalents, came to 1,556,678 men—a smaller proportion of the military manpower potential than the 1,082,119 enlistments in the Confederate service.

The lessons of recruitment for future wars were plain: the necessity to initiate national conscription at the start of a war; to include Blacks as well as whites on equal footing; to shun commutation, substitution, bounties, and short terms of service. Above all, individualism and states rights must be subordinated to national authority.

"Amend the Constitution—it is the way to unity and peace," argued Ashley of Ohio in calling up the proposed amendment abolishing slavery throughout the United States. This theme, echoing Lincoln's own exhortation to the Congress to act, promptly encountered objection from Democratic leaders. Pruyn of New York retorted that slavery lay beyond reach of constitutional amendment. Mindful of the Republican platform of 1860 and Lincoln's willingness in 1861 to guarantee slavery by constitutional amendment, Voorhees charged the Republicans with bad faith.

Not unity but continuing division would be the outcome, the Hoosier orator forecast. "The party now in power will seek to enfranchise the liberated negro, to make him a voter, a juror, and eligible to hold office." Even more virulent racialism was voiced by Fernando Wood: "the Almighty has made the black man inferior . . . and you cannot wipe out the distinction." The recent Democratic nominee for the vice-presidency, Pendleton, threw his prestige against the amendment.

While the House dawdled two states made decisive moves toward freedom. In Tennessee a Unionist convention proposed a popular vote on state abolition to be held on Washington's birthday. A constitutional convention in Missouri, with only four dissenting votes, approved abolition; and without waiting for ratification, the zealous governor proclaimed the proposed ordinance to be in effect. The lower chamber of the state legislature greeted the news with applause and sang "John Brown's Body." In Washington "Sunset" Cox argued that state action made a constitutional amendment unnecessary.

Advocates of abolition pleaded for action as an instrument of nationality, of keeping peace in the future, of morality in exterminating an evil institution, and of retribution upon the South for starting the war. The House heard with special alertness Rollins, from a Missouri slavekeeping constituency, speak for passage.

The result was in doubt. It was the same House that had failed in June to muster the requisite two-thirds majority. On the last day of January, the day set for the last struggle, the galleries of the House filled. But the seats of eight Democrats were empty. The roll call on the great act of liberation advanced. At its end the announcement was made—the amendment had passed. The galleries rose to their feet, soldiers shouting and cheering, while ladies floated their handkerchiefs. Republican members embraced one another and in a delirium of joy waved their hats and canes. For some time the speaker was unable to bring order. Nothing more could be done on the immortal day; and the House adjourned.

Sober analysis of the vote, however, showed that the famous victory had been won by the thin margin of two votes. Eleven Democrats had voted yea, together with the eight absentees subtracting strength from the opposition party. Thirteen Border men had voted yea; the Kentucky delegation had divided three for and six against. Every nay vote in the House had been cast by a Democrat.

Beyond the long-range effects of the presidential election, Lincoln's appeal, the progress of the armies and of state emancipation, four more immediate factors in passing for amendment may be noted. Seward exerted his influence among New York Democrats, six of whom voted yea. Lincoln manipulated the patronage; and to the anger of the opposition, Speaker Colfax insisted on having his yea counted. Finally, Cox had weakened the principal argument of his party by admitting that the amendment was constitutional, though inexpedient.

"The day opened a new dispensation," wrote an eyewitness to the historic occasion, Samuel Bowles, editor of the Springfield *Republican*. "Today," he continued on February 1 from his Washington vantage point, "a negro has been admitted to practice in the Supreme Court. And the work goes on, or rather has just begun."

A few days later, subscribers to the *Independent* read the classic lines written by Whittier after hearing the bells ring on passage of the amendment:

> It is done
>> In the circuit of the sun
> Shall the sound thereof go forth.
>> It shall bid the sad rejoice,
>> It shall give the dumb a voice,
> It shall belt with joy the earth.

Seward, counting ratifications by eight Southern states not represented in Congress, proclaimed the amendment in force.

"Emancipate, Enfranchise, Educate," exhorted the Black preacher to an audience that filled the House of Representatives on the second Sunday in February 1865. Invited by the chaplain, the preacher had violated an unrepealed law that prohibited any Negro to set foot in the legislative chambers. Born a slave, the Reverend Henry Highland Garnet was notorious for a militant speech he had delivered at a Negro convention back in 1843 when he had called upon slaves to revolt. Now less militant, he asked the members of Congress to forward racial equality, especially giving the freedman the vote and an education.

The Black community in Washington lay under congressional authority and awaited Federal action. Sumner continued his crusade to desegregate the street railways of the District of Columbia. In previous sessions, when requests for franchises had come before the Senate, he had successfully incorporated clauses forbidding exclusion of Negroes from the cars. Now he sought a blanket ban for the District. A vote taken in Committee of the Whole failed, 19-20. Immediately renewing his fight in open Senate, he saw Republican stalwarts like Hale, Lane, Doolittle, and Morrill switch sides, gaining a victory, 26-10. Thereafter, but not ever after, Washington Negroes had the right to ride the horse cars. When, testing the statute, the venerable Black abolitionist Sojourner Truth was roughed up by a hostile white conductor, who was trying to push her out of a car, she had him arrested and fired.

Four more steps toward equality may be noted. The House passed a resolution condemning as an "odious discrimination" a military order requiring Negroes leaving Washington to have a pass. It called upon the president to revoke the order; all the negative votes but one were cast by Democrats. The House, which in 1862 had laid on the table a bill to remove the disqualification of Negroes from carrying the mails, now joined the Senate in removing this example of discrimination. The scandalous reluctance of Congress to grant full retroactive equal pay to all Negro regiments promised equal pay when they enrolled was at last swallowed in the dying hours of this session. And fourthly, notwithstanding earlier approval of the Thirteenth Amendment, amid strong opposition, Congress passed a joint resolution assuring Negro soldiers that their wives and children should also be forever free. Every affirmative vote but one in the two chambers was cast by Republicans; Winter Davis opposed in a close House vote, 45 members not voting.

While Congress was making these striking moves, elsewhere in the North the evolution of a new postwar aim—racial equality—could be discerned. From Massachusetts to California abolitionists attacked segregation in schools, churches, and transportation, exclusion of Negro testimony, and discriminatory "Black laws." The way was being prepared for civil rights guarantees in the Reconstruction era.

In a series of measures enacted during the war, Congress had laid a foundation, albeit a frail one, for the Negro's future. It had established the principle of Federal support of Negro schools, of equality before the law, of equal access to public transportation, of economic opportunity, of equal eligibility to military service. It had shrunk from integrated schools, equal suffrage, and economic assistance and remedial education essential to a long-enslaved people. What it had done for Blacks had often been done either under military necessity or with caution and without conviction as to human equality. The future of race relations in the United States remained murky.

"What is to become of them?" asked a military aide in midwinter 1863, after seeing destitute freedmen in the South. From early in the war Negroes had found refuge within Union lines. With the advance of the blue-coated armies in the South, dimensions of the problem of what to do about the Southern Negroes grew.

Colonization was ever a chimera, though some men pursued it until the end of the war. Other solutions must be sought. At Port Royal, South Carolina, an experiment in freedom successfully combined governmental and private assistance toward Negroes who were paid wages by the treasury department for cultivating abandoned lands and were educated for freedom by Northern teachers and missionaries who volunteered their services. In the Mississippi Valley, army authorities, with the cooperation of philanthropic organizations, undertook to employ and assist Negroes. Freedmen's aid societies, with substantial contributions from British counterparts, and the American Missionary Association offered organized private aid to Southern Negroes.

But a wider vision than any of these efforts and a sustained program were every day becoming more exigent. Tattered, hungry, and uneducated, Negroes by the thousands, unprepared for freedom, needed the assistance of the Federal government that was liberating them. If freedom came to all Negroes in the Confederacy, upward of three and a half million would stand in want of a long-range program.

The United States government, devoted to the dogma of individualism, was ideologically unready for the immense task. To draft a blueprint for the Negro's future, the American Freedmen's Inquiry Commission was created in the War Department. Its initial report in the summer of 1863 occupied bold ground in advocating temporary Federal guardianship of the freedmen.

Legislation implementing recommendations of the commission came before the House in December. Approved by a margin of only two votes by the House, a bill establishing a freedmen's bureau in the War Department encountered Sumner's objections in the Senate. By a 21 to 9 vote, the Senate placed the bureau under the Treasury, where the ardent anti-slavery Chase might be expected to keep an eye on its operations. The lower chamber non-concurred, and the freedmen were neglected until the next session of Congress.

When in the winter of 1864-65, with months having passed and legions of Negroes in need, Sumner resumed agitation for a bureau under the Treasury, he met Democratic opposition organized by Indiana's Hendricks and Western Republican opposition led by Iowa's Grimes. An ardent sectionalist, who had not voted on the earlier bill, Grimes appeared suspicious of a bill that might throw all its advantages to Blacks and the East. The abolitionist Hale, who also had not voted on the earlier bill, snapped he was tired of coddling Negroes at the expense of whites. Against a solid Democratic opposition, joined by 14 Republicans and Unionists, the bill failed in the Senate.

To establish some kind of a bureau, with less than a fortnight left in the session, Sumner yielded leadership to Wilson, who headed a joint committee that embraced but one Democrat. This legislative device—the conference committee—so very valuable in enacting the legislation of the Civil War, wrote "an entirely new bill."

The outcome was extraordinary. In spite of the earlier wrangling, the new bill was adopted by both houses without a division. The president approved it the same day. The law established a Bureau for the Relief of Freedmen and Refugees in the War Department. The Bureau would have "control of all subjects relating to refugees and freedmen from rebel states." It would supervise and manage all abandoned lands; and it would provide temporary subsistence, clothing, and fuel, and assign land.

These features were unremarkable; what was remarkable was a series of provisions not seen in previous versions. The bill covered *white* refugees as well as Black. It abandoned all provisions suggesting supervision of the freedmen by arranging contracts or supervising their labor. It provided for allotments of forty acres of land on a rental basis for three years, after which they might be purchased. It refused to open up the public domain in the Southern states to freedmen and refugees.

Novel as this venture in Federal relief was, it was at the same time in many respects short-sighted and racist as well as dilatory. The Bureau was to operate only during the war and one year thereafter. Available lands, acquired by abandonment and confiscation, would amount to no more than 800,000 acres and would be distributed to white loyalists as well as Blacks. Education was left largely to private philanthropy. Capital for farming and purchasing land was not made available; indeed, Congress made no initial appropriation of money for the Bureau.

Behind this thin facade of philanthropy lay a lack of vision of the magnitude of the work, a spirit of improvisation, a powerful economic tradition of self-help, and a grim racism. The members of the American Freedmen's Inquiry Commission had announced they were agreed on one thing: all governmental measures for Blacks must be temporary. There were no precedents to draw upon. "The natural laws of supply and demand should be left to regulate rates of compensation and places of residence," said the Commission. Racist fears that all Southern lands, abandoned and public, might be awarded to Blacks inhered in the radical changes in the bill's final version. The noted reformer Samuel G. Howe, a member of the Commission, privately believed that "the free operation of 'natural laws' might lead to the extinction of the Negro in the entire continent" of North America. That Blacks were not suited to the temperate zones was believed by many white Americans, who with this notion readily reconciled freedom for Blacks with a vision of white America.

Reconstructing the Union was the quintessential war aim. To save the Union was Lincoln's unfailing purpose. To preserve the Union with the rights of the states unimpaired had been Congress' intention as announced in the Crittenden resolutions of July 1861. The problem of reconstruction did not loom on the political horizon suddenly in the summer of 1864, but in fact had been under discussion from early in the war.

The North had waged war on the constitutional theory that the Union was indestructible; no state had a right to secede. Early in 1862 rival views of reconstruction emerged. After Grant's victories in Tennessee, Lincoln instituted a conservative policy of military reconstruction under executive control. Proceeding on the theory that Tennessee had never seceded, because it had no power to do so, Lincoln named Andrew Johnson its military governor. Subsequently, he appointed military governors for Louisiana, North Carolina, and Arkansas.

Meanwhile, a radical policy with respect both to states and Negroes was urged upon the House. This policy looked to reducing the rebellious states to territories, freeing the slaves, and placing reconstruction under congressional control. Stevens said the Southern states were "out of the Union"; and Sumner told the Senate the Southern states had committed "suicide." Territorialization, however, failed to attract widespread support; and the prevailing view in the Thirty-seventh Congress by the time it adjourned was described by one of its members as "progressive restoration." Congress intended to recognize the continuing existence of the Southern states, to cooperate with the president in the restoration of them, but, under the constitutional clause by which the United States guaranteed to every state a republican form of government, to exercise ultimate control over the process of reconstruction.

When the Thirty-eighth Congress opened in December 1863, military governments existed in four Southern states. Union successes in July at Vicksburg and Gettysburg and in November at Lookout Mountain and Missionary Ridge gave hope that the tide of war had turned. A broad policy of reconstruction seemed necessary.

In a proclamation of amnesty, dated the same day as his Annual Message, Lincoln announced his policy of reconstruction. Behind his words lurked the hope of undermining military resistance in the Confederacy and of quickly restoring the seceded states. Pardon and property rights would be generously extended to all who would take a prescribed oath of future loyalty, with exception of certain Confederate leaders and property in slaves. Whenever ten percent of the 1860 electorate had taken this oath, they might set up a new government, which must be republican in form; and the president promised to recognize it.

As to the status of Negroes, Lincoln said he would not object to state measures which, having provided for the freedom and education of Negroes, might be "consistent as a temporary arrangement, with their present condition as a laboring, landless, and homeless class." Having gone so far in exerting executive authority, Lincoln next acknowledged the constitutional right of Congress to seat members sent from the states. And further to disarm legislative objection, he pragmatically remarked that while this plan was the best he could devise, "it must not be understood that no other possible mode would be acceptable."

At first the majority of Republicans in Congress, contrary to historical mythology, appeared to approve the president's plan. What seemed important was his combining reconstruction with emancipation. But Lincoln's haste in reconstructing Louisiana, allowing the election of state officials before a new antislavery constitution was written, alarmed many members of Congress. Stevens spoke for a growing number when he insisted no state should be readmitted until it had by its own constitution forever prohibited slavery. Distrust of Southern whites while the war was raging was understandably strong, and opposition to the minimal requirements of Lincoln's plan mounted. Ten percent of the 1860 electorate was thought too small a base for a new government. An absolute prohibition of slavery and a guarantee of the public debt were necessary. Congressional assent to recognition of new state governments must be asserted. "The question of reconstruction," Fessenden told the Senate, "should properly be settled by Congress."

Congressional policy culminated in the first session of the Thirty-eighth

Congress in the Wade-Davis bill. This measure broadened the base of the new governments by requiring a majority, not ten percent, of white male citizens to form them. In the process of reestablishing state governments, more stringent loyalty oaths were exacted and a greater number of rebels was excluded than under the executive plan.

The heart of the proposed law lay in the requirement that slavery be forever prohibited in the new state constitutions and in the execution of the constitutional duty of the United States to guarantee a republican form of government. A new constitution must also repudiate the rebel debt. Upon adoption of the constitution by the qualified voters, the president must recognize the new government, "after obtaining the assent of congress."

Behind this bill lay a variety of motives, high and low: the desire to insist upon congressional prerogative, distrust of the South, the guarantee of freedom to Negroes, and the intention to postpone reconstruction until after the presidential election, if not after the war. The oft repeated assertion by historians that the Republicans were mainly concerned about preserving the tariff and other aspects of the economic reconstruction wrought during the war requires further proof than yet adduced.

The bill did not represent aggressive radicalism. The chief architect appears not to have been either Wade or Davis but Ira Harris, a conservative senator from New York and former jurist, who in a bill presented in 1862-63 had formulated the material points of this congressional policy on reconstruction. The House rejected a radical preamble and passed the bill by a solid Republican vote. The Senate, having rejected Negro suffrage, proceeded to emasculate the House bill; and after the House nonconcurred, the upper chamber passed the bill, with five Republicans absent and another seven in the negative. The generally moderate character of the bill may be measured by noting that it did not provide for territorialization of the states, nor for confiscation of rebel property, nor for the ballot for Blacks.

The point is especially worth emphasis that, although the bill proposed the use of national power beyond what had been contemplated by the president, it stood on the idea of a *federal* Union, with reform to be carried out by *state* constitutional conventions. States rights were not dead. The states had not committed suicide; they were not to be relegated to territories. They were to act as elements of the federal system to remove the cause of disunion and civil war.

Still, the differences between Lincoln and the Republicans in Congress were substantial. The Wade-Davis bill was a congressional alternative to executive reconstruction. It was also a legislative rebuke of the president. On the day of adjournment, Lincoln went to the Capitol to sign bills. The irrepressible Zachariah Chandler asked the president if he intended to sign this bill. "The important point," he cried, "is that one prohibiting slavery in the reconstructed states."

"That is the point on which I doubt the authority of Congress to act," answered Lincoln. He refused to sign the bill and within a few days took his case to the people. He was unprepared, he said, to set aside the free governments of Louisiana and Arkansas or to declare a constitutional competency in Congress to abolish slavery in states. With customary pragmatism he denied being inflexibly committed to any single plan and deemed the system for restoration in the bill "as one very proper plan."

It was perhaps Lincoln's good fortune that Congress had adjourned. James G. Blaine believed that the president's extraordinary course met with almost unanimous Republican dissent. He thought that if Congress had been in session, "a very rancorous hostility would have been developed against the President." The Wade-Davis bill had signified a nearly unanimous Republican view.

Wade and Davis, for their part, soon voiced their violent opposition in a caustic "Protest." They reviewed the differences between their measure and the president's policy; and then in angry words and ugly threats denounced the pocket veto as a "blow . . . at the rights of humanity," concluding by inviting the supporters of the government to "consider the remedy for these usurpations, and, having found it, fearlessly execute it."

Their vehement language instead of injuring Lincoln injured the authors. Their hidden purpose to unseat Lincoln as the party nominee failed. Davis was defeated for reelection. The party united in early September, as we have seen, and reconstruction was not an issue in the fall contest.

His position strengthened by reelection, Lincoln in his last Annual Message invited a rapprochement with Congress over reconstruction. Though the door to amnesty was still open, he warned the South that more rigorous measures might become necessary. Though presidential reconstruction was continuing, he pointed out executive power would diminish by cessation of the war; moreover, the admission of members was a congressional question.

The session ended in stalemate. Champions of congressional prerogative thought they had won a victory when the two houses passed a joint resolution "declaring certain States not entitled to representation in the electoral college." Lincoln cleverly deflected the rebuke by signing the resolution, remarking he did so in deference to Congress, adding with gentle sarcasm his disclaimer that by signing the resolution he had expressed any opinion of his own on it.

Two legislative questions on reconstruction were to be decided: enactment of a general reconstruction law and admission of Louisiana. The House labored for over two months on a revision of the Wade-Davis measure, which failed when 19 Republicans voted with the Democrats to shelve it. If the House in this session was unable to pass a new reconstruction bill, the Senate was able to prevent the readmission of Louisiana. Trumbull as chairman of the Judiciary Committee brought up a joint resolution to recognize the Lincoln government as the "legitimate government" of the state.

Sumner led the opposition. He insisted, first and foremost, that Negroes be accorded the right to vote, and next that Congress exercise the authority in the work of reconstruction. If Louisiana should be admitted, then Arkansas was next. After that there would be no stopping the advance of presidential reconstruction, lenient with rebel leaders, lax toward Negro suffrage, and long on executive authority. Sumner mobilized an incongruous coalition of radical Republicans and Democrats, making a vote impossible. The admission of Louisiana was abandoned.

When Congress adjourned, it had not worked out a policy on reconstruction in cooperation with the executive. Most congressmen seemed unaware of the imminence of peace and the urgent need to provide for civil governments in the South. The lawmakers would not meet again until December. "Nine months is an age in these times of rapid events," warned the *National Intelligencer* four days after the session ended. Hostilities in fact ceased a few weeks later, leaving the executive in charge of reconstruction.

In his last public address, two days after Appomattox, speaking to serenaders, Lincoln defended his reconstruction policy. He took note of the constitutional controversy over whether the seceded states, "so called," were in the Union or out, dismissing it as "a merely pernicious abstraction." Citing Louisiana as an illustration of his policy, he answered other criticisms of presidential reconstruction. The sole object of reconstruction, he posited, was to get states again into a "proper practical relation." Though some persons charged that ten percent of the voters was too small a nucleus, this fraction had succeeded in forming a new, free state government. Though it dissatisfied some persons that the vote had not been given to Blacks, the new constitution provided equally for public schools for Blacks and whites and empowered the legislature to confer the vote on Blacks. Better, he thought, to take gains and foster them, rather than destroy them. In homely barnyard analogy, he asked, "Concede that the new government of Louisiana is only to what it should be as the egg is to the fowl, we shall sooner have the fowl by hatching the egg than by smashing it?"

As to Negro suffrage, the "fundamental condition" which Sumner wanted to impose upon Louisiana, Lincoln remarked, "I would myself prefer that it were now conferred on the very intelligent, and on those who serve our cause as soldiers." This public statement of personal preference was bolder than his letter of a year earlier to the Union governor of Louisiana, wherein Lincoln had "barely" suggested for the governor's "private consideration" that such Negroes be given the vote. Still, it must be observed that Lincoln's policy on the Negro remained unchanged: though he held a personal preference about extending the ballot to selected Negroes, he would not make this a condition for the restoration of a state. Whether he would have embraced universal Negro suffrage, the creed of the radicals in 1867, cannot be known. What seems certain is that his alleged letter to James S. Wadsworth espousing civil and political equality of both races is spurious. Lincoln was neither an equalitarian, nor a white supremacist, but a pragmatist. What seems certain also is that he would have hewn to the line that in his judgment would have advanced the national interest.

Peace was the "fundamental condition" to reconstruction as well as to shaping the Negro's future. The problem of peace terms, it will be recalled, had arisen during the election of 1864. Lincoln in a famous letter to Greeley had insisted upon "restoration of peace, the integrity of the whole Union, and the abandonment of slavery" as his terms. Privately, he said he would not allow insistence upon abandonment of slavery to stand in the way of peace.

His Annual Message of December 1864 seemed to retreat from his insistence upon abandonment of slavery in his statement that the Southern people "can, at any moment, have peace simply by laying down their arms and submitting to the national authority under the Constitution." But in presenting this as the single condition of peace, "I retract nothing heretofore said about slavery," he continued.

His meaning became more clear in the conference he held two months later with Vice-President Stephens of the Confederacy. Lincoln was inflexible upon the ending of hostilities and the restoring of national authority. Abandonment of slavery, however, he put in a revealing light. As for his Emancipation Proclamation, the courts must decide its legal status. He himself thought it would cease to operate when the war ended. It applied, he believed, only to those slaves who had come under its scope during the war—only about 200,000. The courts might in time rule it applied everywhere. He favored gradual emancipation; and he had issued his proclamation to save the Union.

Seward, who accompanied Lincoln, told the Confederate commissioners that Congress had just approved the Thirteenth Amendment. According to Stephens, Seward, without contradiction from Lincoln, pointed out the Southern states could defeat the amendment. Lincoln interposed, asking Stephens to tell the people of Georgia to ratify the amendment "*prospectively*" to take effect in perhaps five years.

Believing both North and South were responsible for slavery, Lincoln said he favored a government indemnity as high as $400 million to owners for the loss of their slaves. He could of course make no promises about congressional appropriations.

He could give assurances about the confiscation and penal laws, for these lay under his authority. He would execute these laws "with the utmost liberality."

Finally, as to the political status of the Southern states, they would be "immediately restored to their practical relations to the Union" upon cessation of fighting. Congress held the power to admit representatives from these states; unable to make any promise, he thought Congress would admit them.

This conference, held in the presidential steamer the *River Queen* anchored in Hampton Roads, gives us perhaps the fullest available outline of Lincoln's thinking about peace. Unyielding upon saving the Union and stopping the fighting, he displayed magnanimity toward the persons and property of the enemy. He favored gradual emancipation, compensation to slaveowners, amnesty toward insurgents, and rapid restoration of the Southern states without punitive action or revolutionary change.

Two evenings later, back in Washington, Lincoln described to his cabinet the above plan, "looking to peace and re-union," to be submitted to Congress as a joint resolution. "It did not meet with favor, but was dropped," Welles laconically wrote of the unanimous disapproval. Lincoln earnestly desired to achieve an early peace and to conciliate the South. He had failed at Hampton Roads, for Jefferson Davis on hearing of the conference had refused any terms but Confederate independence. He had failed at his cabinet meeting, for his advisers believed his terms harmful, if rejected, and impossible to get through Congress.

The arbitrament of arms, not negotiation and conciliation, ended the war. At Appomattox on April 9, 1865, General R. E. Lee, his forces shrunk to fewer than 30,000 men, his rations short, his army virtually encircled, accepted the surrender terms of General U. S. Grant, given in the generous spirit of Lincoln's peace terms. Final capitulation of Confederate forces followed over the next six weeks. The war for the Union had been won. The war for Southern independence had been lost.

Lincoln did not survive to reconstruct the Union. His peace terms were not adopted. On the main issue of the war—preserving the nation—he had prevailed. On the emerging issue of reconstruction, he left a partially formulated plan which was not followed. His last, best legacy to the nation he had rescued was the eloquent peroration to his Second Inaugural: "With malice toward none, with charity for all; with firmness in the right, as God gives us to see the right, let us strive on to finish the work we are in; to bind up the nation's wounds; to care for him who shall have borne the battle, and for his widow, and his orphan—to do all which may achieve and cherish a just and lasting peace, among ourselves, and with all nations."

CHAPTER THIRTEEN

A New Federalism

A new nation, it is often said, emerged from the flames of the Civil War. Before Sumter the republic had been beset by the firedragons of state sovereignty and sectionalism. The republic was not reduced to rubble, though slavery—the main tinderbox of sectionalism—was wiped out. The house was no longer divided, and a new sense of its spaciousness animated its dwellers.

After Appomattox men could look to the national government with less apprehension and greater trust. Lowell in his ode commemorating the returning soldiers and the Harvard dead wrote:

Bow down, dear Land, for thou hast found release!

. . . .

What were our lives without thee?
What all our lives to save thee?

>We reck not what we gave thee;
>We will not dare to doubt thee,
>But ask whatever else, and we will dare!

The victory on the battlefield put the quietus to the theory of secession. Four years after the war in the language of finality, the Supreme Court decreed that the Union was indissoluble and perpetual. The destruction of slavery, which in 1860 the Republican platform had pledged to maintain as an inviolate right of the states, was the most spectacular sacrifice to the new nationalism.

Beyond this, a spate of congressional measures greatly expanded the activity of the central government. A protective tariff had in 1832 touched off the nullification controversy in South Carolina. Branded as a violation of the delegated tax powers of Congress, protectionism for three decades threatened domestic tranquility. The Civil War entrenched protectionism, and with little important remission the national government in the era after the war exercised broad economic power.

The authority of the Federal government to charter national banks had been assailed by Jefferson, Jackson, and Tyler; and attempts to exercise it had been abandoned. The war years gave birth to a system of national banks chartered by the national government; they were authorized to issue bank notes based on the national debt, and the state banks were stopped from issuing bank notes. This time the national banks endured, sustained by the Supreme Court in 1875 and strengthened by the Federal Reserve system in the twentieth century. Fear of fiat money and faith in hard coin had long prevented the Federal government from claiming the power to force public acceptance of paper money as legal tender. The Supreme Court, under Chase, with some ambivalence to be sure, upheld the constitutionality of the Legal Tender Act. Before the end of Reconstruction, Greenbackers were clamoring for more paper money.

Few citizens before the war had contributed directly to the treasury. By the war's close everyone and everything was taxed. As a contemporary observed, the government seemed to be operating on the principle of the Irishman at Donnybrook Fair: "Whenever you see a head, hit it." The Civil War tax on incomes was directly challenged in the Supreme Court in 1881; but unanimously the justices sustained this exercise of national power.

"What clause in the Constitution authorized Congress to give away lands?" demanded a Southern states rights opponent of a homestead bill in the debates before the war. Buchanan had vetoed a homestead bill, contending that Congress had no power to donate land to individuals or states. Federal aid to internal improvements in 1830 had met the veto of Andrew Jackson in the memorable Maysville road bill. The Civil War Congress set aside constitutional objections and liberally donated land to individuals and railroads. The postwar generation acquiesced to the constitutionality of the Homestead Act. It was aid to the Union Pacific Railroad that was challenged in the Supreme Court, which stoutly upheld Federal aid to the great transcontinental: "It was a national work, originating in national necessities, and requiring national assistance."

The draft, Daniel Webster rumbled in the House of Representatives in 1814, was unconstitutional, inconsistent with "free principles." If a conscription law should be passed, he warned, "It will be the solemn duty of the state governments to protect their own authority over their own militia and to interpose between their citizens and arbitrary power." Conscription was legislated by Congress and upheld by various Federal courts during the Civil War. Not until the First World War did the Supreme Court rule on the question, reaching the conclusion that the nation's power to conscript was included in the congressional authority to raise armies.

Thus it was that in a notable series of measures, long the subject of controversy in American history, the national authority was staunchly asserted. In a rather different fashion, national power was extended through the Habeas Corpus Act, the partition of a state without its consent, the bold use of the presidential office, the growth of Federal bureaucracy, and amendment of the Constitution.

The Habeas Corpus Act of 1863 provided for removal of certain suits from state to Federal courts at the expense of states rights. The violence done to Virginia in establishing West Virginia was a nationalistic act of war which only by a legal fiction had the consent of the state of Virginia. Both of these blows at states rights won vindication in the Supreme Court.

The executive branch of the government, reduced to near impotence by Pierce and Buchanan, metamorphosed into a quasi-presidential dictatorship. Lincoln justified his extraordinary role in two ways, claiming in an emergency he could, first, exercise congressional power, trusting that Congress later would ratify his action; and, second and more important, he held the president's war power. "I conceive that I may in an emergency do things on military grounds which cannot be done constitutionally by Congress," he once remarked. Armed with this philosophy he overrode states rights and congressional prerogative in order to save the life of the nation.

The centralizing process of the Civil War may be seen in the growth of the Federal bureaucracy. The civil service nearly quintupled during the four years of fighting, with 136,236 civilian employees in the War Department alone. Beyond this, new titles with new areas of governmental authority attested to the growing magnitude of Washington's activities: Military Director and Superintendent of Railroads, Commissioner of Agriculture, Commissioner of Internal Revenue, Judge Advocate General of the army and later one of the navy, Provost Marshal General, Comptroller of the Currency, Commissioner of Immigration, and Commissioner of the Freedmen's Bureau. Never had the national government been so effectively and extensively organized.

The new relationship between the states and the nation was written into three constitutional amendments. The first of these destroyed the right of a state to maintain the institution of slavery. The Fourteenth Amendment not only made Negroes citizens of the United States, thus overturning the Dred Scott decision, but it also for the first time defined national citizenship: "All persons born or naturalized in the United States, and subject to the jurisdiction thereof, are citizens of the United States . . . " National citizenship now became primary, and state citizenship, derived from mere residence, secondary. "No State shall" were the opening words of the next portion of the Fourteenth Amendment as it proceeded to circumscribe traditional rights of states. Finally, the Fifteenth Amendment stripped both the states and the United States of the power to deny or abridge the right to vote on account of race, color, or previous condition of servitude. The power to enforce these articles against the states was given Congress in each amendment. The Negro, hapless cause of division and civil war, now proved to be a force promoting nationalism.

Notwithstanding all this, the degree of nationalism attained through the war for the Union may be overstated. The author of a study of Lincoln and the war governors entitled his final chapter, "The Death of States' Rights." Lincoln had made a nation, he wrote, "But States' rights were dead."

This verdict is greatly exaggerated. If one reviews the outcome of many aspects of the new nationalism, he perceives the persistence of states rights. In the realm of banking, for example, the national banking system did not destroy state banks, leaving to them the deposit function. Nor did it, in prohibiting state bank note issue, arrogate the power to the national government. Instead, it conferred the authority upon the national banks, which of course were privately owned. With regard to the income tax, the Supreme Court, reversing itself in 1895, declared the tax unconstitutional. The Habeas Corpus Act proved a fruitful source of controversy between state and Federal courts, leaving to future generations the adjustment of differences. The Supreme Court soon enough found a rationalization to erode national authority over the Negro's civil rights and his use of the ballot. With an uncertain hand the Supreme Court first gave the states a limited concurrent right to regulate interstate railroads and later took away the right.

The states survived the War between the States. A new federalism, with the balance shifted away from the states to the nation, emerged from the war and its aftermath. Much of the old antagonism between state and nation was swallowed. The Agricultural College Act under which the national government granted lands to the states represented a Federal partnership. Once a state had received its land, it assumed responsibility for the college with a minimum of responsibility to the Federal government. Centralized banking, such as set up in the first two Banks of the United States, simply did not exist under the National Bank Act. Civil War laws, erecting barriers of minimum capital requirements and prohibitions on mortgage loans, failed to achieve a truly national bank system.

Whatever may be said about Lincoln as nationalist and even dictator, he never intended in his war against secession to annihilate states rights. He did not believe in state suicide. He and Sumner had different conceptions of the future Federal Union. "While Mr. Sumner is very cordial with me," Lincoln remarked during a time of disagreement between them, "he is making history in an issue with me on this very point. He hopes to succeed in beating the President so as to change this Government from its original form and make it a strong centralized power." Lincoln's view, in a nutshell, was that under the Constitution states had rights but not sovereignty. Nationalism had its limits. The Civil War had demonstrated that what might be termed a centripetal federalism offered a better system of equilibrium for the diversities of mid-nineteenth century America than either states rights or a nation-state.

One of the most vivid lessons of the Civil War was the vitality of American political institutions. The Constitution had withstood the test. Though written, it had proved to be not excessively rigid. Though strained, it had not been subverted. Though civil rights had been in some instances infringed, they had not been permanently impaired. Given the special nature of the crisis—an internal war—they had been surprisingly respected. The Constitution had shown itself equal to the emergency.

Similarly, the Supreme Court cooperated toward the winning of the war. Southern and Democratic in the late 1850s, it had contributed to the outbreak by its notorious Dred Scott decision. The Republicans during the war refashioned the court, naming three associate justices, expanding the number of judges to ten, and toward the war's end appointing a new chief justice. The Court did not curb the extraordinary power assumed by the president. Taney's negative opinion in the Merryman case was not a Supreme Court opinion, but that of a circuit judge who was also chief justice, and it was refuted and disregarded by Lincoln. When Vallandigham sought Supreme Court review of his case, the Court refused jurisdiction. When litigants challenged Lincoln's theory of the war in the Prize Cases, the Court sustained the president. When in the fall of 1864 the aged author of the Dred Scott decision died, Lincoln replaced Taney with a stout antislavery man, Salmon P. Chase, with important implications for the future. In the generation after the Civil War, the Lincoln court maintained with few exceptions both administration and congressional measures undertaken during the war.

The role of Congress stands in an interesting light. With regard to essential war measures, it gave the president what he needed. "The purse and the sword have been confided to him almost without hesitation," remarked the *National Intelligencer* the day of his second inauguration. On issues of emancipation, confiscation, and reconstruction there were important differences, but these were not obstacles to winning the war. Rather than acting without executive leadership on "non-war" measures, as sometimes said, Congress frequently received presidential prodding, as on such measures as railroads, legal tender, the agricultural bureau, national banking, and contract labor. Rather than either dominating the president or doing its work independently of him, it sometimes acquiesced in his leadership, thus exhibiting a pattern of considerable complexity. Postwar congresses by dominating national policy more than made amends for the attitude of the war years.

The party system, though assailed by sectionalism and secession, kept a viable two-party capability. The Republican party dominated Civil War politics, less so in the second half of the war than in the first. Though it included factions—radicals, sectionalists, moderates, and conservatives—broadened its base, and changed its name, the party retained an essential unity. Party was the most important determinant in legislative voting.

As for the Democrats, they scarcely deserve the reproachful term Copperhead. Fessenden's remark about Senate Democrats, "They have given us a large proportion of their votes," is apposite. Conservative in their outlook on the Constitution and on property rights, somewhat more racist than the Republicans, the Democrats, who also had factions, by and large represented the loyal opposition. Kentucky, as we have seen, perhaps presented the most consistently obstructive bloc in Congress.

In perspective, the years of the Civil War were a time of abnormal tensions, taking expression in political institutions and often operating springs of positive action. The Republican party, which controlled Congress and usually the state governments, and the presidency were the two outstanding political institutions. Sometimes in cooperation and sometimes in competition, they conduced to an energetic and successful war. Northern unity was maintained, though with difficulty, and being maintained it enabled the North to win the war.

The Civil War, vindicating majority rule, matured American democracy. It excised the cancer that threatened the nation's life. It deepened the people's sense of their nationality. It widened the field of government. It ushered in a new federalism.

The postwar generation knew a new spirit of vastness, of organization, of power, of hope, and of challenge. Oliver Wendell Holmes, Jr., wounded at Ball's Bluff, Antietam, and Chancellorsville, looking back on his generation reminisced: "Through our great good fortune, in our youth our hearts were touched with fire. It was given us at the outset to learn that life is a profound and passionate thing ... we ... learned that whether a man accepts from Fortune her spade and will look downward and dig, or from Aspiration her axe and cord and will scale the ice, the one and only success which it is his to command is to bring to his work a mighty heart."

Perhaps the greatest lesson of the Civil War lay in its revelation of the inner sources by which the American people nourish their political institutions.

Guide to Further Study

There is no one-volume general history of Northern politics during the Civil War; this work aims to fill that gap. Excellent works which, among other matters, treat this subject include: J. G. Randall and D. Donald, *The Civil War and Reconstruction* (Lexington, Mass.: 1969); J. F. Rhodes, *History of the United States from the Compromise of 1850 [to 1877]*, 7 vols. (New York: 1893-1906); A. Nevins, *The Ordeal of the Union*, 8 vols. (New York: 1949-1971). J. A. Rawley, ed., *Lincoln and Civil War Politics* (New York: 1969) offers some historians' controversies. E. L. McKitrick, "Party Politics and the Union and Confederate War Efforts," in W. N. Chambers and W. D. Burnham, eds., *The American Party Systems* (New York: 1967) is brilliantly suggestive.

Essential to the subject are the *Congressional Globe* for

1861-1865 and *The Official Records of the War of the Rebellion*, 128 vols. (Washington: 1880-1901). F. Freidel, ed., *Union Pamphlets of the Civil War*, 2 vols. (Cambridge, Mass.: 1967) collects an important form of political literature. Three invaluable compilations of documents and statistics are: *American Annual Cyclopaedia and Register of Important Events* (New York: 1862-1866); W. D. Burnham, *Presidential Ballots, 1836-1892* (Baltimore: 1955); and *Historical Statistics of the United States* (Washington: 1960).

Newspapers of special value include the *Springfield Republican, The Liberator, New York Herald, New York World, New York Tribune, The Evening Post* (New York), *National Intelligencer, Chicago Tribune,* and *The Times* (London).

Diaries that provide an inner history include: H. K. Beale, ed., *The Diary of Edward Bates, 1859-1866* (Washington: 1933); T. C. Pease and J. G. Randall, eds., *The Diary of Orville Hickman Browning*, 2 vols. (Springfield, Ill.: 1927-1933); D. Donald, ed., *Inside Lincoln's Cabinet: The Civil War Diaries of Salmon P. Chase* (New York: 1954); T. Dennett, ed., *Lincoln and the Civil War in the Diaries and Letters of John Hay* (New York: 1939); H. K. Beale and A. W. Brownsword, eds., *Diary of Gideon Welles*, 3 vols. (New York: 1960).

Histories by contemporaries, each valuable for its view, comprise: J. G. Blaine, *Twenty Years of Congress*, 2 vols. (Norwich, Conn.: 1884-1886); S. S. Cox, *Three Decades of Federal Legislation, 1855-1885*, 2 vols. (Providence: 1885); H. Greeley, *The American Conflict*, 2 vols. (Hartford: 1866); and John Sherman, *John Sherman's Recollections*, 2 vols. (Chicago: 1895).

R. P. Basler, ed., *The Collected Works of Abraham Lincoln*, 9 vols. (New Brunswick, N.J.: 1953-1955) is definitive and indispensable. Poetic insight may be found in the Civil War writings of Walt Whitman, J. R. Lowell, J. G. Whittier, among contemporaries, and the incomparable, *John Brown's Body* by S. V. Benét.

There are political biographies of nearly every important figure. Their very abundance makes it impossible to list them here, with a few exceptions. For Lincoln three works require citation: J. G. Nicolay and J. Hay, *Abraham Lincoln: A History*, 10 vols. (New York: 1890), written by his secretaries; B. P. Thomas, *Abraham Lincoln* (New York: 1952), the best one-volume life; and J. G. Randall and R. N. Current, *Lincoln the President*, 4 vols. (New York: 1945-1955), the most scholarly.

Two notable biographies of cabinet members are: G. G. Van Deusen, *William Henry Seward* (New York: 1967) and B. P. Thomas and H. M. Hyman, *Stanton* (New York: 1962). I. Katz, *August Belmont* (New York: 1968) and J. A. Rawley, *Edwin D. Morgan* (New York: 1955) portray the Democratic and Republican national chairmen respectively. David Donald, *Charles Sumner*, 2 vols. (New York: 1961-1970) is in a class by itself. W. Salter, *The Life of James W. Grimes* (New York: 1876) is a model among old-fashioned lives; A. D. Kirwan, *John J. Crittenden* (Lexington, Ky.: 1962) is judicious; a work of painstaking research into the life of C. L. Vallandigham is F. L. Klement, *The Limits of Dissent* (Lexington, Ky.: 1970).

The historiographical problem of the radical Republicans may be said to have begun with T. H. Williams, *Lincoln and the Radicals* (Madison: 1941), who was challenged by D. Donald, *Lincoln Reconsidered* (New York: 1956), and by various articles and papers by G. M. Linden and A. G. Bogue. H. L. Trefousse, *The Radical Republicans: Lincoln's Vanguard for Racial Justice* (New York: 1969) sees the radicals not as opportunists and materialists but as idealists.

Historical interpretation of the Democrats may be followed in R. H. Abzug, "The Copperheads: Historical Approaches to Civil War Dissent," *Indiana Magazine of History* 66 (1970) and R. O. Curry, "The Union As It Was: A Critique of Recent Interpretations of the 'Copperheads,' " *Civil War History* 13 (1967). L. P. Curry, "Congressional Democrats, 1861-1863," *Civil War History* 12 (1966) finds the Democrats to be the loyal opposition.

Chapter 1

Standard histories of the 1860 election are: E. D. Fite, *The Presidential Campaign of 1860* (New York: 1911) and R. H. Luthin, *The First Lincoln Campaign* (Cambridge, Mass.: 1944). E. Foner, *Free Soil, Free Labor, Free Men* (New York: 1970) delineates the ideology of the Republican party before the Civil War. M. F. Holt, *Forging a Majority* (New Haven: 1969) analyzes the social bases of the formation of the Republican party in Pittsburgh, embodying the "new political history." The historians' controversy over the German-American vote in 1860 is presented, with an able introduction, in F. C. Luebke, ed., *Ethnic Voters and the Election of Lincoln* (Lincoln, Nebr.: 1971).

Lincoln's handling of the secession crisis is probed in: D. M. Potter, *Lincoln and His Party in the Secession Crisis* (New Haven: 1942); K. M. Stampp, *And the War Came* (Baton Rouge: 1950); R. N. Current, *Lincoln and the First Shot* (Philadelphia: 1963).

Comparative studies of presidential cabinets are: B. J. Hendrick, *Lincoln's War Cabinet* (Boston: 1946) and R. W. Patrick, *Jefferson Davis and His Cabinet* (Baton Rouge: 1944).

One source of Lincoln's political strength is evaluated in H. J. Carman and R. H. Luthin, *Lincoln and the Patronage* (New York: 1943). J. A. Rawley, "The Nationalism of Abraham Lincoln," *Civil War History* 9 (1963) explores Lincoln's overriding concern for the Union. A. Bestor, "The American Civil War as a Constitutional Crisis," *American Historical Review* 69 (1964) is important.

Chapter 2

Phillip S. Paludan, "The American Civil War Considered as a Crisis in Law and Order," *American Historical Review* 77 (1972) seeks to explain why men rushed to fight in terms of the concept of law and order. E. C. Smith, *The Borderland in the Civil War* (New York: 1927) is the fullest general account. C. L. Wagandt, *The Mighty Revolution: Negro Emancipation in Maryland, 1862-1864* (Baltimore: 1964) is a scholarly study of one loyal slave state's travail in ending slavery. J. G. Randall, *Constitutional Problems under Lincoln*, rev. ed. (Urbana: 1964) is a model of erudition.

Chapter 3

L. P. Curry, *Blueprint for Modern America: Nonmilitary Legislation of the First Civil War Congress* (Nashville: 1968) is a careful study of the Thirty-seventh Congress.

The working of Congress is better understood after reading: D. S. Alexander, *History and Procedure of the House of Representatives* (Boston: 1916); N. W. Polsby, "The Institutionalization of the House of Representatives," *American Political Science Review* 62 (1968); A. McCown, *The Congressional Conference Committee* (New York: 1927); and H. White, *Executive Influence in Determining Military Policy in the United States* (Urbana: 1925). See also C. A. Berdahl, *War Powers of the Executive in the United States* (Urbana: 1921).

Standard monographs on their subjects are: S. Ratner, *American Taxation* (New York: 1942) and F. W. Taussig, *The Tariff History of the United States* (New York: 1931). H. M. Hyman, *Era of the Oath. Northern Loyalty Tests during the Civil War and Reconstruction* (Philadelphia: 1954) breaks new ground.

Chapter 4

B. Hammond, *Sovereignty and an Empty Purse. Banks and Politics in the Civil War* (Princeton: 1970) is a magisterial work stressing centralization of authority. Charles Beard's interpretation of a monolithic business community operating through the Republican party is attacked by R. P. Sharkey, *Money, Class, and Party* (Baltimore: 1959) and I. Unger, *The Greenback Era* (Princeton: 1964).

The Union war debt falls into perspective in R. T. Patterson, *Federal Debt-Management Policies, 1865-1879* (Durham: 1954) and M. A. Robinson, "Federal Debt Management: Civil War, World War I, and World War II," *American Economic Review* 45 (1955). M. Friedman, "The Role of War in American Economic Development," *American Economic Review* 42 (1952) and D. T. Gilchrist and W. D. Lewis, eds., *Economic Change in the Civil War Era* (Greenville, Del.: 1965) are important.

A. H. Meneely, *The War Department, 1861* (New York: 1928) is a masterly study. F. A. Shannon, *The Organization and Administration of the Union Army, 1861-1865*, 2 vols. (Cleveland: 1928) and J. F. Leach, *Conscription in the United States* (Rutland, Vt.: 1952), the one critical, the other sympathetic, offset one another. E. C. Murdoch in *One Million Men: The Civil War Draft in the North* (Madison: 1971) and elsewhere brings a fresh perspective. There is no comparable body of research on the navy; and my account is pieced together from a number of sources.

Chapter 5

R. M. Robbins, *Our Landed Heritage* (Lincoln, Nebr.: 1962) is authoritative. Sectionalism as a determinant of political behavior is analyzed in: E. D. Ross, "Northern Sectionalism in the Civil War Era," *Iowa Journal of History and Politics* 30 (1932); P. W. Gates, "Western Opposition to the Agricultural Act," *Indiana Magazine of History* 37 (1941); and A. G. Bogue, "Senators, Sectionalism, and the 'Western' Measures of the Republican Party," in D. M. Ellis, ed., *The Frontier in American Development* (Ithaca: 1969).

Chapter 6

J. M. McPherson, *The Struggle for Equality* (Princeton: 1964) demonstrates that the abolitionists were political activists during the Civil War and Reconstruction. B. Quarles, *Lincoln and the Negro* (New York: 1962) traces its theme with understanding. C. M. Green, *The Secret City. A History of Race Relations in the Nation's Capital* (Princeton: 1967) relates a grim story. J. H. Franklin, *The Emancipation Proclamation* (New York: 1963) is a highly readable account. D. Cornish, *The Sable Arm* (New York: 1966) details the narrative of Negro troops in the Union Army. A pioneer article by an eminent Negro historian is C. Wesley, "Lincoln's Plan for Colonizing Negroes," *Journal of Negro History* 4 (1919).

Chapter 7

F. Wood, *Black Scare* (Berkeley: 1968) brings out a long-neglected aspect of Civil War politics. E. D. Adams, *Great Britain and the American Civil War*, 2 vols. (New York: 1925) is full and scholarly. V. H. Cohen, "Charles Sumner and the *Trent* Affair," *Journal of Southern History* 22 (1956) depicts the senator's role in keeping the peace.

Chapter 8

Two first-class works on state politics are W. E. Parrish, *Turbulent Partnership: Missouri and the Union, 1861-1865* (Columbia, Mo.: 1963) and R. O. Curry, *A House Divided: A Study of Statehood Politics and the Copperhead Movement* (Pittsburgh: 1964). G. C. Sellery, *Lincoln's Suspension of Habeas Corpus as Viewed by Congress* (Madison: 1907) remains standard. A. Cole, *The Era of the Civil War, 1848-1870* (Springfield, Ill.: 1919) is an excellent, broad-gauge history of Lincoln's home state. E. L. Thornbrough, *Indiana in the Civil War Era, 1850-1880* (Indianapolis: 1965) probes a pivotal state. S. I. Kutler, *Judicial Power and Reconstruction Politics* (Chicago: 1968) has material on the Supreme Court and Civil War politics.

Chapter 9

F. B. Woodford, *Father Abraham's Children* (Detroit: 1961) includes an account of the Detroit race riot. For the New York City riot, see A. P. Man, Jr., "Labor Competition and the New York Draft Riots of 1863," *Journal of Negro History* 36 (1951) and James McCague, *The Second Rebellion* (New York: 1968). There is no adequate study of the spring and fall elections of 1863.

Chapter 10

Herman Belz, "The Etheridge Conspiracy of 1863: A Projected Conservative Coup," *Journal of Southern History* 36 (1970) is an excellent account. E. N. Wright, *Conscientious Objectors in the Civil War* (Philadelphia: 1931) is standard. J. P. Davis, *The Union Pacific Railway* (Chicago: 1894), though old, is useful. G. O. Virtue, "Marxian Interpretation of the Civil War," *Nebraska History* 30 (1949) is a pioneer rebuttal to Charles Beard and others, which deserves to be better known. C. Erickson, *American Industry and the European Immigrant, 1860-1885* (Cambridge, Mass.: 1957) throws new light on the contract labor law.

Chapter 11

W. F. Zornow, *Lincoln and the Party Divided* (Norman: 1954) is a general scholarly account. E. C. Kirkland, *The Peacemakers of 1864* (New York: 1927) is a political study. J. A. Rawley, *Turning Points of the Civil War* (Lincoln, Nebr.: 1966) has a chapter on the election of 1864. O. O. Winther, "The Soldier Vote in the Election of 1864," *New York History* 25 (1944) is informative.

Chapter 12

Lincoln's views on equal rights for Negroes in 1864-1865 have been the subject of scholarly debate; see L. H. Johnson, "Lincoln and Equal Rights: The Authenticity of the Wadsworth Letter," *Journal of Southern History* 32 (1966); H. M. Hyman, "Lincoln and Equal Rights for Negroes: The Irrelevancy of the 'Wadsworth Letter,'" *Civil War History* 12 (1966); and L. H. Johnson, "Lincoln and Equal Rights: A Reply," *Civil War History* 13 (1967).

A capital study is H. Belz, *Reconstructing the Union: Theory and Policy during the Civil War* (Ithaca: 1969). D. Donald, *The Politics of Reconstruction, 1863-1867* (Baton Rouge: 1965) finds the solution of Republican voting in Congress in the need to win votes at home at the next election.

"The Peacemaker" is the title of a chapter in R. N. Current, *The Lincoln Nobody Knows* (New York: 1958). On the same theme is L. H. Johnson, "Lincoln's Solution to the Problem of Peace Terms, 1864-1865," *Journal of Southern History* 34 (1968).

Finally, the student who wishes to keep abreast of the progress of research on Civil War politics may consult *Civil War History*, a scholarly quarterly published by The Kent State University Press.

Index